THEATRE

in a cool climate

Acknowledgements

Our thanks to Corinne Beaver, Jane Noble, Hilary Wilson, Irene and John Slatter, and to our publisher, Judith Scott.

Vera Gottlieb and Colin Chambers

Vera Gottlieb would also like to express deep appreciation to George Hamilton, Adrian Tookman, David Lipkin, Andrew Platt, and their respective teams at the Royal Free Hospital, London, including Phyl Morris-Vincent, Leslie Mattin, Kate Jones, Mila Constant, and the Community Team of BP4.

THEATRE

in a cool climate

Edited by
Vera Gottlieb and Colin Chambers

Amber Lane Press

Published in 1999 by Amber Lane Press Ltd, Church Street, Charlbury, Oxford OX7 3PR
Telephone and fax: 01608 810024

Printed and bound by the Guernsey Press Company Ltd, C.I.

Introduction, collection and editorial matter copyright © Vera Gottlieb and Colin Chambers, 1999. Chapters copyright © individual authors, 1999. The right of the contributors to be identified as the authors of their work has been asserted by them in accordance with Section 77 of the Copyright, Designs and Patents Act 1988. Excerpts from Sir Richard Eyre's address to the British Academy in 1998 and Professor George Steiner's opening lecture at the Edinburgh Festival in 1996 are quoted with the permission of the authors.

A CIP catalogue record for this book is available from the British Library

ISBN: 1 872868 26 6

Contents

PAUL SCOFIELD

Foreword

I T IS MY PRIVILEGE to introduce a book whose contents and whose distinguished contributors appear to me to embrace every possible aspect of theatre, its art, its practitioners, its administration and the harsh climate of its present economic situation.

I am an actor and it is only from that view-point that I can speak with conviction. The theatre is a corporate undertaking which demands the presence of the audience and the presence of the actors, it is a living 'in the flesh' representation of life; no other form of entertainment can light the fire which can, in a moment, blaze between playgoer and performer. The state of the theatre is healthy. There is always something to be seen and relished in its offerings, it has its troughs and its crests, you can be bored by it, or it can be a revelatory experience, an enlargement of perception. The play itself, the text, is the bed-rock of the performance, an actor or director cannot use his craft to the utmost without the insights and the passion of the writer behind him. It is the essential spring-board of the entire process, and the actors' sensitivity and understanding of this essence, and the director's 'eye of the audience' are the means whereby it emerges into palpable flesh and blood.

There can be a moment in a play when an audience, which has begun the evening singly, in pairs or groups in their rows of seats, all quite separate from each other, when they, in that moment become a unity. They have been entered by a recognition, the sharing of an insight; the actor can feel this and becomes a part of their one-ness.

That for me is what the theatre is for, and the reader will find echoes of my assumption in the ensuing pages, together with the expression of other views and wider perspectives.

Vera Gottlieb and Colin Chambers

Introduction

> Wandering between two worlds, one dead
> The other powerless to be born.
>
> *Matthew Arnold*

THIS BOOK AROSE out of the sense that an informal snapshot of contemporary theatre, written by a diversity of practitioners, would be of interest both now and in the future – an interest related not only to the approaching end of a century but also to the beginning of a new millennium. This invites a kind of stocktaking, which was missing in 1899 or 1900, and may have been a lost opportunity for today's reader in looking back at what some theatre practitioners thought at that time.

Every contributor writes as an individual and yet – quite independently – as one of a pair within a specialism, to increase perspectives and approaches. And each has been invited to express a subjective perception, although in much of what they write, similar values are either explicit or implicit, depending on how he or she has approached the aims of the book. These aims may be roughly defined as: analysing or describing the recent and current theatrical situation from the viewpoint of their own discipline and, more generally, as people working in the theatre at large; to express how they might wish theatre to develop as we approach the new millennium; and, as a third part of this 'freeze-frame', what a practitioner of today might both fear *and* hope for the nature and function of theatre as we enter the twenty-first century.

9

Each of our eighteen contributors, within the nine chapters by writers, actors, directors, designers, critics, producers, managers and literary managers, has approached this differently. We have tried to edit lightly in order to ensure that the individual voice is not ironed out to create a single tone for the book as a whole.

It is also worth remembering that had professional theatre practitioners put their ideas down on paper in 1899 or 1900, most of the specialisms included here would have been absent since they did not exist as such: namely the roles of director, designer, literary manager, producer or even the manager of today. Concepts such as 'directors' theatre' or 'designers' theatre' belong to the twentieth century.

Actors, writers and critics have existed since the inception of theatre, but the work done by Cleo Sylvestre and Simon Russell Beale as actors, or Harold Pinter and Winsome Pinnock as writers, and Irving Wardle or Joyce McMillan as critics, has obviously altered to meet the needs of their contemporary theatre – and indeed has helped to *create* that theatre. It would be interesting to have a crystal ball in order to see how these and the 'new' jobs may develop as the roles fulfilled by Peter Hall, Richard Eyre, Katie Mitchell, Paule Constable, Alison Chitty, Venu Dhupa, Genista McIntosh, Leila Jancovich, Ella Wildridge, Colin Chambers and Jatinder Verma will no doubt alter in the future.

During the course of the twentieth century we have seen the development of film, radio and television, with a resulting crossover from one medium to another by actors, writers, directors, and designers. Several writers have in fact made a deliberate decision to write for one or more of these media, given the potential mass audience which they may reach. Moreover, the relationship between actor and audience has changed according to the medium, with, for example, a new emphasis on stars, and with the potential – sometimes realized – of bringing art to popular culture, and of popular culture absorbing art. This also raises major questions of control over one's own work, a control which varies according to the medium, and indeed raises other questions about what is now a huge industry – and one which is much more international. Sales of a British television serial or series or an independently produced film for Channel 4 may make an actor better known internationally than any number of theatre tours abroad; conversely, a writer working in television may be better known for work done in the theatre. The same is often the case with film, both media being dominated by actor and director.

Over the last hundred years, starting with cinema and followed by radio and then television, the lines of demarcation between forms of expression have been redrawn, sometimes negatively, at other times positively. And this is inseparable from the specific periods which contextualize the work. Thus Matthew Arnold's words in his *Culture and Anarchy* in 1869 suggest a continuum of thinking, and a shared awareness (if one may put it that way) between the nineteenth and twentieth centuries that 'something' is missing.

In 1851, with the Great Exhibition, the Victorians unashamedly and nationalistically exhibited their own produce, industry and ingenuity. They also sold space to other countries, which enabled America, for example, to demonstrate the latest inventions yet at a *British* exhibition, thus reinforcing the sense of Britain as 'the workshop of the world'. The legacy of this international trade fair can still be seen in such great London institutions as the Victoria and Albert Museum or Science Museum. Exactly one hundred years later, with the Festival of Britain in 1951, the postwar aims of reconstruction were clear – and unusually supportive of the arts and British culture. This, in turn, has left us with the legacy of London's South Bank arts complex. In contrast, the Millennium Dome – currently causing so much controversy – may provide a metaphor for our times of 'wandering between two worlds'. This major structure, conceived and built at great expense, is intended to celebrate *something* – but we do not know *what* or what function it may ultimately serve, if any. The British are currently caught between 'heritage' and 'future' with no very clear sense of direction, and in this confusion the arts, as ever, are struggling to survive.

The title of this book, *Theatre in a Cool Climate*, reflects this situation, yet it would be quite wrong to suggest that the views expressed are essentially pessimistic. Surprisingly, most of the contributors, in their snapshot of today and thinking for tomorrow, are – to use Richard Eyre's phrase from his chapter – 'travelling in hope'.

1

HAROLD PINTER

Pinter's Landscapes – or 'It Never Happened'

Harold Pinter's plays include: The Birthday Party, The Dumb Waiter, The Hothouse, The Caretaker, The Homecoming, Landscape, The Lover, The Collection, Old Times, No Man's Land, Betrayal, One for the Road, Mountain Language, Party Time, Moonlight *and* Ashes to Ashes.

This interview with Harold Pinter and the Editors took place in London on 22 January 1998.

GOTTLIEB: We are delighted that you are prepared to talk about the theatre today, and in the future. Is that because you have strong feelings about what's going on with theatre now?

PINTER: No. Absolutely not. I'm prepared to talk around this area if that's what you want but if you mean an *overall* state of affairs and my *overall* view, I don't possess one, so I have very little to say, but it rather depends on what we talk about.

CHAMBERS: You don't possess an overview of what's happening in the theatre at the moment?

PINTER: No. I don't. Nor do I possess an overview of what's happened to theatre in the last fifty years, for the simple reason that I've been working quite intensively in theatre in one way or another for virtually fifty years

13

now, so I must be one of the oldest of your contributors, if not the oldest. I actually started working in the theatre as an actor in 1949, so we're almost there. But, as I say, it's a long time – and I've been working very hard, burrowing away in one guise or role or another: writing, acting and directing, so I'm not in a position to take an overview. I've been too busy.

GOTTLIEB: Are there changes that you've seen over the fifty years, which you've welcomed or have worried you at all? Particularly about the *context* of your work?

PINTER: Some changes I have welcomed and others worry me. I welcomed the subsidized theatre, started in the Sixties. Peter Hall invited me to write plays for the RSC, which I did, and this association was very important for me. I enjoyed the work there and the atmosphere.

CHAMBERS: It is dangerous to look back at history and ask what might have happened 'if' . . . but do you think that your own writing *and* that of your contemporaries would have been able to develop in the way that you have *without* subsidy?

PINTER: I'm afraid I really can't speculate.

CHAMBERS: It *is* speculation, but there aren't many other models to look at. If one makes the American comparison, that they didn't have the same subsidy or burgeoning of writers – might one make some assumptions?

PINTER: To try and answer . . . I can give you a precise example, in my own case, of my first two plays. My first professional production – of *The Birthday Party* [1958] – was a commercial production which wasn't exactly the biggest hit of all time! Then I wrote *The Caretaker* [1959] and Michael Codron again produced that and *The Caretaker* went very well. Then, at Peter Hall's invitation, I went to the RSC for the first time about 1962, for a double bill of my play *The Collection* [1962] and Strindberg's *Playing With Fire*. Then I wrote *The Homecoming* [1964] and again Michael Codron wanted to produce it – and this *is* in answer to your question – but I made a crucial decision. I decided that I would prefer it to be done at the Royal

Shakespeare Company, because I thought it wouldn't suffer from that terrible tension you get in the commercial theatre about what the critics are going to say the next day and *therefore* how long it is going to run. I thought it wouldn't apply to the subsidized theatre, and anyway I liked working with Peter and the whole set-up. Nevertheless, those facts did still apply . . . you're always wondering what the critics are going to say. It's part of the whole thing. Peter Hall did a terrific job and I recall that nobody else on the Planning Committee of the Royal Shakespeare Company wanted to do *The Homecoming*. But he overrode the Committee and staged it in the Aldwych. Obviously the situation is different now.

CHAMBERS: Can you imagine anybody *now* doing David Mercer's *Belcher's Luck* as the RSC did in 1966, in a theatre with more than 1000 seats?

PINTER: You said, I believe, that you were concentrating on theatre, as distinct from any of the other media?

GOTTLIEB: Yes, but television drama can come into it, given the cross-over.

PINTER: Well, as you know, I've been considerably involved in television over the years. And it was only a couple of years ago that I did a production of *Landscape* [written in 1968] with Ian Holm and Penelope Wilton at the Dublin Festival; then it came to the National and ran at the Cottesloe for a while, and I was invited to do it by the BBC as a television production.

GOTTLIEB: Invited to direct it?

PINTER: Yes. And I did direct it. The BBC had done ten of my plays over the years. *Landscape* is a 35-minute play, just two people sitting at a table, and that's it. Then three years later I directed my last play *Ashes to Ashes*, and I was very keen to do it . . . to televise it, to record it, because very few people saw it. The Royal Court Theatre Upstairs is so small there were only about a hundred people in every night. I thought the BBC would provide an opportunity for a much broader audience. But there was no chance.

GOTTLIEB: Why not?

PINTER: The BBC were not interested. They simply rejected it. They obviously thought it would only appeal to a minority audience.

GOTTLIEB: Was that the reason they gave you?

PINTER: They didn't give any reason – I never had a single letter from anybody to say, 'for such and such a reason we can't do it'. The answer was just 'no'. So things have certainly changed. It could be called a growing philistinism, don't you think?

GOTTLIEB: This relates to one of the aspects we've been talking to other contributors about – the use of the word 'luvvies'.

PINTER: Ah, yes.

GOTTLIEB: This has come up – not in a frivolous manner – but because it seems so indicative of the times. You used the word 'philistinism', but it's also indicative of an almost articulated disdain, dislike. Even fear of anything that smacks of artists, 'the intelligentsia' – anything which might convey real confrontational thinking.

PINTER: Yes. Absolutely. That is the way they do it – the word 'luvvies' is a way of demeaning artists.

GOTTLIEB: Would you relate this philistinism specifically to the BBC or to television, or is it broader?

PINTER: Oh, broader. I told you that story about *Ashes to Ashes* and television because it seemed to me pertinent . . . and part of what has developed, which is precisely that kind of attitude – that loathing, even fear, of what you call the artist, if you like. Art. So the thing to do about it is to mock it, or refuse it, or kick it in the teeth. I've recently spent some time in Italy [doing *Ashes to Ashes*] and in Greece, and I'm going to Paris shortly. I'm preparing a production in Paris of *Ashes to Ashes*. In Italy, and certainly in

Greece, I found an entirely different state of affairs. People are politically well-informed, sophisticated, and the general tone is of intellectual curiosity and political responsibility. It is palpable and concrete there, and this also applies to the press. In Athens the press is totally different – *and* in Italy.

GOTTLIEB: The 'unpolitical' stance then seems unique to this country. If so, then how far has this attitude impacted on your career? By and large the critics have not seen your plays *as* 'political'. I'm wondering about the dynamic between intention – and reception.

PINTER: That's rather complicated. I would say audiences have been unable to avoid the political in one or two of my plays – particularly in the Eighties. They couldn't avoid that, but they've avoided a lot of other facts, and I must tell you that I don't regard myself as at all a 'popular' playwright in this country . . . I have a much more substantial audience in other countries.

CHAMBERS: Arnold Wesker says the same – that he doesn't have an audience here.

PINTER: Yes. I'm sure Edward Bond would also say the same.

GOTTLIEB: You mentioned the plays of the Eighties which in my view, and clearly in yours, were overtly political, but my memory is that some critics felt this was a temporary aberration on your part.

PINTER: Their assertions were quite inaccurate.

GOTTLIEB: There is a very clear movement and professional development from the early plays, to the present.

PINTER: Well, I believe so too. I've been through this a lot and I'm sure you don't want it in any great detail, but there's no question in my mind that *The Birthday Party* and *The Dumb Waiter* [1957] and *The Hothouse* [first produced in 1980], all of which I wrote before 1960, are essentially political plays. So I believe there's a consistency in my work. Obviously I've been 'elsewhere' at other times . . . one 'travels' . . . that's the whole point of being a writer . . .

CHAMBERS: Yet there is a denial by most of the critical community about this. You can't win. They deny the political nature of the early works and when they *cannot* deny the politics of the later plays, then they argue that it is less good as art. It is a very British perception: if they can see the politics, they believe it can't be any good as drama.

PINTER: Yes – quite. Rather similar to your field – Chekhov, I mean.

GOTTLIEB: Yes, to draw an obvious parallel, Chekhov's not usually considered a political dramatist in this country, yet it would be impossible for Russians, or the French, Italians, Greeks, not to read him that way while not at all negating the art.

CHAMBERS: Or the Germans.

PINTER: That's right.

GOTTLIEB: Not in terms of any 'party politics', but 'political' in the broadest sense, of asking questions about where we are – what is happening to us.

PINTER: That's right. The world we live in.

CHAMBERS: On the Continent that's assumed about any writer whose work has survived.

GOTTLIEB: Equally in Ireland – you find the Continental view, not the British view.

PINTER: Yes, that's absolutely right.

CHAMBERS: When I've been in Dublin, a play by Brian Friel or Frank McGuinness stimulates talk in the theatre bars of a completely different order to the talk in an English theatre. There's intellectual vigour in the debate of issues.

PINTER: Yes. As you know, I've had two festivals of my work in Dublin, one in 1994 and one in 1997, and with both experiences, that was exactly the case. The talk is of a different nature. So I'm afraid I think we live in a very short-sighted country, and also a rather sullen country.

GOTTLIEB: Is this new? Is this something that's developed over the last seventeen or eighteen years? Or, putting it directly – would you relate it to Thatcherism?

PINTER: Yes, I think so. I think that with Thatcherism we had a disaster here. It *was* a disaster and *remains* a disaster. And we're not out of Thatcherism. As a comparison with something I often talk about – McCarthyism in the States. I don't think for a moment that McCarthyism is dead. It's never died. But people talk about it as an historical phenomenon which is long gone. Nonsense. It was rooted in the very texture of American life.

GOTTLIEB: Control through the Hollywood studio system –

PINTER: No, I'm talking more generally – not just the entertainment business. I'm talking about the *nature* of American society. After the First World War, for example, in 1919 there were brutal riots against blacks and 'lefties', and the trial and execution of Sacco and Vanzetti in 1927 – all part of the larger landscape. Very strong and endemic so it never went away, and in the Thirties – I'm giving you a run-down of American politics in about two and a half minutes – but the Thirties, in the dustbowl of the Midwest, the Southern States . . .

GOTTLIEB: *Grapes of Wrath* country?

PINTER: Yes, and the only answer given to the workers is in that great line in *The Grapes of Wrath*, when the Preacher and Tom Joad are caught in the ditch at night by policemen with torches and clubs – and the Preacher says:

'Fellas – you don't know what you're doing! You're killing innocent women and children,' and they say – [*Pinter then made the sound of kicking some-one.*] That's the answer to that. And they actually kill him. That really embodies the world as it actually was – and remains. It hasn't gone away. I've just been reading an account of how only last year in New York, a black woman driver was going towards Harlem – took a right turn when apparently she shouldn't have. Just a traffic infringement – the police car followed – cornered her, and then a policeman got out with a gun, the woman apparently crouched – or moved to the other side of the car – whereupon he shot her. Then six other police also shot her. This is New York. *Now.* Well, what can you say?

CHAMBERS: It's not the same of course, but look what happened at Stoke Newington police station. I think the police have paid out something like a million pounds' compensation to a number of individuals. And that's to those who managed to get it together somehow – to get through the whole system. It's not as extreme, obviously, as in America.

PINTER: No . . . but nevertheless . . . or maybe you don't know, but a couple of years ago in Stoke Newington, the Kurdish Community Centre were doing a production of my *Mountain Language*. Did you hear this? They were rehearsing *Mountain Language* – all refugees and amateur actors. One or two of the actors were walking about outside the Community Centre, in uniform, you know, and with guns which they'd actually hired from the National Theatre. And then the police came along – although the *local* police knew all about it, knew they were doing a play. Before they knew what was happening, there were 200 police, *armed* police, surrounding the building, and helicopters. The police then put them all up against a wall and wouldn't allow them to speak their own language, so it seems as if the police knew the play they were doing . . . and wouldn't allow them to explain. They didn't actually beat anyone up, but they were nonetheless very brutal. They broke down the doors of the Centre, which they needn't have done at all, you know, kicked them in – and finally somebody managed to say: 'We're doing a play!' So they managed to get the point across. And when I went down to see them all, and to see the production a few days later, they were still really shocked. They thought they were back in Turkey.

CHAMBERS: Did you go because of the trouble?

PINTER: I was going to see it anyway, because I'm very much engaged with the Kurdish situation – in fact the Kurds have always thought *Mountain Language* is *about* the Kurdish position. It's not exactly that, but they have rather taken it over.

CHAMBERS: It *is* open to that interpretation.

PINTER: It is. But language, the whole idea of freedom and the whole question of freedom to speak, and constraints of this nature are really widespread. And apply not just in simple terms about speaking your own language but more about *what* you're saying, which I think certainly applies . . . I mean, there are forms of censorship and constraint and repression which are much less extreme but perhaps much more insidious in this country. So I was interested anyway to see what the Kurds were doing, but *particularly* given this police action. I was very concerned to meet all of them, and they were still absolutely terrified.

GOTTLIEB: There is now a kind of collapse of language of opposition. Perhaps since Thatcher virtually took over some of the language – words like radical, like revolutionary. Words that we thought belonged on one side suddenly were being used in a different way.

PINTER: Yes, yes.

GOTTLIEB: Language hijacked by the 'other side', and I think this may have put a number of artists in a difficult position because there seems to be a loss of language, a vacuum, for articulating opposition. This has not happened with *your* work. As a poet 'of' rather than 'in' the theatre, you have found a way of maintaining your dialogue, *and* using language in your own way – poetic. Metaphor, image, symbol. And the silence around the 'unsaid'.

PINTER: Well yes, I hope so. I believe that to be the case.

CHAMBERS: I think the question of Thatcher, and the point about the language of discourse affecting many of us, is that you've managed to operate in a way where you have controlled another sort of language which she hasn't been able to touch.

PINTER: Quite. Yes. But I must tell you something which you may or may not find relevant but I feel somehow it does reflect something – not to do with my own *language*, but to do with my own position as an *independent* person. About a year before the 1997 election, I was – interestingly – actually offered a knighthood by Mr Major. And I declined. I think it is relevant, isn't it? I remember when I received the letter in the post, I thought, 'Ahaha, you know . . .' [*Laughs.*] I was amused because it's the classic thing, isn't it? Neutralizing the opposition.

CHAMBERS: And when you declined – did you give reasons?

PINTER: Yes. Well, I wrote only one or two sentences. I thanked them for the honour, courteously, but said I was unable to accept such an honour from a Conservative government. Yours sincerely . . .

GOTTLIEB: If Tony Blair and the New Labour government were to offer it, how would you respond?

PINTER: Aha. [*Laughs.*] I'm not interested in knighthoods. And he's not going to do that anyway.

GOTTLIEB: We've been talking about Thatcherism, and obviously that took the customary British suspicion of the intelligentsia further, but it wasn't new, was it? I mean it was there in the Thirties, wasn't it?

PINTER: Oh yes, it's always been there.

CHAMBERS: What was frightening was how easily she tapped into it. The Falklands is the most obvious example, not *directly* related to the intelligentsia, but it happened apparently without anything – just a couple of headlines in newspapers and on television – and the country was baying.

PINTER: Yes. Absolutely.

GOTTLIEB: Also the invasion of Grenada, which for me was shocking, yet seems to have been forgotten.

PINTER: I haven't forgotten.

GOTTLIEB: No, I'm sure, but internationally –

CHAMBERS: So-called serious newspapers don't write about it any more and it's not debated in the press.

PINTER: You know – I do. I've written a series of political articles. Over many years, really. The last one was in the *Guardian*. I wrote one about the United States in which I mentioned Haiti, and Grenada and Panama, for example. And all the things that are forgotten. My article was in fact called *It Never Happened*. The *Guardian* actually changed the title to *Picking a Fight With Uncle Sam*, which was stupid! Ridiculous! They're always at that kind of thing, you know. Anyway, they *did* publish it. One of my phrases or one of my paragraphs was: Did the US do this? Did this take place? Were this number of people killed in East Timor? Did all this ever happen? The answer is: 'No. It never happened. Even *while* it was happening, it wasn't happening.'

GOTTLIEB: When I was in Moscow researching Chekhov material, an actor friend asked me: 'What about your civil war?' And I said: 'I'm sorry, what civil war?' and he looked aghast, and said: 'Ireland'. I realized that I had been so infected by the current climate that although I cared about Northern Ireland, I hadn't actually seen it in those terms. That description has never been applied by our press. Yet it *is* a civil war – which relates to what you were saying about 'it never happened'?

PINTER: That's right!

CHAMBERS: It's part of the insidious form of censorship, which we carry in our own heads – a tricky area.

GOTTLIEB: Yes, self-censorship.

PINTER: It's censorship by omission, isn't it? Deliberate omission. What you read in the papers is so highly selective.

CHAMBERS: How does it influence the theatre, which I suppose it must do? There is the example of censored television drama, but I've never in all my time at the RSC known anybody turn down a play for obvious political reasons – not overtly. But there's hardly a major production in the British theatre marking the anniversary of Brecht, the greatest theatre theorist and practitioner of our century. *That* is a form of censorship.

PINTER: Yes. A coralling of thought.

GOTTLIEB: Have you come across this in relation to your own plays? It *is* different because, thankfully, you're alive and well and can fight. Brecht can't. Have you ever found yourself restricted by something almost intangible?

PINTER: I don't think I have. Everyone keeps saying this is a free country, and I agree: it should be. So I'm going to act freely and independently, which I do. And also write exactly what I write, whatever it is, and I hold strongly to that view and am often clobbered for it. It's inevitable.

GOTTLIEB: So when you stick your head up about something overtly political, then people take issue with you?

PINTER: Yes. I don't really understand my own position in this country. It's very difficult for me to make any kind of objective judgement about it. But I think my very existence in the theatre, *and* in relation to politics, does annoy and irritate a lot of people. However, it would be inaccurate and self-indulgent of me to deny there is also a great deal of very positive response.

GOTTLIEB: Where you annoy people, is that because they can't easily label you? One can clearly label Edward Bond, or Trevor Griffiths and indeed Arnold Wesker. But it *is* much harder to put you in any very clear category.

PINTER: Yes. I think that may very well be so.

CHAMBERS: All those writers have been demeaned. In their different ways they've all been marginalized – in some way been kept off centre stage.

PINTER: We have a really profound establishment here, which has been around for a very long time, with profound traditions, and one of the essential elements of those traditions is mockery of the artistic or the intellectually curious. Certainly the politically curious, or politically questioning.

CHAMBERS: Yet it goes further than mocking or marginalizing some artists, doesn't it?

PINTER: Yes. I believe there's a very strong brutal element in this society, which you were talking about in Stoke Newington, for example. Police action. Don't let us forget the police also were given so many powers by the last Conservative government – more and more, all absolutely accepted by the then Labour opposition. And that opposition, now the Labour government, has actually taken on *all* those laws, which are essentially repressive laws. Some of them are actually totalitarian, and our jolly old Labour government has taken over the lot.

GOTTLIEB: May we finish by looking at a different angle? What do you hope for as we approach the millennium?

PINTER: What do I hope for? [*Long pause.*] I want to keep on my toes, in more ways than one. I hope that we can find enough solidarity so that people like you and me can keep on our toes together.

GOTTLIEB: So is it, do you think – as we enter the twenty-first century – a question of damage limitation? Or are there more positive things that we can do?

PINTER: Well, I hope there are more positive things . . . which is to keep the critical consciousness awake. So when I talk about being on one's toes, I mean being on one's *critical* toes. I think it's essential to keep one's critical faculties sharp. Otherwise you're throwing in the towel. If you do that you destroy yourself and help to destroy others. That's why I also feel, for example – just one last thing about 'the world'. . . [*Laughs.*] . . . and that is I have *very* strong feelings about this piece I wrote which I mentioned to you earlier: *It Never Happened.* I finished by saying – I think this *is* relevant – that people say: 'Oh yes, yes, yes – we know all this, everyone knows what the US is like and fuck it anyway – who cares?' And I say 'Sure,' as they say, 'Sure, but the dead are still looking at us, steadily, waiting for us to acknowledge our part in their murder.' And I believe that. That's what I feel.

2

WINSOME PINNOCK

Breaking Down the Door

Winsome Pinnock's plays include A Hero's Welcome, Leave Taking, A Rock in Water, Talking in Tongues *and* Mules. *Her work has been produced at the Royal Court Theatre Upstairs, the Lyric Theatre, Hammersmith and the Belgrade Theatre, Coventry, and she is the first black British woman to have a play performed at the Royal National Theatre. She has also written for film and television (*Bitter Harvest, Chalkface *and* South of the Border). *She has won the George Devine Award, a Unity Theatre Trust award and the Best Play Award in London Weekend Television's Plays on Stage scheme. She has been Writer in Residence at the Royal Court and the Tricycle Theatre and for Clean Break Theatre, and was Senior Visiting Fellow at Cambridge University.*

THE END OF THE TWENTIETH CENTURY has seen a remarkable resurgence of interest in new writing in the theatre. It has witnessed the emergence of an exciting generation of playwrights – among them David Eldridge, Rebecca Prichard, Conor McPherson and Che Walker – who have captured a new and younger theatre audience. This renewal, despite continued problems of funding, has been co-opted, alongside other popular art forms, by the current Labour government in the marketing of the idea of a new Britain or 'Cool Britannia'. Crucial to this marketing is the idea of Britain (and London in particular) as a successfully multicultural society led by the desires and ideas of the young.

How real is this idea? In terms of theatre's role in society, the rise of this new generation of playwrights has been seen negatively in some quarters, as a demise, as marking the end of political theatre. The gay community, for example, has criticized Jonathan Harvey for not writing an issue play on the age of consent amongst gays when in *Beautiful Thing* he chose instead to write a gentle romantic comedy about a love affair between two gay teenagers. Peter Ansorge, writing about contemporary theatre in his book *From Liverpool to Los Angeles*, goes further. He claims that *Beautiful Thing* started life as a film idea and that, failing to find a commission, was then turned into a stage play. He cites this as proof of the fact that contemporary playwrights are no longer committed to political theatre, or to a theatre that has as its central focus a distinct desire to analyse and comment on contemporary society in all its aspects; he sees the contemporary playwright as a careerist seeking success in Hollywood.

Ansorge does not consider the fact that contemporary playwrights move between the different media with some ease because they have inherited a theatre tradition – significantly from the political playwrights with whom he adversely contrasts them – where the barriers between the media have been successfully broken down and where the traditional theatrical conventions of linear narrative and unity have long been discarded. Furthermore, the success of *Beautiful Thing*, and the subsequent film, seems to suggest a certain coming of age of the so-called 'gay' play, or, indeed, of any play that is qualified by a prefix – be it, for example, a 'black' or a 'woman's' play. It suggests a coming of age of a gay playwright who was shrugging off the pressure to write an angry polemical play in order to use the inroads made by the activist playwrights who preceded him to say whatever he wanted to. In fact, the demise of companies such as Gay Sweatshop would seem to be the proof of the success of those activist theatres, which no longer seem to serve a purpose.

In terms of the theatre itself, the new playwrights have introduced a new theatre aesthetic – one that is more influenced by the aesthetic of popular culture, and in particular of film, than by plays of the past; the American film industry has had a huge impact on theatre writing, with plays such as *Mojo* by Jez Butterworth being labelled Tarantinoesque. Critics have mistakenly compared the explicit depictions of onstage violence in Sarah Kane's *Blasted* and *Cleansed* to the graphic uses of violence in the conventional Hollywood narrative, where violence is used to create suspense and plot, and violence as entertainment is offered up for consumption rather than reflection. The influence of film on this new theatre is also exhibited in its theatre language, with many new playwrights using the demotic – the language of popular culture giving their plays a certain accessibility. As with the impact of form, this again can be seen as stemming from the influence – and success – of activist or political theatre where companies such as Red Ladder, 7:84 or the Women's Theatre Group made use of popular culture and adopted the narrative structures of television in order to capture and politicize an audience that did not ordinarily attend the theatre.

Importantly, the popular culture that has influenced these new playwrights is, in turn, dominated by black culture; the language of the street has been appropriated by the mainstream and has become the first language of music, dance, fashion and visual art. Black rhythms of speech, a kind of street argot, have become the benchmark for all youth culture. In the theatre, for example, in Rebecca Prichard's *Yard Gal* (Clean Break Theatre Company), Che Walker's *Been So Long* (Royal Court) and the plays of David Eldridge like *Serving It Up*, the characters, both white and black, rich and poor, share a common street patois.

For playwrights such as myself, who have struggled in our work to find a place for the multiracial, to explore the difficult subjects of racism and, with our own working practices, to redress the imbalance of black artists within the theatre, this should seem like a moment of triumph. However, within the theatre – itself a microcosm of the society it reflects – the idea of the multicultural is notably absent. There is a significant lack of equality and opportunity for black playwrights, performers and directors, as the history of British black theatre shows.

Black theatre – that is, theatre created by or for black performers and geared to attract an audience from the black 'communities' – was founded by migrant performers from the former British colonies in resistance to the racism they encountered from mainstream (i.e. white) theatrical institutions. 'Black theatre' is a contentious label because it is difficult to find an accurate meaning for it. The use of such labelling creates a segregation within theatre that I, personally, am opposed to, and yet it reflects and articulates the reality of a division within theatrical institutions in which black or 'other' performers are viewed solely in relation to their supposed difference. Also, it is a useful term with regard to this chapter, albeit a rather simplistic way of viewing a group that comprises various diverse elements.

Black performers have, of course, been present in Britain for several hundred years, but I am concerned here with the powerful black theatre movement that took place during the second half of the twentieth century with the major immigration from the West Indies – the so-called 'Windrush Years', named after the SS *Empire Windrush* which on 22 June 1948 brought the first migrants from the West Indies to Britain.

During the first wave of the black theatre movement, direct resistance to racism was not the main aim of the dance troupes and groups that sprang up. Their commitment was to performance, although the beginning of a link between performance and resistance in the tradition of black British theatre can be seen in the founding of the Notting Hill Carnival. Started by the black communist activist Claudia Jones, the carnival (in those days a festival of performances by black artists – singers, dancers etc.) was a response to the Notting Hill riots of 1958 in which a black man, Kelso Cochrane, had been killed. It was during the late Sixties and Seventies, with the rise of various political movements – the American Civil Rights Movement, the Black Panthers, feminism – that black playwrights started to use the theatre as a means of resistance. Some theatre groups, such as the Keskidee Centre in Islington, north London, rooted themselves in the black communities, working directly with black youths from the surrounding council housing estates and mirroring the work of political theatre companies such as Red Ladder which was formed in 1968. (I grew up in Islington on the Priory Green council housing estate, and the Keskidee was central to the social life of young black youths, particularly males.)

Black theatre companies flourished during the Seventies and Eighties, again as a result of the inequality faced by black people in Britain in general and by black performers and writers in particular. Racism continued to dominate the lives of black migrant families, epitomized by the 'sus' laws, which saw the police using ancient vagrancy laws to stop and search young black men at random on 'suspicion'. Blacks were constantly viewed as criminals – a schoolfriend of mine was mistaken for a known prostitute, kept overnight in a cell and eventually released without apology. Theatre companies such as Carib, Talawa, Temba, Black Mime Theatre, Umoja and the Black Theatre Co-operative were the only companies to consistently employ black performers or to produce plays that explored the experiences of black Britons. Such companies also collaborated to produce an annual Festival of Black Plays and were able to demonstrate how, despite pressure from lack of funding, their combined strengths could help to sustain the black theatre movement.

Some of the playwrights of the time described themselves as West Indian, and their theatrical aesthetics drew directly on West Indian culture, using ritual and the carnival tradition – plays such as Mustapha Matura's *Play Mas,* set in Trinidad during Carnival, and Edgar White's *Nine Night,* which uses the ritual of grieving the dead. Several white writers of the Seventies and early Eighties also tackled the theme of racism, such as Michael Hastings in *Gloo Joo*, David Edgar in *Destiny* and Barrie Keeffe in *Sus.*

During the Eighties, however, a new kind of black playwright emerged – the black playwright who, usually, was British-born but who had inherited a West Indian cultural tradition from his or her parents. For these playwrights – writers such as Michael Ellis, Michael McMillan, Jacqueline Rudet, Bernadine Evaristo and myself – issues of identity were of pressing concern, the idea of being trapped between certain dualities: migrant/native; 'black' culture/'white' culture; being caught between two cultures and belonging to neither. These pressures found their way into the plays, as did a growing anger at continued racism. A good example is *Strange Fruit* by Caryl Phillips (born in St. Kitts), which presents this alienation through the searing anger and pain of the main character as he returns to England where he was brought up after attending his grandfather's funeral in the Caribbean. In my own case, the confusion of identity motivated the writing of *Leave Taking*, a play which looks at the conflict between a West Indian mother and her two English daughters. I was interested in the use of both dialect and 'standard' English in the play. Having been dissuaded from using dialect in my own everyday life, it was liberating – and an act of defiance – to use it on stage within a play that could easily fit the confines of a traditional proscenium theatre. Such plays were beginning to question the idea of Englishness, and to explore the idea that the rituals and traditions of West

Indian culture alone might not be enough, or even appropriate, to describe the experiences of second-generation blacks.

As one of the playwrights to emerge in the Eighties, I would say that I, like others of my generation, did not feel that my work should only be produced by the black theatre companies but that they should have a place within the mainstream. When a play by a writer like myself is presented on a mainstream stage, the profile of the visiting audience is radically changed. I noticed, when *Leave Taking* was produced by the National Theatre, the presence of black audience members who had probably never ventured into that particular theatre before. For an artist whose aim is to reach as many people as possible, theatre elitism is extremely problematical, but my own experience demonstrates that the theatre remains elitist only because it is allowed to be so. When a so-called 'black' play is produced at a theatre, the marketing department will call on its list of black institutions and invite them. The message is that they are only invited to see plays by black artists and are not otherwise welcome.

The Eighties were also notable for the global visibility of the black woman writer. Black American women such as Toni Cade Bambara, Toni Morrison, Maya Angelou and Alice Walker, taking their lead from one of the famous slogans of the feminist movement – 'the personal is political' – were writing about the politics of the personal aspects of black women's lives. The confessional tone of some of the novels written by these women proved to be a literary breakthrough, which has, even recently, been appropriated by white male novelists such as Nick Hornby. The work of such black women writers was popular and accessible, and, although they spoke ostensibly to and for black women, they also cut through the boundaries of race and gender.

Taking a cue from this perhaps, as well as from the growth in numbers of white women writing for the British theatre – writers such as Caryl Churchill, Timberlake Wertenbaker, Sarah Daniels and Claire McIntyre – the Theatre of Black Women was formed by Bernadine Evaristo and Patricia Hillaire. The company produced plays by performer and director Paulette Randall and poet Jackie Kay. The founders of the company were themselves poets, performers, writers and directors. Because the members of the company were multi-skilled and worked within various media, they were able to experiment with theatre form. They were influenced by the most prominent black woman playwright of the time, the American Ntozake Shange – another poet – who describes her play *For Colored Girls Who Have Considered Suicide When the Rainbow is Enuf* as a choreo-poem in which performance (the physical, the visual) and language are of equal importance, reminiscent of Samuel Beckett's use of physical poetry.

When the plays of Caryl Churchill and Timberlake Wertenbaker became successful, the literary manager of the Royal Court stated that the theatre had started to receive more unsolicited scripts from unknown women playwrights. The success of those two writers had aroused a certain confidence in writers who had not yet broken through but who felt that there was a possibility that they might. Similarly, the success of the black American female novelists demonstrated the commercial viability of the black woman artist and eventually opened up opportunities for black women artists in Britain. When I started writing in the early Eighties I felt that there was a certain receptiveness among theatre managements for the work of a black playwright. Without the confidence afforded by the strength as it was then of the black theatre scene and the emergence of black women writers, I may not have imagined the possibility of breaking through as a playwright.

As we approach the new millennium, the contemporary black theatre scene seems to be very depressing. Of the London-based black theatre companies cited above that sprang up in the Seventies and Eighties only two – Black Theatre Co-operative and Talawa – remain. The others lost their funding during the Thatcher years along with numerous political (i.e. left-wing) theatre companies. There were many conferences in 1998 that debated both the death of political theatre in general and the demise of black theatre in particular. Very little seems to have changed since the foundation of the early black theatres. Despite the marketing of 'Cool Britannia' as a new and exciting multicultural society, it is not unusual to watch play after play in which not a single black or Asian performer appears. It is a common experience to leave a contemporary theatre and return to a world that, on the surface, bears little resemblance to what one has just seen.

Yet there are at present many more black playwrights, performers and directors than there have ever been, many of whom have gained valuable experience in both mainstream and fringe productions. It is still more difficult, however, for black theatre practitioners to sustain a career in the theatre than their white counterparts. Black writers are often confined to fringe or studio theatres, generally for a very low fee, and it is usually difficult for them to secure more mainstream theatre work or the lucrative television commissions. I am usually only approached to write for television when there is a black character in the programme, as though a black writer cannot write for white performers or vice versa. After ten years' experience of writing for the professional theatre, including contributions to film and television, there are still some producers who tell me that I am not experienced enough to work on particular projects. However, it must be noted that Liselle Kayla, who wrote *Us Girls*, a six-part situation comedy about three generations of black women, is one of the few black writers to write for the popular television soap series *EastEnders* on a regular basis.

Structural problems within the theatre itself also conspire against the development of plays by black and Asian playwrights. The theatre is director-led, and it is a director's passionate response to a play that determines whether or not it will be produced. Because there are so few black directors with permanent placements at theatres, plays by black playwrights are often just not picked up because there is no one to respond to their subject matter. When a theatre management does decide to put on a play by a black playwright they will often offer it to the assistant director – the most inexperienced director in the theatre – and it will usually be performed in a studio. Although many assistant directors are highly talented, they are, in most cases, being allowed to cut their teeth on the black playwright's work. This denies the playwright concerned the valuable dramaturgical input of an experienced director. It seems as if there is an unspoken rule that an experienced director does not direct a 'black' play, probably because it is seen as a career setback.

Despite the demise of so many black theatre companies, the Nineties have seen a couple of breakthroughs by individual practitioners. One major theatre success was Ayub Khan-Din's *East is East,* which focuses on the relationship of a flawed Asian businessman with his white English wife and his clan of mixed-race offspring. He longs for a Pakistan that he cannot return to and his frustration at failing to force the family to conform to tradition explodes into sudden acts of violence. While the conflict between the father and his children is at the centre of the play, the children themselves do not question their identity. What is notable is their certainty about who and what they are and their constant assertion of their Englishness. The play was produced at the Royal Court's Theatre Upstairs and, after a successful run, transferred to the Theatre Downstairs. It was one of only two plays by black or Asian British playwrights to find its way on to the Royal Court's main stage in the Nineties. The other was 'Biyi Bandele's adaptation of Chinua Achebe's *Things Fall Apart*. (Plays by black American playwrights Anna Deveare Smith and George C. Wolfe were also seen Downstairs.) *East is East* subsequently transferred to the Theatre Royal, Stratford East, one of the few theatres in London that can lay claim to the description multicultural, both in terms of the plays produced and the audience that attends the performances. It is interesting that *East is East* looks at the different aspects of the meaning of 'mixed race' in terms of a mixed marriage, a white woman who has chosen to live with Pakistani culture, which has altered her own view of herself as an Englishwoman and of the children, the products of an interracial marriage.

I stated earlier that popular culture was dominated by black youth culture. It should also be noted that this, in turn, is led by artists of mixed race, particularly in music. Tricky, Goldie and Roni Size are all artists who contend with notions of the hybrid and work with the fusion of disparate styles.

Jenny McCleod is another black playwright to have emerged in the Nineties. Her play *Raising Fires* (Bush Theatre) was set during seventeenth-century Britain and looked at the way in which a young woman is scapegoated as a witch and accused of starting a series of freak fires. In a cast of nine, only one character (the young woman) is black and at the time that the play was written (1994) McCleod stated that race was not a factor in her plays, that she did not write plays in order to provide job opportunities for black actors. Although McCleod later revoked this statement, it is still an interesting position for a black writer to take, and one that questions the idea that there can be such a thing as a 'black' play.

The tradition and history of black theatre means that it was a theatre of protest, one that explored notions of race, identity and Englishness and that it was situated in opposition to mainstream theatre. This position of resistance was upheld in order to achieve equality for black writers who would then be free to write whatever they wanted. The work of black playwrights should not be defined solely by their race. It is interesting to note that Jenny McCleod went on to write a novel, following the lead of one-time playwrights such as Caryl Phillips and Fred D'Aguiar. Although his new play was performed at the National in 1999, Hanif Kureishi has stated in the past that the theatre had ceased to be the medium through which he could tell the stories that he wanted to tell. Maybe these writers have simply realized that, as plays by black writers are usually produced in the studios with inexperienced directors, they have little chance of breaking through the glass ceiling. Perhaps the novel liberates them – especially from the constraints of having to write for small casts and limited settings – and allows them to explore their ideas with a greater degree of complexity. Whatever the reasons, the novel – as well as the feature film – has benefited from a theatrical brain drain of black writing talent.

My own plays have met with a degree of success and have been produced within mainstream theatres such as the Royal Court Theatre Upstairs and the Royal National Theatre. When I first started to write plays I was very conscious of some kind of political agenda. I wanted to write plays where black women were the heroines and I also wanted to chart the various developments of a multicultural society. Even if I had not consciously written with this in mind, the plays when produced would, I believe, always find themselves situated within a social context that meant that they would have some political implication whatever they were about, simply because so few plays by black playwrights are produced. This fact alone means that every play by a black playwright, whether or not issues of race and identity are its subject, is weighted with the absence of other plays, the absence of other playwrights. The play becomes representative, and it could not be otherwise when there is very little to complement or contradict it. I am currently writing a play in which there is a narrative that does not centre on issues of race or identity, but I will not be surprised if, because of my choice to cast the play mainly with black actors, it is viewed as a 'black' play.

Once again, black playwrights are having to create alternative spaces in order to be heard and in the process they have started to question the very notion of the 'writer' or the 'playwright'. Many have chosen to see themselves as performers, prioritizing performance over text. Companies like Moti Roti often use the idea of visual art in their performances, undertaking 'interventions' – performances or installations that are situated within various communities in order to incite debate and reflection.

It has been said that the rise of the black comedy circuit has replaced black theatre, with comedians such as Curtis Walker appropriating the subject matter of theatre, such as questions of identity and racism. In the Nineties a group of experienced and notable black performers – Brian Bovell, Gary MacDonald, Michael Buffong, Robbie Gee, Sylvester Williams, Victor Romero Evans, Roger Griffiths and Eddie Nestor – who were performing in a documentary play about black veterans of the Second World War and the Falklands War, formed the comedy group The Posse. The group peformed topical sketches and songs and produced two full-length plays. This populist comedy drew in a large black audience and was, in the main, light entertainment, although at times there were subtle explorations of homosexuality, date rape and sexual politics in relation to the black community. The Posse was soon joined by the Bibi Crew, a group of women performers who also used the comedy sketch show to explore various current topics. If black theatre has not yet been properly integrated into the mainstream, then black comedy and comedians, such as Gina Yashere, Curtis Walker and Angie Le Mar, have succeeded, simply by dint of creating their own mainstream.

The collaboration between performer, director and writer is the lifeblood of the theatre. In the case of black theatre practitioners, the wealth of talented performers is highly visible. However, there is a lack of material to accommodate that talent. Alby James, erstwhile artistic director of the now defunct Temba Theatre, went on to establish a programme of workshops for a handpicked group of new playwrights. It is only by interventions such as this that black playwrights will receive the 'nurturing' (a word that is overused in theatre but which suggests some acknowledgement that playwrights are both born *and* made) that will enable them to build writing careers. Taking part in these workshops are writers such as Jenny Davies and Dona Daley, whose first play *Weathering the Storm*, a love story set during the 'Windrush era', was produced by the West Yorkshire Playhouse in 1997.

As the twentieth century comes to its end, I have been attending conferences where black theatre practitioners have been expressing their frustrations at the continued lack of opportunity or equality for black artists. The demise of so many of the black theatre companies is often cited as proof of the depression of the current scene. However, many of the artistic directors of those companies are still working in theatre: Denise Wong, former artistic director of Black Mime Theatre, is based at Birmingham Rep, for example. It is important that black directors penetrate the mainstream. It is only their presence there that may change the artistic decisions made by theatre managers, who can cite the lack of interest on the part of their directors for the absence of work by black artists. Many black playwrights remain committed to writing for the theatre despite the odds – among them 'Biyi Bandele, Jenny McCleod, Roy Williams, Bonnie Greer and myself.

The new millennium may witness the maturing and development of such artists and the presentation of their works on the main stages of the British theatre. As theatre is a microcosm of its society, and truthfully reflects what is happening therein, when this starts to happen then Britain's multicultural society will begin to come of age.

3

SIMON RUSSELL BEALE

A Good Investment

Simon Russell Beale began his acting career at the Traverse Theatre, Edinburgh. He has spent many seasons with the Royal Shakespeare Company, playing a range of leading parts from Ariel, Edgar and Richard III to Konstantin in The Seagull, *Lord Are in Edward Bond's* Restoration, *Oswald in* Ghosts *and Marlowe's* Edward II. *His leading roles for the Royal National Theatre include Mosca in* Volpone, *Guildenstern in* Rosencrantz and Guildenstern Are Dead *and Iago. As well as performing a great deal on the radio, he has also made several notable appearances on television, including Widmerpool in* A Dance to the Music of Time.

IN 1998 I DID A LONG TOUR of *Othello*. The Royal National Theatre production visited Austria, Poland, Japan, South Korea, China, New Zealand, Australia and the United States of America. I mention this not only because it was an exhilarating experience but also because touring a Shakespeare play around the world raises a number of questions about the nature of our work in Britain.

Our hosts, needless to say, were invariably generous and enthusiastic. But, of course, they were not uncritical. Whether they were vociferous New York schoolchildren, serious Shanghai drama students, super-sophisticated diplomats and businessmen based in Tokyo or festival-hardened Australians, they understood us to be representing, however inadequately, a great tradition, and reserved the right to judge us by the very highest standards.

Tradition is a dangerous word. I have worked for most of my professional life at the Royal Shakespeare Company and the Royal National
Theatre, both companies with a proud sense of their own history. Any
actor taking on any role in any Shakespeare production at Stratford or on
the South Bank invites comparison with actors of the past. This happens
whether he or she likes it or not, and no actor can avoid acquiring some
knowledge of how earlier productions looked and sounded. I never saw
Olivier on stage but I have an acute sense of what sort of performer he was.
On the rehearsal room floor this vague sense of following in great footsteps
is something I find very exciting. It keeps me on my toes. I hope it stops
my being arrogant, while providing me with a quite specific set of challenges.
The weight of tradition becomes an obstacle to good work only when certain
performances are perceived to be, in some way, canonical, or when one's
own performance becomes predominantly an essay on the work of previous
actors. Otherwise, our awareness of the history of our work serving as a
reminder of its great worth can only be a good thing.

This is, of course, sentimental, though not irrelevant. A sense of
tradition has a practical value, since watching and working with older
and more experienced actors is supremely important.

The formal training of an actor is necessarily an inexact science.
Unlike classical singers and dancers, there is no all-embracing method
that an actor can use to construct a technique. I first became aware of the
excitement and value of watching another actor work during rehearsals of
my first professional Shakespeare production. I had left university with
a fairly rigid and puritanical view of how Shakespeare should be done:
clarity was all-important, any hint of overt emotion was a sign of self-
indulgence. I guess I am still a bit of a puritan but I remember being bowled
over by one particular performance, which was, quite simply, operatic.
Gillian Barge, playing Paulina in *The Winter's Tale*, showed me that an
actor can be expansive and true, natural and rhetorical.

Over eight years at the RSC I learnt, even if it was only subconsciously,
from many others – from watching Alec McCowen's cool precision or
John Wood's intellectual excitement or Susan Fleetwood's rigorous lack of
sentimentality. In consequence, I firmly believe that young actors must
be given the chance, if they wish, to develop slowly yet freely within the
relatively safe environment of a secure yet experimental company.

Perhaps we could learn from Eastern Europe. During the tour of *Othello* I was invited to watch a performance of *Uncle Vanya* in Warsaw. The shabby studio theatre where I saw the play was a part of the huge Ministry of Culture building that I believe was a gift from Stalin to the city. The cast were, I think, members of the Polish National Theatre. Despite production values that we in Britain would have found woefully inadequate, the presentation of a bored, enclosed and desperately unhappy community was absolutely watertight. The actors had no need of anything beyond their own imaginative skills and their obvious belief in the project. I had the impression that this was a very recently developed production, but when I returned to London a friend told me that he had seen the same show a few years previously. I should have guessed. The performances all had an ease and a quiet confidence that could only have come from a long period of careful work. To achieve such effortlessness an actor needs time – as the members of the Maly Theatre of St Petersburg also proved on their visit to London in 1998, when they brought an adaptation of Dostoyevsky's *The Possessed*, which they had rehearsed for three years and that has stayed in their repertoire for nearly a decade.

The idea of tradition can also be perverted. As we saw in the Eighties, our theatrical tradition, seen as part of a necessarily vague idea of a national cultural heritage, was a potentially worrying idea. I joined the RSC in the mid-Eighties, at a time when a fiercely successful Conservative Party was in the middle of its time in office. As is now recognized, the attitude of that Tory government to the arts in general and the theatre in particular was, even at its best, careless. Theatre, especially Shakespeare productions, seemed to be regarded either as vaguely interesting museum pieces that represented past glories, or glamorous adjuncts to big business – an attitude that assumed that the best productions should be slickly presented and pose no threatening arguments.

This led, inevitably, to the rise of the star designers – or, rather, of star designs. To be perfectly honest, I feel that theatre designers have been unfairly branded as representative of a cynical, style-led theatre in the Eighties. Of course mistakes were made, and certainly actors often felt relatively powerless in the face of designs that had to be finalized before rehearsals had even started. But, equally well, I remember the excitement of going to the English National Opera and seeing designs that were not only beautiful but set out deliberately to challenge preconceptions. I feel also that there is a place for luxurious theatre. Matthew Warchus's production at the National of Ben Jonson's *Volpone* (a play concerned primarily with the power of money) revelled in its conspicuous consumption, but both designer and director never forgot that the design was successful only if it underlined the playwright's severely moralistic argument.

Richard Hudson's costumes for *Volpone* were made, for the most part, from rich and no doubt expensive fabrics that nevertheless, through the use of dark colours and elegant cut, presented a surface sobriety – a type of sartorial hypocrisy perhaps. His set developed from an accurate understanding of the play as a type of farce, where quick exits and entrances were essential. He built a series of small rooms that revolved on the Olivier stage and successfully reduced a huge acting area to a manageable size. It seemed to me a confident, sensitive and highly successful design.

There is no denying, though, that there was pressure on the classical companies during the Eighties to produce safe theatre. The reaction of those who worked in the classical theatre was twofold.

Firstly, they insisted absolutely that productions of classical plays were a chance for rediscovery and that dramatic techniques should never be allowed to stagnate. Secondly, and more pragmatically, that if we were part of the business life of this country, our contributions should be rewarded financially by greater initial investment. The economic argument has been well-rehearsed and, one hopes, won. However, the effect of constant worry about our economic and artistic worth was that every practitioner in theatre felt defensive. It always felt better to play safe. Only in the last few years have people working in theatre become simply unapologetic about their role.

That is what we should take with us into a new century dominated by electronic media: a confidence that theatre, regardless of its wide-ranging effect on television and film, is valuable in itself. Live performance can only become more important, because it has no satisfying substitute. And its role in the health and vitality of any world-class city is undeniable. A moderately sophisticated New Yorker would find it astonishing that there was ever any doubt about that.

I realize that, up to this point, I have been writing with Shakespeare productions foremost in my mind. This is, I suppose, inevitable, given the companies I have worked with and the productions I have done. Inevitable, too, in that his writing remains still the most demanding and ultimately satisfying for actor and director. This seems to be recognized all over the world. One of the most acute impressions resulting from the tour of *Othello* is that Shakespeare really is a global writer – a focus for debate and experiment for practitioners in many different types of theatre. That is why his work cannot be presented as part of an English theatre package without faint embarrassment, but why, equally, British actors feel privileged to know that his plays are a central component of a flexible national tradition.

Access to Shakespeare productions across the world will become easier, of course, and opportunities for the exchange of ideas greater. Seeing a scene from *Macbeth* played by two stars of the Beijing Opera is a forcible reminder that, however hard one tried and even if one wanted to, Shakespeare has grown too big and has proved too hospitable to be seen solely as a playwright of his own time and place. It would be marvellous, though, to capitalize on the fact that Shakespeare was, we think, born in England and wrote, we know, in English and establish in London or Stratford a centre for the study of his work by practitioners of all nationalities and in all media disciplines. After all, academics have the Shakespeare Institute and the Shakespeare Centre and other specialists have the Globe Theatre. Why not pool our resources and create something really grand?

Shakespeare's plays have also provided a focus for the challenge that theatre in Britain now exists in a multiracial, multicultural environment. In my first two years at the RSC, the casting of a black actor in a classical role (Hugh Quarshie as Banquo, for example) was still regarded as something unusual and provoked, extraordinarily enough, outraged reaction in some members of the audience. That situation has now happily begun to change. We are not yet colour-blind, but practitioners and audiences are heading in the right direction. Again, my involvement in *Othello* has taught me a great deal about the problems facing black actors in Britain. I talked long and hard with David Harewood, who played the title role, about the peculiar demands made of him in a predominantly white theatre. Even his unquestioned talent cannot necessarily ensure his sense of ease, and although the battle to include black actors in mainstream theatrical productions was fought by older actors than him, a subtler process is now at work. I hope I will not be accused of putting words into his mouth, but I sense in him a desire to use his knowledge of black history and his understanding of black culture as an active component of his work. In fact, David dislikes the term 'colour-blind', which I used earlier, since it implies an absolute, inevitably white, standard that should be followed by actors of whatever colour. As he says, 'I don't want you to ignore my colour; I am asking you to look at it.' In other words, mere assimilation is not enough. Black theatre companies have, of course, been exploring the relationship between different and equal traditions for many years now. They have shown that if care and respect are exercised in the process of casting, rehearsal and performance a new and rich world of theatre is possible. I hope that mainstream classical theatre is strong enough to welcome the exhilarating challenge posed by their work. In a multiracial Britain we must have a genuinely multi-racial theatre.

Shakespeare provides us with a perfect bedrock for this type of exploration and experiment, not only because his plays are so adaptable, but also, paradoxically, because he is too big a writer not to make precise demands of his actors. There *are* rules to be obeyed, although they are few and simple. One of the problems facing British actors who no longer enjoy a huge network of well-financed repertory theatres is how to learn those rules and where to practise. Repertory theatres can no longer afford to put on a good number of plays with large casts, and although useful work by groups like Cheek By Jowl provided younger actors with good experience under a great director like Declan Donnellan, the main burden of training has fallen on the two big national companies. This means, inevitably, that it is not easy for any actor to exercise their right to fail. In this context, the development of workshops like the Studio at the National, where the process is ultimately more important than any final product, is essential. (It is also essential that a young actor willing to put in the time to learn properly and good enough to be regarded as a healthy investment, should be given a decent salary.)

What is exciting (and it's an obvious thing to say, I know) is that learning never stops. The demands of theatre audiences used to the natural-ism of television and film, for instance, have to be met not necessarily by imitation but by a careful and constant review of the way we present poetic or rhetorical drama. Production values, too, have been affected by what we all see in the cinema.

What should never change is a confidence in the value of a vigorous tradition of presenting Shakespeare and other difficult and demanding writers. One of the benefits of using Shakespeare as a benchmark in any debate about theatrical technique is that the incalculable influence of his writing is evident in the work of later naturalistic and non-naturalistic playwrights. A knowledge of how Shakespeare's language works helps any actor in a direct way with the plays of poetic writers like Samuel Beckett, Howard Barker or Frank McGuinness. Equally, the precision that his plays demand exercises intellectual muscles needed in more naturalistic theatre – the plays of Chekhov, Ibsen or David Hare, for example. Acting in Shakespeare's plays creates confidence. And that confidence is best encouraged, it seems to me, by a careful cultivation of the company ethos. Unfortunately, just as actors need time and space to develop, companies, whether big or small, need money. One can only hope that people will realize what a good investment they are.

4

CLEO SYLVESTRE

'Fucking Shakespeare – Fucking Marvellous!'

Cleo Sylvestre made her West End debut in Simon Gray's Wise Child *at Wyndham's Theatre, then joined the National Theatre to play Nurse Norton in Peter Nichols'* The National Health *while simultaneously appearing in the TV soap* Crossroads. *She spent three years at the Young Vic, becoming a member of the Board in 1991. She has worked on TV, radio and in regional theatres throughout Britain. In 1999 she acted in an episode of* Tube Tales, *directed by Jude Law, and in* Three, *a short film directed by Isaac Julien. A Board member of the Freeform Arts Trust and a judge for RIMA Awards and Plays on Stage, Cleo Sylvestre is also co-director of The Rosemary Branch theatre in Islington, north London.*

DURING THE EARLY DAYS of the Young Vic there was a thriving street market in The Cut, where the theatre is based. Those of us in the company would patronize the stalls, regularly buying our fruit and vegetables from the barrow boys. One day, while I was selecting a cauliflower during my lunchtime break from rehearsals, the stallholder said: ''Ere Cleo, what sort of things do you do in that theatre?' So I told him – Shakespeare, plays for young children in the studio, and modern plays. Something for everyone, in fact. 'Why don't you come along sometime?' I asked. He looked at me somewhat quizzically and, having been brought up on a council estate near Euston, I recognized that familiar sign of 'Not for the likes of me.'

A couple of weeks passed and one evening after the show (*Othello*) I was 'unwinding' along with the rest of the cast in our local pub, the Windmill. There was a tap on my shoulder. It was the cauliflower seller. ''Ere Cleo, just been to see the show. Fucking Shakespeare – fucking marvellous!' From then on he was a regular visitor at the Young Vic. The power, magic and language of the theatre had gained yet another supporter.

Nowadays the street market has all but disappeared and the opportunity to communicate with a checkout person in a busy supermarket, above the incessant pinging and ponging of the electronic scanners and tills, rarely exists. As we hasten towards the millennium with our mobile phones, digital TVs, PCs, websites, modems and mouses (or is it mice?), when we can, at the push of a button or flick of a switch, be connected to almost any part of the world, are we nevertheless losing the ability to communicate on a more personal level? Communication, after all, is one of the key words of the theatre. Yet, even as an optimist by nature (either that or plain foolish to still be a jobbing actress after all these years), I do sometimes feel that we actors are in the process of becoming an endangered species. Radical steps must be taken if we are not to die out completely.

At the risk of stating the obvious, none of us actors, playwrights, directors, designers, technicians and producers have a future in theatre unless we have an audience and keep it. Alas, perhaps now even more than ever, there is a huge divide between those for whom theatregoing is an integral part of their life, i.e. a necessity and a ritual, and those for whom it is a luxury and a choice. The universal appeal of the theatre means that it can be appreciated, enjoyed and experienced by prince and pauper alike, but in today's climate, for many, theatre has to take a back seat. What 'choice' do senior citizens living solely on a state pension have, between saving up to pay their gas, electric or phone bill or buying a decent seat to see a show, albeit at a concession? Do I, as a widowed mother of three on a limited income, buy tickets to a play or purchase a new pair of trainers for one of my children? And what about the audiences of tomorrow?

Given that drama is no longer part of the school curriculum, it follows that countless children are being denied their baptism into the theatre. Why waste valuable time performing or watching plays when there are league tables to consider? Schoolchildren all over Britain are encouraged to use and relate to computers but are denied the magic, visual and emotional stimulation – not to mention spiritual enhancement – that theatre can bring. Thus it follows that unless a child is from a theatregoing household it will have precious little way of gaining access to it. There is no place on pie charts or graphs for recording quality of life, even though more and more children are facing the prospect of never having regular or full-time employment when they leave school. How do we wean tomorrow's audience off Game Boys and computers? Are we approaching a situation where the physical act of theatregoing becomes redundant?

Banking, shopping and research are just three of the huge range of activities that can be carried out from the confines of one's home using a PC, so why not a trip to the theatre? Surfing the net, hey presto! 'Which theatre shall I visit?' Click. 'Adelphi, Apollo, Arts . . . I think I fancy – here it is – the Old Vic.' Click. 'Now then, what play?' Click. 'Mmm, I've always regretted not having seen *The Entertainer*. Here it is.' Click. 'Just like *Armchair Theatre* used to be.'

Synonymous with the name of the late, much-lamented television producer Sydney Newman, *Armchair Theatre* was devised to put plays on television and nurtured a whole generation of actors, playwrights, directors and technicians during the late Fifties and early Sixties. These were exciting times indeed. Those involved in the arts were encouraged to be experimental and stretch their creativity. Theatre was still very popular despite competition from the relatively new medium of television and the relationship between the two was symbiotic. It could still be so if we did not live in an environment dominated by market forces and those who seem hell-bent on force-feeding the public a cultural diet akin to fast food. Tell them so often that that's what they want and in time they'll come to believe it.

Assuming the theatre is going to survive in the twenty-first century, where is the next generation of actors going to come from? Training is costly and local authorities are more and more reluctant to award grants, so unless students have families wealthy enough to pay their fees and maintenance they will have to get a well-paid job in order to survive. How many incipient Barrie Rutters or Sheila Hancocks will the theatre lose if this discrimination is allowed to continue? No doubt the powers that be will say: 'Use some initiative – go and get some individual sponsorship.' But when the multinationals have no compunction about exploiting the earth's resources and manufacturing goods that are frequently of no value to one's physical or spiritual well-being, are they likely to be altruistic and sponsor a penniless drama student without demanding that they prostitute their artistic integrity? We have become acclimatized to watching sponsored stage and television productions and, more often than not, seeing the corporation's name or logo cropping up at every available opportunity. So we can have *Hamlet* sponsored by a tobacco company, *A Doll's House* courtesy of a toy shop, *Hay Fever* in conjunction with a drug company. Why not? For centuries drama and all the arts have relied on patronage and the show 'must go on' – but at what cost?

So what does the future hold when you've finished your training? Not much chance today of being fortunate enough to spend a few months in a repertory company with a regular group of actors putting on a different play every two to three weeks, grappling with a huge range of parts, some of which you'll shine in, and the others – well, the less said the better – getting to know the theatre's usual patrons, learning to live with nylon sheets in the digs that you've booked into, or familiarizing yourself with the town in which you're playing. Working in rep was not always a bed of roses but it was stimulating, uplifting and exciting. It gave the actors a chance to experiment, to utilize the hours spent on voice work and learning stagecraft and then, night after night, to discover fresh insights into their role or the play they are performing.

For me, one of the most appealing things about acting is that it is organic and in a constant state of flux. What is it that happens to a play or the performers that can transform a piece overnight from the merely good to the sublime? Is it the audience, the actors or what? Fortunately I don't think we will ever know, and that is the sheer magic of theatre and acting.

So many reps have disappeared over the past few years and the tendency for most of those that remain is to employ actors on short-term contracts; or they get in soap stars in a bid to attract a new audience. The soap star phenomenon in theatres is a relatively new one. Not so long ago actors were reluctant to appear in soaps as they felt this might have an adverse effect on their stage careers. Indeed, many theatre directors and producers were loath to even consider employing someone whose soap appearances had made them a household name, fearing that the public would not take them seriously on stage. Not any longer. As theatres struggle to keep their heads above water, soap stars are lining up to throw them a Mae West. So where does this leave the jobbing actor who would usually be playing these parts? Probably down at the local Job Centre signing on and trying to prove that they are 'actively' looking for work.

Fringe theatre has managed to perform a dual function for the actor. For established actors, earning a living mainly from television or film, it provides the opportunity to stretch themselves and to work with new writers and directors, knowing that they can still pay the mortgage thanks to their earnings from the media. To the jobbing actor, fringe work offers the same artistic opportunities with the potential bonus of maybe, just maybe, being 'seen' by that well-known TV director or casting director – and being offered *the* job or part they've been waiting for.

Financially, though, the jobbing actor has a lot to contend with. When rehearsing for a fringe play, JSA (Job Seeker's Allowance) can no longer be claimed since technically the actor is not available for work. Yet the actor *is* working and in his or her *chosen* profession – and this becomes a 'Catch 22' scenario since the actor is not usually being paid as there either is no money or very little money around. This is difficult to explain to the bureaucrats, whose brief seems to be to get everyone off JSA and retrained so that maybe, one day, they will earn a regular wage. How many middle-aged actors have had to turn down an offer of work on the fringe because they have been forced onto a ReStart course to train as computer operators, telephonists, retail salespeople or whatever when they have very little chance of finding jobs in those areas and it's not what they want to do anyway?

The young jobbing actor suffers a similar fate at the Job Centre, and it is now becoming more and more difficult for them to get any stage experience at all so long as the fringe door is constantly slammed shut. Some of the most innovative and exciting work of recent years has originated on the fringe, which is also responsible for reaching out to a brand new and uninitiated audience.

To those who view actors as spongers or work-shy, fringe theatre provides a prime example of our dedication. We frequently find ourselves working under adverse conditions, rehearsing in cold, damp rooms, trying to learn lines and research the character we are playing and, possibly, doing some outside temporary work just to pay the bills. Obviously, if an actor has a family then the problems are greatly increased. Who will look after the pre-school child? And there is usually no *financial* incentive to appear on the fringe. It truly is a labour of love.

Profit-share is a phrase familiar to those of us who work or have worked on the fringe.

The phone rings:

'Hello. Can I speak to Cleo Sylvestre?'

'Speaking.'

'Oh, hello, you don't know me but I was given your number by X. I believe you've worked together?'

'Yes, that's right.'

'Well, I'm a director and I've got this very exciting new script which I'm putting on at the Lady Hamilton in Deptford. It's a relatively modern fringe venue. Do you know it?'

'Can't say that I do.'

'Anyway, there's a part which I would very much like you to consider playing, if you're available, and like it, of course. It's a profit-share production so I'm afraid there's no money in it to speak of, but we can give you £10 a week towards travel expenses. If there's any money left over after we've paid the venue and production costs then you'll have a share of it. It should do well, the writer attracted a lot of attention with his first play, so the critics are bound to review it. Would you like to read it and then perhaps we can meet up?'

The subtext to this scenario, however, would read something like this:

'Exciting new script': Still in development and to be worked on and improved by the actors during rehearsals.

'The Lady Hamilton in Deptford': A back-street pub, nowhere near the Underground and a good twenty minutes' walk from the bus stop, in an area where you wouldn't want to linger late at night.

'A relatively modern fringe venue': There is a separate loo for the actors so they don't have to wander through the pub in costume if they get caught short.

'A part which I would very much like you to consider playing': I really wanted Whoopi Goldberg but she's busy filming and probably wouldn't consider doing a fringe play anyway.

'It's a profit-share production': Can you afford to subsidize yourself for a four-week rehearsal period and a three-week run? Because by the time we've rented the venue, paid for posters, props, set, etc. there's unlikely to be any money left to split between the cast of five, the director, stage manager, designer, writer and lighting designer.

'The critics are bound to review it': Dream on! What critic from the national papers is going to have the time or inclination to schlep to some obscure venue to review an experimental production instead of going to a glitzy First Night in the West End? Well, yes, it does happen, but not too often.

So what does the future hold for the fringe? Having been involved in the running of a fringe venue for eighteen months I feel that it can and should be able to survive, especially as this type of theatre has always been prepared to take risks and can offer innovative and exciting work to new and often uninitiated audiences. Unfortunately, in all too many pub theatres there is a distinct 'us and them' feeling. Actors and audiences are frequently given the cold shoulder by the landlord and the locals, yet there is no reason why we cannot all co-exist. Many pubs are struggling to compete with the video and television culture, so you would think that they'd welcome whatever extra custom, however small, the theatre brings in. And the breweries could help by charging a peppercorn rent until the theatre is in profit, and then they could calculate a more realistic figure, perhaps percentage-based. The news that many breweries are converting their theatre spaces into hostel accommodation doesn't bode well. Some actors make a notable 'contribution' to the brewing industry – so you might think they'd get something back in return.

If fringe theatres with similar objectives but in different areas could link together it would help cut the cost of productions. For example, three similar-sized venues, well distanced from one another, could each mount a production which then rotated to the other two. This carousel would mean that actors would benefit from a nine-week instead of a three-week run, audiences could choose the venue that was most convenient for them, and the theatre would only have to meet the costs of one production. Furthermore, the critics might be more inclined to review a production with a longer shelf-life. In essence, the future of the fringe lies in our own sheer determination to make it survive.

For any form of theatre work, auditioning always plays a major part in the jobbing actor's life. Over the past few years, however, things have taken a dramatic turn. Directors are no longer very keen on listening to set audition pieces, but usually prefer to work with the actor on a section of the play in question. This is a turn for the better. But even bigger changes are happening. Some months ago my agent rang:

> 'Cleo? It's Elaine. Now, please don't take offence, but I've just had a very strange enquiry from Theatre Y [a well-known mainstream London venue]. I don't like to ask, but have you got a criminal record?'

> 'No, not that I can think of. Why?'

> 'Well, they're thinking of you for a new play they're about to do and just wanted to know.'

> 'Sorry, Elaine, I guess I'll have to miss out on that one.'

A few days passed and she rang again:

> 'Cleo, they've been back on the phone about the play at Y. Haven't you even had a driving offence?'

It turned out that they were casting the part of a criminal and they could only get funding if they employed someone with a record. So much for acting.

More and more the ordinary actor is being superseded by the personality. Sports celebrities, pop stars, politicians – you name them – they're all there treading the boards, monotonously reading their memoirs on the radio, presenting TV shows, doing all those jobs that formerly went to dedicated actors.

All is not lost, however, and recently there has been a welcome area of growth for some actors. Many businesses, hospitals and local government offices now use actors for role-playing as part of their training programmes. We may be called upon to be aggressive, to react to bad news or to be the victims of racism or sexism – whatever scenario is required. Whilst obviously not the same as acting in a play, nevertheless role-playing may be of great value to the actor and of even greater benefit to the recipient. As the scenarios are not normally scripted, it allows the actor to develop his or her improvisational skills. At the same time, it affords the client the opportunity of working with a professional who can stop in the middle of a role-play for a discussion and then pick up exactly where it broke off. For many employers and employees this can only raise the profile of acting and, ideally, win a few more supporters for the theatre and its contribution to everyday life.

Actors and acting are still not taken seriously enough in Britain. 'Ah, but if you're an actor you must expect to spend most of your time out of work,' is a comment we frequently hear. 'But why?' I find myself wondering. Some of the poorer countries – such as Romania or Mexico – encourage and support the arts and realize the valuable contribution its practitioners make to the cultural, spiritual and even economic well-being of the country.

If the people won't go to the theatre, then make the theatre go to the people. There has been a mushrooming of faceless, bland and antiseptic shopping malls/arcades/precincts since the beginning of the Eighties. These mind-boggling tributes to featureless municipal architecture, assaulting the senses with their interminable Muzak, plastic plants and identical shops – no matter which town or city you are in – have a lot to answer for. They are helping to sound the death knell for the theatre and should carry a government health warning. Why can't they have live musicians playing, or actors, jugglers and acrobats providing entertainment instead of the ubiquitous inflatable bunnies at Easter and, humiliation of humiliations, actors dressed in grotesque, lurid costumes prancing around? Those responsible for such cultural violation should be sentenced to a lifetime wandering around the Lakeside Shopping Centre. The planners have missed an opportunity to bring theatre back to the market environment. The presence of performers in such bleak surroundings would humanize the place. No doubt those responsible would be tempted to exploit the themed idea but for someone with flair and imagination arcade entertainment could offer an exciting challenge as well as providing work for resting actors.

As we move closer to becoming a themed society, actors are losing out all over the place. What would an actor rather play: Shakespeare's Henry VIII or an overweight Tudor monarch masquerading as Henry VIII at a banquet laid on for Japanese and American tourists? Many have no artistic choice; they have to go for the themed pound as it's the only option available if they are to keep their financial heads above water.

Surely the day will come when bureaucrats and Government will be cured of their cultural myopia and place the arts once again at the centre of our day-to-day existence. What better way could they begin than to revive Theatre-in-Education and hand back to children all over the country their lost – or indeed stolen – dramatic birthright. Then, once more, they could experience the marriage between poetry and passion, magic and mystery, truth and trickery that theatre alone can bring.

Vast advances in technology have been made over the twentieth century, but particularly over the last few years with the use of the microchip. There is no reason why theatre should not embrace this and be enhanced by it. The odds, however, always seem stacked against the actor. This is partly because of the increased trend for casting personalities and partly because, with the exception of musicals, cast lists today rarely reach double figures. Commercial and fringe managements prefer to mount small-scale productions – understandable given that the lower the costs, the lower the loss if the show fails. This in turn encourages writers to produce work for small casts since that way it stands a greater chance of performance. And yet again the actor loses out, and if you're female, of a 'certain' age and class, and from a non-white ethnic background – forget it. Today the plum roles for women in mainstream theatre are nearly always the prerogative of the white middle class – despite all the drastic cultural changes in society over the last couple of decades.

So what has theatre to look forward to? More realization, I hope, that what it has to offer is unique. Our senses are in danger of becoming numbed by a society where brutality, lust, greed and corruption are a part of everyday life. Combine all those ingredients and put them on stage. Give me a good 'Jacobean' play any day and let's support and encourage all those actors who are 'waiting in the wings'.

5

RICHARD EYRE

Michelangelo's Snowman

Sir Richard Eyre directed his first production in Leicester in 1965. He was Associate Director at the Royal Lyceum Theatre, Edinburgh in 1967 and Director of Productions from 1970–72, and was Artistic Director at Nottingham Playhouse from 1973–78. In 1981 he became Associate Director of the National Theatre, where he has directed 27 productions, and was its Artistic Director from 1988–97. He has also directed productions for the Royal Court, the West End and Broadway, and the Royal Opera House. He has directed many films for television and was Producer of 'Play for Today' for the BBC from 1978–80. His memoir, Utopia and Other Places, *was published in 1993.*

This is an abbreviated version of the lecture given by Sir Richard Eyre as an Honorary Fellow of Goldsmiths College, inaugurating the annual Marjorie Frances Lecture in the Drama Department, Goldsmiths College, London University, on 28 November 1996.

I CAN'T BE SURE that I'm not wasting my time standing here, and I'm not entirely confident that I might not be wasting yours. Is there any point talking about theatre at all? My sympathies are with the dancer Pavlova when somebody asked her what she meant when she was dancing. 'If I could tell you,' she said, 'I wouldn't dance it.' But undaunted – and perhaps as a surrogate for doing the thing itself – we have talks, speeches, seminars, discussions, manifestos, demonstrations and petitions, which make the thing we are cherishing – the medium of theatre – seem like a small butterfly in the hands of a clumsy giant.

Recently there was a conference on the theatre hosted by the University of Texas, which holds the world's largest collection of playwrights' manuscripts. The title of the conference was 'Shouting at Night'. It claimed to be a quote from Michael Gambon in answer to the question: 'What do you do for a living?' In fact, to be pedantic, it was the answer given by the son of a fellow actor when asked by another child what his father did for his living. 'He shouts at night,' said the boy.

This ironic job description would seem to pander to the case for the prosecution advanced recently in the *Sunday Times* by a cultural policeman who regularly issues mental health warnings against the theatre. 'The trouble is,' he says, 'that actors act on stage. They grimace. They gesticulate. They strike poses. In the classic repertoire, they declaim; in modern drama they've been trained to "project" . . . Anybody spending an evening in the British theatre would be excused from thinking that "histrionic" and "hysteric" were the same thing.' This from a critic who will contentedly and uncritically consume the camp daftness of most Hollywood movies, appearing to be immune to their endemic hysteria and histrionics.

It is not hard to detect the smell of prejudice here, and all prejudices are the enemy of reason. To those who dislike the theatre there is something more at stake than mere preference for one art form over another, and I'm reluctant to get drawn into the sort of beauty contest beloved of arts editors, brandishing the superior virtues of theatre over fiction, or film, or football, or even food. For me the attraction of theatre lies in its 'theatreness' – those unique properties that make it distinct from any other medium – its use of space, of light, of speech, of music, of storytelling. Theatre always prospers under the logic of plot, and it always thrives on metaphor – a room becomes a world, a group of characters becomes a whole society. Everything about the theatre depends on the relationship of a performer to a group of spectators in the present tense. In short – it's live and it's unreproducible.

Even at its very greatest, the art of theatre is ephemeral; it lives on only in the memory, melting away after the event like a snowman. After a rare snowfall in Florence, Piero de' Medici is alleged to have commissioned Michelangelo to make a sculpture in snow: Michelangelo's

Snowman. It was said to have been his greatest work, but you had to have been there to have seen it – it was as frail, as mutable, and as vulnerable as a theatre performance.

Film is robust. The audience can make love, they can riot, they can leave the cinema, and the film will continue: the only thing that can subvert it is the failure of the projector. Theatre, on the other hand, is endemically fallible: it depends on the whole audience being willing to give their constant consent. This was painfully demonstrated for me at a matinee of *John Gabriel Borkman* at the National a few weeks ago. Paul Scofield, as Borkman, had delivered his heart-breaking final speech, a hand of iron had gripped his heart, he'd died and lay stretched out on the bench as the two sisters who had loved him all their lives – played by Eileen Atkins and Vanessa Redgrave – finally held hands after a lifetime of animosity. The two black silhouettes stood isolated against a canvas of falling snow, and as the lights started to dim to blackness in a breathless silence the voice of an old woman was heard: 'They've got a lot of clearing up to do.'

We live in an age which has become – and to some extent rightly – at best sceptical and at worst cynical of any sort of public social obligation or ceremony. A generation has been weaned on the intermittent demands of television and video games and empowered by the use of the remote control to become hanging judges, impatient with any idea that takes more than a few minutes to develop, and intolerant of space between words, of stillness, and of silence. In the cinema, that haven of solitary, dreamlike disengagement, we're wrapped in a screen that often extends beyond the angle of vision; our point of view is manipulated by moving the camera, changing the size of shot, cutting from one angle or subject to another, accompanied by sounds that surround the body and, like acupuncture, penetrate and stimulate the willingly supine brain.

Theatre, however, is all in wide shot and offers a spartan soundtrack. It maintains a stubborn dependence on plot, and looks archaic and demure when set against such contemporary obsessions as graphic design, fashion photography and body-piercing jewellery. Theatre will always be unfashionable because of its form, its need for order in narrative and in structure, and it will always appear to lag behind a society that is conspicuous for its formlessness. Theatre's concern with the frailty of being human will always look defenceless when set against the films of Arnold Schwarzenegger, or the confident certainties of politics or journalism.

To like the theatre you must always travel in hope, but you must also recognize that the 'choice' of going to the theatre – or indeed to the opera, to an art gallery – is a 'choice' that has not been offered to most people in this country. Most young people are not taken to the theatre by their parents or their schools or their colleges. Many people feel that theatregoing is not for them, they don't feel comfortable in the buildings, and if they feel anything at all about the theatre they feel disenfranchised.

The consequence of this disaffection is that the right wing urges that we stop subsidizing the arts and allow the open market to determine the future of theatre; and the left wing (if it's still a vocal element in politics) agrees with the right that the theatre is an irredeemably elitist activity, irrevocably distanced from the tastes and concerns of the working class. And the Labour Party demonstrates to us that New Labour means New Philistinism, avoiding in public any mention of the arts or culture, and in private any discussion that might lead to a policy initiative. Struggling in the middle of this political miasma we, the theatre practitioners, the evangelical utopians, defend our patch and are swept into the turbulent eddies of arguments with funding bodies whose hearts can't agree with their heads. They urge charging 'what the market will stand' for tickets, and advocate 'more developed marketing' to target the middle-class audience, while at the same time pressing for greater access and audience development.

Deprived of the power to engender real access – by reducing the price of all theatre tickets and funding education so that the arts become a genuine 'choice' – we are urged to go out and multiply, to spread our work through television. This is like urging a wine-maker to popularize the drinking of burgundy through encouraging people to drink Ribena. Any televised version of a theatre performance shot on however many cameras from the back of the auditorium could only have a virtue as an archive or as an educational tool. If a piece of taped theatre is viewed in the context of TV drama, it will always appear clumsy and undernourished. It can never be regarded as anything but a wholesale dilution of the theatrical original. This bogus 'access' can only succeed in making thousands more people doubt that a visit to the theatre is worth making.

The only hope and the only argument for theatre that can be made has to be made through the art itself, and since it is an art form that even at its crudest requires buildings, technical equipment, technicians, front of house staff, stage management, directors, writers, and above all performers, the consideration of money is one that can't be primly ignored. I'm fond of the story of Shaw visiting Sam Goldwyn in Hollywood to discuss the possibility of one of Shaw's plays being made into a film. Shaw listened for some time in silence as Goldwyn expounded on the brilliance and profundity of his play. Then he spoke: 'The problem with you, Mr Goldwyn, is that you care only for art. Whereas I care only for money.' If we want a theatre that takes artistic risks, sustains the best of tradition, develops new talent, feeds the commercial theatre, and does all this at seat prices which do not exclude all but the very rich, then we have no alternative but to seek state support. If we think all these aims are worthless, then by all means let's dispense with subsidy.

But in the end, if all the mechanics of social engineering are achieved and fine-tuned, if, as Chekhov said, 'the people are brought up to the level of Gogol, instead of Gogol brought down to the level of the people', and if the financial ecology of the theatre becomes stable, the case for the survival of theatre can only be made through the art itself. It has to live up to our propaganda for it.

I often feel like Flaubert when people start talking about the state of the theatre. He said that when the talk turned to literary topics he felt like a former convict listening to a conversation about prison reform. One of the attractions of theatre for me is how it resists theory; whatever you think, feel or say about the theatre, the only test is in performance. Even such a compulsive theoretician as Brecht conceded this: 'In the theatre,' he said, 'the proof of the pudding is in the eating.' No one expresses this better than Paul Scofield in a letter he wrote to a friend of mine who had – ever hopeful – asked him if he would do a poetry reading and talk about his work. This is what Paul wrote:

> I have found that an actor's work has life and interest only in its execution. It seems to wither away in discussion, and become emptily theoretical and insubstantial. It has no rules (except perhaps audibility). With every play and every playwright the

actor starts from scratch, as if he or she knows nothing and proceeds to learn afresh every time – growing with the relationships of the characters and the insights of the writer. When the play has finished its run he's empty until the next time. And it's the emptiness which is, I find, apparent in any discussion of theatre work.

I am tempted to take Paul's statement at face value and concede the impossibility of debating the aesthetics of an ephemeral art – to own up to the absurdity of talking about Michelangelo's Snowman – but I am too much the politician, and have been coerced in my role over the last ten years into evangelism. I am suspicious of all manifestos, and none more so than in the theatre, but unless we fight for our art it will wither. We must, I believe, make theatre which exploits the 'unreproducible' elements of theatre, which proclaims the virtues of its liveness and its uniqueness, which combines the elements of time, space, light, speech, music and story-telling; a theatre which ravishes the eyes and ears and enchants the soul. For me the best motto for a theatre practitioner is that provided, perhaps surprisingly, by Kafka: 'If theatre is to affect life, it must be stronger, more intense than ordinary life. That is the law of gravity.'

If you believe in the prevailing credo of contemporary art, then you believe that art progresses in a deterministic fashion. You must therefore believe that the theatre is an outdated art form, a skeleton clothed in the dusty costume of past grandeur. Theatre is immune to the creed of modernism, which would claim that art forms, traditions and beliefs become either 'wrong' or 'irrelevant'. In this century painting and sculpture have frequently been pronounced dead and their afterlife has been celebrated in conceptual art and in installations. The visual arts have become increasingly self-referential and increasingly the property of an audience which defines itself by its exclusivity, and which despises comprehensibility as puerile populism. I recently heard a contemporary sculptor derided by a respected commentator on contemporary art for his 'outdated humanism'.

The theatre, on the other hand, has 'progressed' over this century from the poetic realism of Chekhov's plays to the – how shall I put it? – poetic realism of David Mamet's plays. And every other 'ism' in the theatre

– naturalism, expressionism, absurdism, Brechtianism – can be found, latent or full-blown, in the plays of Shakespeare. But art doesn't progress; it evolves, and in the theatre the evolution is always, irrespective of technological advances, more an evolution of content rather than form. Theatre can never dissolve its reliance on the scale of the human figure, the sound of the human voice, and the disposition of mankind to tell each other stories.

If you ask me 'What is the future of theatre?' I have to answer that I live at the centre of a Ptolemaic solar system around which the planets revolve, and I am no more able to give you an objective picture of the theatrical universe than I am to conjugate irregular verbs in Serbo-Croat. I can tell you that there are two unarguably indispensable components in making a piece of theatre – the actor and the writer. The director (a largely twentieth-century invention) will often seek to be considered the primary creator, but however inventive, however imaginative, the creative pulse in the theatre will always be derived from the people whose souls are at stake: the writer and the actor. Directors and designers are the builders not the architects.

Real changes in the theatre have always been made by writers, the demands of their content obliging those who stage the plays – and, indeed, the musicals – to seek new modes of presentation. The people who have most significantly transformed the theatre of the twentieth century are Chekhov and Brecht, and Rodgers and Hammerstein, and to me it is transparently obvious that if the theatre is to keep moving forward what is most urgently required now is the motor of another playwright – or composer – of genius. Money helps to fuel the vehicle, but money alone never produced any art worth having. 'Artists,' said Gorky, 'can't be forced like rhubarb.'

One can't legislate for talent; it is inequitable and unpredictable. It's a commonplace to observe that the theatrical landscape of the US is a wasteland, and yet out of this desert have emerged the most gifted writers of the English-speaking world of the last fifteen years: David Mamet and Tony Kushner. If God plays dice with the universe nowhere is it more apparent than in the distribution of talent; all that money can do to help is allow it to breathe, be educated, be trained, be exercised, be recognized and be enjoyed.

All theatre has a tendency to decline to the condition of trivia – ephemeral, impermanent, frivolous. Every now and then someone comes along and shakes up that notion – in the seventeenth century it was Shakespeare, Jonson and Molière; in the nineteenth it was Goethe, Schiller and the Duke of Meiningen; in the early twentieth century we had Ibsen, Chekhov, Stanislavsky and Nemirovich-Danchenko, Meyerhold, Brecht, Shaw and Granville Barker; and in the late Fifties and early Sixties we had Joan Littlewood, George Devine and, in recent years, Peter Brook in Stratford and in Paris. All of them demonstrated, implicitly or explicitly, the notion that the theatre was an art, a forum, a faith, something to be fought for. At the Royal Court George Devine engendered a system of values that gave the theatre of his time a goal: to be 'about something', to be ambitious for the work before the career, and to be unsanctimoniously unembarrassed about being serious – in short, he taught self-respect.

If it can be said that sexual intercourse began in 1963, it can as plausibly be said that modern British theatre started with the production of *Look Back in Anger* in 1956. It is only possible to understand the essential and sensationally liberating effect of John Osborne's play by understanding how, as Arthur Miller said at the time, the British theatre was 'hermetically sealed off from life' – and from the American theatre. The arrival of *Look Back in Anger* ushered in a whole generation of playwrights who felt encouraged to take the theatre seriously and felt licensed to allow their plays to reflect the life that they observed around them.

From my Ptolemaic observatory I'm encouraged to feel that the genetic link from John Osborne remains unbroken: the DNA chain links Osborne to Arnold Wesker to Edward Bond to Tom Stoppard to Peter Shaffer to Harold Pinter to Charles Wood to Peter Nichols to Alan Bennett to Alan Ayckbourn to Trevor Griffiths to Christopher Hampton to David Edgar to Caryl Churchill to David Hare to a new generation of writers who carry little ideological baggage and no allegiances to any school of playwriting, past or present. Many of the older generation of writers not only continue to write new plays, but they defy the conventional graph of a playwright's progress, ascending rather than declining. They connect with a group of writers who are young, ambitious and cocky, and keen to repudiate the notion of the theatre as dull, demure and unpopular. To name four who have had conspicuous success: Jonathan Harvey,

Jez Butterworth, Patrick Marber and Martin McDonagh. Their attitude
to the theatre – half sceptical, half opportunistic – can be summed up by
what Martin McDonagh said when I asked him why he wanted to write
for the theatre: 'I wanted to write the sort of plays that I'd like to see in a
theatre, if I wanted to go to one.'

This profusion of new writing is a phenomenon unknown in the
rest of Europe, where the creative motor is provided by the director, and
the writer is generally a functionary of the directorial conceit – in both
senses of the word. In Eastern Europe the theatre enjoyed – if that's
not too painful a description – an extraordinarily potent life under the
Communist regime. Theatres were well funded and although the repertoire was severely restricted, and imaginative new plays virtually unknown,
classical plays became the vessels of dissent; allegory became a political device.
But that form of carrying messages, and the power that it displayed, born
out of the repression, became envied and mimicked by directors in the rest
of Europe. It's a habit of mind now amongst European directors and
designers to see every text of whatever origin as an opportunity to display feats of design and *mise en scène*, the writers' intentions becoming
barely discernible through a fog of expressionism.

When I took my production of *Richard III* to Germany I was
surprised that the production, which had been regarded as an example of
'directors' theatre' by some British critics, was seen as revolutionary. 'It
put the actors at the centre,' said the German critics. Of course there are
brilliant exceptions to my generalizations: Peter Stein, Lev Dodin and
Giorgio Strehler are three of them. All autocrats, they seek to enfranchise
the actor even if they prefer the writer to be inconspicuous or, preferably,
dead. When I directed a play of Eduardo de Filippo a few years ago, I said
to his widow, Isabella, that I had heard that Strehler's production of the
play had been brilliant. 'Brilliant, yes,' she said, 'but it was no longer
Eduardo's play.'

Of course it's possible to argue that Strehler had improved de Filippo's
play and I sometimes think that in this country a proper respect for the
writer and the text becomes a charter for unimaginative direction and
inanimate performance. It's an often repeated story, at least by directors,
that John Dexter said to Arnold Wesker when directing a play of his, 'Oh
do shut up, Arnold, or I'll direct this play the way you wrote it, then we'll

all be in trouble.' When I directed the same de Filippo play, Isabella remarked about a particular passage (to which the audience responded enthusiastically): 'I don't know if that is right, Richard. You see, Eduardo was not an expressionist, he was a Sicilian.' It's a moot point. I believe there should be a collaboration, a dialectic between parties that are not altogether equal: the writer has initiated and created the work, the director is realizing it, not redesigning it.

There's not a director alive that doesn't have a (perhaps necessary) streak of immodesty in him or her, a desire to be the auteur of the event. In Britain we have seen the classical canon, particularly the plays of Shakespeare, recycled and re-examined for the last thirty years. But what started as an endeavour to reclaim a repertoire largely lost to us has become a spiral of repetition, and the spiral is a diminishing one; big theatres demand big audiences to preserve their financial ecology, and ever more frequent productions of the small number of always popular Shakespeare plays become necessary. The fabric starts to wear thin from over-use: the director's imagination gets stale, the audience's enthusiasm dwindles.

However, from my astronomer's perch I'm encouraged by the obvious appetite and talent of a number of young directors who are more interested in developing their abilities than furthering their careers, even if I find the determination of some of them to eschew new writing short-sighted and sanctimonious. There is much talk of 'site-specific' work, and 'finding new spaces', spoken with the born-again zeal of the artist who believes that art is re-animated by changing the frame of the picture rather than the content. 'Create new forms of expression!' is the cry of the century, but, for me, what's new in art always lies in the subject matter and in the intensification of forms which are already in existence. In the theatre that subject matter will inevitably be preoccupied with the fate of human relationships.

In the last ten years I have been most encouraged and inspired most by the work of Tony Kushner and of Robert Lepage. What they have in common is this: they are eclectic, inventive and stylistically daring, but their style is always determined not by cross-referencing to fashion or other art forms but by the stories they want to tell. They both attempt, like the best art, to make sense of the world. The first half of Tony Kushner's play *Angels in America* is subtitled *The Millennium Approaches*, and that's what it's about: the lurking fascism in US politics, the effects of the death of Communism, the rise of fundamentalist religions, the spread of Aids, the cancer of racism; death, hope, fear, love. Its unpredictable poetry slaloms between expressionism and naturalism, visionary wit merges with ardent polemic, acute pain rubs shoulders with genial farce.

Robert Lepage is similarly unafraid of large subjects. His recent show *The Seven Streams of the River Ota* embraced Hiroshima, the Holocaust and Aids, and contrived to do so with a humane wit and a beguiling grace. An amazing number of theatrical and filmic devices were combined alchemically with no sense of ostentation; the stylistic vocabulary of film, video, ballet, sitcom, Shakespeare and Japanese theatre, made a syntax accessible to a generation weaned on the remote control, the rock video and TV naturalism, but was always at the service of the telling of the story.

I always feel optimistic when I look at Robert's work, and when I talk to him about the theatre. He is confident of creating theatre which can have meaning for a new generation, and if he is pessimistic about an art form, it is film rather than theatre. He said this to me recently:

> In the next four or five years we'll be amazed how theatre and film will have to live together, because film cannot continue in the form it is, in the way it's presented. People want direct life, three-dimensional interaction, and that's something that belongs to the theatre. Our field of work is telling stories and if we want to be exciting theatre storytellers we have to be interested in film, television and novels, because those forms of storytelling are changing how we tell stories. You have to have the humility to say, 'This subject deserves this, or this,' not try to imprison it or stifle it because you have a style, a way of doing things.

It's this openness and eclecticism that I find so liberating. In the middle of *Seven Streams*, following a succession of scenes where the space, and the time, seamlessly expands and contracts, there is a scene in a room in Amsterdam played in real time, entirely naturalistically; the euthanasia of a man infected with Aids. It is immensely simple, immensely touching, and is no less 'theatrical' than the cascade of visual images and surrealistic scenes that have preceded it.

In the theatre we must use what is necessary to say what we want to say; there should be no hierarchy of form. David Hare's *Skylight*, a two-and-a-half hour play set in real time in one location, can be as potent as a seven-hour play that moves from Hiroshima to New York and from wartime to the present day. Both use the theatre to tell stories that have power, resonance and relevance to the way we live our lives. As long as the theatre has the desire and ability to do that – to entertain as much as enlarge the imagination – I won't mourn for its decline, or feel that we are failing to solve the question: 'What direction does the theatre go in?'

Picasso, who had an answer to most things, had the answer to this. He told a friend that Giacometti's work was becoming increasingly monotonous and repetitive. The friend defended Giacometti, talking of his intense desire to 'find a new solution to the problem of figuration.' 'There isn't a solution,' said Picasso. 'There never is a solution. That's as it should be.'

6

KATIE MITCHELL

Liberate, Don't Refrigerate

Katie Mitchell is a freelance director. Her productions for Classics on a Shoe-string, which she founded, include Arden of Faversham, Vassa Zheleznova, Women of Troy, The House of Bernarda Alba *and* Live Like Pigs. *She has directed at the Royal National Theatre* (Rutherford and Son, The Machine Wreckers) *and spent ten years with the Royal Shakespeare Company, where she was an Associate Director and Director of The Other Place. Her RSC productions include* The Dybbuk, Ghosts, The Mysteries, Uncle Vanya, *and* The Phoenician Women, *which won her the 1996 Evening Standard Award for Best Director.*

IT WAS A TRIP to Eastern Europe in 1989 to research training for directors that first awoke me to the real artistic possibilities and social responsibilities of theatre. I had always admired the aesthetic of East-ern European theatre but once there, visiting the distinct and different countries of Russia, Poland, Georgia and Lithuania, I soon realized that their aesthetic was a result of a theatre that had needed to develop a sophisticated visual language in order, amongst other things, to elude the textual censors. So to my surprise I saw a theatre that had a strong political and social role, a theatre that was a gathering place where, through drama, key political, social and spiritual issues of the day had been and were being debated – a theatre, in short, that was actually needed by an entire community. It was a theatre that changed people's lives and articulated their deepest needs and concerns, a theatre with a function. This gave me faith in the theatre's ability to fulfil a proper role in my own country, reaching beyond art for art's sake or art for the sake of entertainment or escapism.

The level of state subsidy there also enabled many theatre companies to work on productions over long periods of time. For example, Lev Dodin's three-part production of *The Possessed* rehearsed for three years from 1989 to 1991, which compares to rehearsal periods for a production in Britain of between three and eight weeks. The difference between the two cultures is, in the words of Theatre de Complicite director Simon McBurney, the difference between working horizontally and working vertically. To work horizontally is to think always about moving forwards on to the next project, driven by ambition and vanity, happy – or, at least, willing – to leave work incomplete once it has passed through the critical net of the first night and the subsequent reviews. To work vertically is to spend more time on less work and focus on deepening and layering the work, tracking it from birth to grave with equal attention at every stage. It is the kind of work that took Peter Brook out of Britain to France because the conditions were not right for it here.

In British theatre the problem for me was – and is – to try to find or create the right conditions that would allow me to practise a theatre that mattered. Sadly, this is a problem that now besets some theatres in Eastern Europe too, having got rid of the censor but also of the generous state subsidy that supported the theatre infrastructure there. When in 1998 I visited Russia again for the first time since 1989 the change in the theatre community was startling. I was on a reconnaissance trip to Siberia for the British Council to explore the possibilities of touring there. The reduction in levels of state subsidy for the arts was not only changing the programming and working processes of some theatres, but also meant that many were having to resort to bizarre methods of raising money. The Opera House in Novosibirsk, the capital of Western Siberia, had rented a large proportion of its foyer space to the Siberian equivalent of MFI, so that you walked past a series of living room furniture suites on the way to your seat. More alarmingly, the Music Theatre in Krasnoyarsk staged what in effect were stripteases in the foyer in order to raise money.

My travels to Eastern Europe instilled in me the firm belief that the only creative way forward for me was to work within an ensemble – a group of actors with whom one works over a considerable period of time. But where does one go to do this in Britain? There are those who have creatively adapted to the existing infrastructure and are achieving this: Tim Supple at the Young Vic, for example, or Mike Alfreds at Method & Madness. Companies like Theatre de Complicite work with a constellation of performers whom they draw on for different productions, and there are still avant-garde groups like Forced Entertainment who have an ensemble of ten years' standing. But these are the exceptions, not the rule. The Royal National Theatre produces repertoire theatre – unless it is offering a straight run of a show like *Oklahoma!* – but its repertoire is not created by an ensemble, and the real sadness about a company like the RSC, which has the ensemble as its main philosophical plank, is that it is simply too large to be one. Although it is possible to create a mini-ensemble for a single production at the RSC, which is one of the privileges of working for the company, many of the actors just don't feel part of an overall ensemble, a sense underlined by the absence of an understanding between the directors of what an ensemble is. There is a danger that the idea is reduced to a financial imperative rather than an enriching and practical reality. I say this knowing how much effort has gone, and is going, into attempting to correct this problem.

As a freelance director in Britain, one is by nature peripatetic, moving from one group of actors to another, each time having to cohere them into using one language, one system of working. I have found recently that I can spend up to 60 per cent of the rehearsal period bringing the actors together into one way of working. The nature of our actor and director training here exacerbates the problem. The debate about directors' training divides, crudely speaking, into two schools: those who claim that it is irrelevant and that either you have the mysterious skill to direct or you have not, and those who insist that training is a crucial prerequisite for the job. Of course, to some extent it does come down to temperament and natural gifts, but there are basic skills, like textual analysis or stagecraft, for instance, which would be of enormous benefit to any director starting off on his or her career. Training for directors here is patchy and mixed, where it takes place at all. I 'trained' by working as an assistant director at the King's Head, Paines Plough and the RSC and picked up skills in an ad hoc, unsystematic fashion.

Although for actors there are more schools and courses, the inadequacy of state funding is already excluding many, and the content is variable, which is both enriching and frustrating not only for the actor but also for the director. Enriching in that it can create a rehearsal environment in which there are many different skills and methods available; frustrating in that it can be like being in a room in which everyone is speaking a different language and it takes a lot of subtle negotiation to 'understand' each other and, therefore, work together. In the Russia of 1989, by comparison, not only did the actors usually receive a four-year training and directors five years, but they often trained together and all worked within one system – the Stanislavsky system. Each course was led by a professional practitioner and, in many cases, the directors spent their first year training as actors before moving on to theory and practical directing exercises. I am not saying that this is the only way of working, and it certainly doesn't reflect the practice in Russia today where drama schools are no longer state-funded and no longer adhere exclusively to one system. But, as a model, what this kind of training means is that actors and directors at least start out with a shared language and working method, even if they choose to depart from it or use other techniques in making their work.

As a freelance director one not only has to start from point zero with the actors on every new job but each time there is a different administrative context as well – and every institution has its philosophy or ideology, which manifests itself in the way it likes to structure the process and presentation of its work. Even at the RSC, where I worked for more than a decade, I still found myself having to negotiate the 'right' conditions for the work with every production. This concerns not only the rehearsals and the performances but also the context in which the work is produced. An audience's experience of the work can be informed as much by the marketing, the theatre's foyers or the programmes as by the production itself. In my experience, institutions, large and small, are frightened of change and tend to want the art to fit into existing structures instead of changing the structures to suit the art. Those who are more courageous often simply can't make the changes because they are not resourced to do so. The effort involved in trying to change the structures can be so huge that in the fight one can end up losing one's enthusiasm for the work and, indeed, for the initial idea that animated it.

Although the way in which the work is actually made and presented can sometimes be negatively influenced by the building one is working in, I have never experienced any form of censorship in terms of the choice of text. And in many cases I have found that theatres have been brave to schedule certain productions, either because of the obscurity of the material, as in the case of *The Phoenician Women* at the RSC, or because of the political content of plays, like Ernst Toller's Christian socialist *The Machine Wreckers* at the National. Recent media debates about plays like Sarah Kane's *Blasted*, which reached the 'heights' of *Newsnight* and the tabloids, are reassuring in that they prove theatre can still hit raw nerves in the community we live in and that courage when it comes to scheduling is important because it creates proper debate about our society. However, the need of theatres to make sense commercially can mean that they do have to play it safe politically more than, I imagine, many of them would like to. We are no longer, for example, in a culture where Peter Brook's *US* could take place on the main stage at the RSC.

I do not doubt the motives of those who run the institutions. I see all too clearly that it is a huge struggle for them to keep their heads above water in the current financial circumstances. The subsidized theatre is now no more protected from the claws of the marketplace than is the commercial sector. But that is no justification for what in some instances appears to be a widening gap between the objectives of the administrative structures and the objectives of the work. The gap does not reflect a conscious desire on behalf of those who run the institutions, rather it is a reflection of historical inevitability and a funding structure that follows buildings not people.

In his essay *Stanislavsky and the Bearer Bonds* David Mamet claims that the active life of any healthy theatrical enterprise lasts at most between five and ten years, and that it is birthed by a group of artists of roughly the same age (normally starting in their mid-twenties) who share artistic, political and spiritual aims. The main reason for the collapse in artistic purpose occurs because the aims that bound the group together when aged 25 to 35 cannot bind them when they are aged 35 to 45. In most instances, despite the collapse of artistic purpose and the departure of some of the core artists, the physical administrative plant is sustained, thereby continuing the form of the company's vision but not its living content.

In Britain we appear to be operating in a theatre culture that refuses to recognize that this is often the reality of any proper artistic endeavour. It keeps the institutional shell alive, forcing the next generation to abide by its dead administrative structures. In the case of the RSC, for example, the structure was put in place in the 1960s and '70s in direct response to the artistic needs and external circumstances of the time. But the artistic objectives of those generations are in many cases not the objectives of my generation and yet we are still having to work within the same framework. I say 'forced' and 'have to' as if we are being dragged to our rehearsal rooms screaming and kicking, which is, of course, not the case. We choose to work in the institutions and we have to accept the responsibility for, and therefore the consequences of, that choice. Perhaps our fault is that we have not found a way of coming together as a generation to discuss the problem with those who run the institutions.

The same problem is true of theatre buildings. Many directors now seem to be increasingly interested in exploring new physical contexts for their work. I'm not surprised at the number of my contemporaries who have tried to take over the Roundhouse, the old train shed in north London, in order to make their work there in new conditions. At heart, this expresses a wish to re-examine the very ritual of theatregoing and also the possibilities of new relationships between actor, audience and environment, both in terms of the performance space itself and of its context in the community. The architecture and location of our existing buildings can, in some cases, create a barrier between certain sections of the community and our work. I know that however much I might want to go to a football match I would be put off by ignorance of the ritual. So, I think, what must it be like the other way round?

I remember Deborah Warner at a talk we gave a few years ago; when asked under what circumstances she would work at the National she jokingly replied: 'If it were closed.' It was a deliberately flippant comment that contains a great deal of truth: if the National were closed it would become a site rather than a theatre building and would, therefore, allow more freedom to experiment with context.

I know that for myself this impulse is part of the subconscious influence from developments in the visual arts in Britain over the last ten years or so, both in terms of high media profile artists like Damien Hirst, but, more importantly, the site-specific and installation work of people like Antony Gormley, Bill Viola, Mona Hatoum and Anish Kapoor. Although there is nothing new about installation and site-specific work in itself, it appears to have become a more dominant and popular form of artistic expression here now. When I visited the *Rites of Passage* exhibition at the Tate Gallery and the Hayward Gallery's *Y* exhibition in 1997 they were crammed with people, especially the young. The work on display challenges the traditional relationship between art and the viewer: one no longer looks at a two-dimensional flat surface, rather it is as if you are *inside* the image, and this provokes you to re-examine your relationship to space, surface, texture and the other people with whom you are experiencing the work. Site-specific work can also mean that you literally have to travel through, and experience, areas of the community that you would not normally see. One short-term exhibition space I visited recently was situated in a flat in a run-down tower block in London's East End. You were given the address but, once at the foot of the block, there were no signs anywhere, nor on the door to the exhibition itself. For the artists involved, the experience of the context was as important as the experience of the work in the flat at the end of the journey.

When designer Vicki Mortimer and I decided to present six short plays by Samuel Beckett at the RSC's The Other Place and later in four European venues, we consciously explored this influence, by stripping the auditorium of seats, dividing it into two 'spaces' with linking corridors and creating, in effect, an installation. And it is not by chance that other theatre directors have crossed, and are crossing, the boundaries between the two forms – Robert Wilson, for example, with his piece *HG* about H.G.Wells at the Clink Street Vaults in south London, and Deborah Warner in her installation at the St Pancras Hotel and in her choice of sites for *The Wasteland.*

Yet this desire is not only related to presenting one-off events. It also reflects the influence of the permanent environments set up by directors such as Peter Brook at the Bouffes du Nord or Ariane Mnouchkine at The Cartoucherie, both in Paris. These are theatre 'homes' for relatively fixed ensembles, where the artists have total control over their environments, rather than theatre 'houses' visited on an ad hoc basis. The Cartoucherie, for instance, is a collection of old warehouses in the Bois de Vincennes, a base not only for Mnouchkine's company, Théâtre du Soleil, but also for a range of performance practitioners, each with their own warehouse around a communal square. The open architecture of the three warehouses that comprise the foyer and performance space of Théâtre du Soleil provides a more or less neutral palette, enabling the company to reinvent the use of space for each show. I am always impressed by the way in which the foyer is radically reconceived in terms of decor and atmosphere in response to each new project being presented. Although, to some extent, Théâtre du Soleil has become an 'institution', enjoying large government support, its theatre space still allows the company to retain a spatial fluidity in response to different projects, which would be impossible in a traditional theatre.

But I am also sure that the search for new forms and new contexts is one of the many possible attempts to deal with the nagging awareness that we are playing to only a very small section of the society we live in. Given the real interests of today's young people, are we in any sense articulating their perceptions and concerns in a form that speaks to them? In his disturbing book *Dark Heart*, which presents an analysis of the causes and effects of poverty in Britain today, Nick Davies claims that a quarter of the population is living in poverty and that the other three-quarters have, since 1979, become more prosperous, experiencing a real increase of 40 per cent in their salaries. So, clearly we are in danger of missing out both on young people and on those who simply cannot afford to come. But there has also been an alarming reduction in support for some theatres from previous theatregoers, for whom the cost of relatively highly priced tickets is not a real obstacle.

Theatre at root is simply a story told by one section of the community to another section, but at the moment the artists and their audiences are almost inhabiting two very different worlds and are in danger of losing the possibility of a proper and mutually creative meeting ground. The critic Michael Billington even predicts that soon only a 'dwindling minority will seek out things called "plays".' In one sense he is right, because this is what is already happening and will continue to happen if the theatre community lets it. But if we can find a way of responding to the social context more responsibly and changing the administrative structures of theatres to channel those new responses then this need not be the case.

When George Steiner gave a lecture to mark the opening of the 1996 Edinburgh Festival, he, like David Mamet, talked about the 'organic form and logic in the birth, evolution and decay of human institutions'. He said:

> To know when to stop is a rare but vivid mark of honesty within excellence. Too many worn-out ghosts of the past or altered cultural ambitions and ideals litter the scene. It is precisely when it is doing well, when its box office is healthy, that an institution should draw a dangerous breath and ask of itself: 'Is my continued existence truly representative of my initial aims? Are current realizations matching the excellence of the outset?' These are not questions to be afraid of. It is the failure of nerve implicit in not posing them which could signal stasis or even decline. Faced candidly, the very self-questioning may generate those changes, those new hopes and fruitful errors whereby the arts are celebrated and renewed within a society.

In the current financial climate it can be hard for any organization to respond to Steiner's inspiring questioning as it lurches from one financial crisis to the next. But I have always worried that money and marketing problems, amongst other things, can be used as a smokescreen to hide artistic decay and paralysis. I also know from my own work how difficult it can be to admit defeat or failure and to destroy everything that exists so far, in order to start again. But the work of any artist who is serious about what he or she does will always be fluid, growing and changing in response to artistic discoveries from within and social changes from without. Until administrative structures find an equivalent fluidity they will end up refrigerating art instead of liberating it and facilitating its growth. More and more practitioners will leave to forge their own forms in other contexts and other countries, and we will play to smaller and smaller sections of our community.

I do not think anything constructive would be gained by throwing any of our theatrical institutions to the wolves of the marketplace, as Gerry Robinson, the new Arts Council of England chairman, threatens. I agree with what Richard Eyre said when he addressed the Royal Academy in 1998: 'If we don't try to make our institutions work, what have we got? They're the only formal evidence of man as a social animal; they're all imperfect but they're the only instruments of society that represent the belief, the hope – the faith, if you like – that we're capable of working together.' But there is no question about the crisis many institutions are now in, and we need to counter the crisis creatively. We need continually to provoke, to challenge and to renew both the work and the structures that support it so that nothing – not context, not form, not content – blocks or jams the vital exchange between the actor and the imagination of the audience that guarantees the survival of theatre and is the reason for its existence.

7

ALISON CHITTY

More, Please!

Alison Chitty is a theatre and film designer. She has worked extensively in the UK, Europe and the USA. She started her career at the Victoria Theatre, Stoke-on-Trent, and was later Resident Designer at the Royal National Theatre for eight years, where she designed many productions, including A Month in the Country, Danton's Death, Venice Preserv'd (*British Drama Award*), Antony and Cleopatra, *and* The Late Shakespeares. *She has designed many operas, most notably* Gawain (*ROH*), *the Olivier Award-winning productions of* Khovanshchina (*ENO*) *and* Billy Budd (*Geneva, ROH, Paris*), *and* Tristan and Isolde (*Seattle*). *Her work in film includes Mike Leigh's* Naked *and* Secrets and Lies (*Palme d'Or, Cannes*). *She is co-director of the Motley Theatre Design Course.*

I TRAINED AT the Central School of Art and Design with Ralph Koltai, a wonderful teacher who taught us always to fight for the best and to keep a sense of humour. He told us never to forget that any group of performers can put on a play without designers and to 'never read the script, it's much too confusing!' – ironic advice that served to reinforce how central the text is to all our work. He taught us by example that the designer is an integral part of theatre and to design what the play is about, not where the events take place. The design element cannot be separated from the overall experience of the performance. Our contribution is the power of colour, texture, imagery – the visual element supporting and illuminating the play.

I had a good time at Central in the late 1960s, where my fees and some living expenses were paid by a government grant. When I graduated I won an Arts Council scholarship for a nine-month placement at the Victoria Theatre, Stoke-on-Trent, working with the director Peter Cheeseman, which expanded to an eight-year commitment to that theatre; it was a terrific apprenticeship. We were a repertory theatre and we put on twelve to thirteen plays a year: one Shakespeare, several other classics, two pieces of theatre for children, and always over 50 per cent contemporary work, which included *Saved* by Edward Bond and *Fanshen* by David Hare; and there was a core team of writers – Alan Ayckbourn, Henry Livings, Alan Plater and Peter Terson – and a constant stream of new ones – Shane Connaughton, Ken Campbell and Tony Perrin. There was a permanent company of actors and a commitment to the development of local musical documentaries. There was even two years of special additional funding when we were able to have a performance on the road every day – in a pub, a prison, a hospital, an adventure playground – at the same time as maintaining daily performances in the theatre. Our work was committed to the district and the community. We had a feeling that we had some political power, and this all made sense to me.

I now realize how important a time this was for my development as a designer. I was beginning to recognize what is now a central philosophy and approach to my work, sorting out passions and defining priorities. In this theatre in the round I learned a respect for text and performers. I began to understand the power of performers and objects in space, their effect on one another, and why the performance space is defined by the action. I began to understand why I was working in theatre: primarily a love of storytelling, born out of childhood years listening to *Children's Hour* with David Davis, radio plays and radio documentaries. I began to see that theatre is a unique way to satisfy an innate need to express our ideas, to sort out and understand our world, ourselves, and our feelings. With theatre we can influence and change people's lives, and we can share how we feel.

I was lucky. When I joined the profession Jenny Lee was the first Minister for the Arts, eight or ten new theatres were being built outside London, repertory theatres were growing and flourishing because their grants were being increased, and the fringe was just inventing itself. Every year there were five or six Arts Council bursaries for young designers. There were permanent head of design and assistant design positions in all reps. The Victoria Theatre itself had a head of design, a co-designer, and an assistant; now, I understand there is only a permanent head of design. The regions are no longer the same training ground for designers. I wonder whether recent governments have understood the repercussions of reduced funding in the regions, which were the training ground in the past for our major theatre, TV and film companies, not only of designers but also of actors and directors.

By the mid-1980s and into the 1990s (under Thatcher and the subsequent Conservative governments) further education establishments and art schools in particular were 'rationalized'. There was the formation of the London Institute, an umbrella organization established to oversee the amalgamation of the large London art schools. There were even stories of proposals for the Central Theatre Design Course to amalgamate with a window-dressing course at the College of Distributive Trades. Some tidy mind no doubt felt we could all mess around with felt and glue for two and a half years and then go our separate ways to work with managers, mannequins, and sales figures, or directors, actors, and plays. Thank God it never happened. *Politics dictates theatre*

What did happen, however, was that the Conservative government brought to an end both full student grants and discretionary awards; then the subsequent Labour government introduced student loans. Pressure was applied for theatre design courses to be full to overflowing, with financial incentives going to the schools for each student enrolled. The courses became overcrowded, and in many cases it was impossible for students to have permanent work spaces, a fundamental requirement for any artist. Now, as I understand it, the dust is settling. Still no government student grants, though there is some movement on discretionary awards. However, the staff-student ratio remains poor. Hours of administration are expected to take priority, so what happens to teaching and tutorials? There is no alternative to what are called 'contact hours' – teaching in small groups, somehow finding a way to fill the bottomless pit of need for one-to-one discussion, argument, criticism and a personal support system.

During this period of change I became angered by what I saw as a system top-heavy with administration, where somehow students and their education were not the most important thing. In 1992, while making my will, deciding where to bequeath my library, I knew it had to go to the Motley Theatre Design Course. I knew that it would always be available to students and that a small core of committed tutors and students would fight for it to survive. Two weeks later, Margaret ('Percy') Harris, who founded the course in 1965, asked me to join her as co-director. She is a determined and passionate theatre person who, with her sister Sophie, and Elizabeth Montgomery, comprised the brilliant trio of theatre designers called Motley. She has a personal approach to teaching – idiosyncratic, uncompromising, and fiercely independent. I accepted.

One of Motley's concerns has always been to assist the students' smooth transition into the profession. Opportunities for young designers at the start of their careers have always been very limited. The establishment of the fringe has created a new way into the profession, and the story is the same for directors, actors and writers. Unfortunately, the fringe route for designers doesn't begin to replace the apprenticeship and opportunities that used to be available in the reps. No stability, no continuity, little or no wages, and low budgets.

In addition, Arts Council funding of the scholarship scheme has been reduced to one-off placements to a theatre or practising designer, and sadly selection is now made by interview, no longer from an annual exhibition. I understand that in 1998 there were 150 applications for a year's placement with a designer, and 40 others for secondment to a regional theatre – 190 young designers looking for some way to start out. However, in a surprisingly generous gesture, some of the responsibility for supporting young designers has been taken by Lady Anya Sainsbury with the formation of the Linbury Prize, which in 1997 attracted 127 young entrants. Founded in 1987, this biennial competition provides an exhibition at the Royal National Theatre for a shortlist of 12 young designers and cash prizes and a job for four competition winners. The Linbury Prize is also indirectly supporting theatre, opera and dance companies, as it provides additional funding to assist with the visual element of a production designed by the prizewinners.

Small efforts by individuals seem to make the most remarkable difference to people's spirits; for example, the 'Designer Director Dating Day' that I coordinate at the National's Studio, which continues the inspiration and initiative taken a decade ago by the director Peter Gill.

At these 'dating' days, 24 designers and directors spend a day together once a year; it's a marketplace. In the morning, 12 directors interview 12 designers – 144 meetings take place. In the afternoon, 12 designers interview 12 directors. 'Who's your favourite painter?' 'Give me ten words to define the word "blue".' 'Who are your favourite theatre designers?' 'What do you think of Joseph Beuys?' In all, 288 meetings and a free lunch, all for 24 phone calls and 24 tube fares! I was thrilled to hear that the idea had been taken up by West Yorkshire Playhouse.

As designers we look for and rely on our colleagues, our collaborators: the directors. But where do they come from? At one time, directors were the successful, upgraded, stage managers; more recently they have come out of universities and their drama societies, then they develop through the haphazard 'training' of assisting many and various other untrained directors. When I joined the profession I'd been given the idea that directors were a breed who knew what they wanted, who embarked on a project with a vision, possibly even of the final product, and that they knew why they wanted to direct a particular play. This suggested that what was required was a designer who was obedient, a servant who just implemented someone else's ideas. Under the guise of collaboration, designers should do as they are told. Fortunately, this has rarely happened to me, although I do know of colleagues who have been confronted at a first meeting by a director with a ground plan of the stage layout.

Designers are still mostly dependent on directors for every job. It is still the norm for theatres to approach directors at the initiation of a project and then for a director to offer a production to a designer. Some designers, frustrated by this, have become directors, and some (like Tom Cairns, David Fielding, Antony McDonald and Ultz) have become director/designers. On the whole, my experience working with directors is that we have worked in a partnership, journeying into the 'unknown' – a structured, controlled, but ultimately messy process that eventually fine-tunes the 'unknown' into a unique 'known', creating a performance that is the theatre experience. Working this way, the final product is discovered during the process. There is a variant of this version, which I've experienced most often with writer/ directors, such as Peter Gill and Mike Leigh. Both these directors had an enormous influence on me. They are extremely different, but both passionately concerned with the human condition and how the story of our lives can be told. Peter Gill in particular introduced me to the Royal Court school of poetic naturalism. Working with them there is always a sense of an intangible 'known', which can be imagined yet only recognized as exactly what we were searching for when it is found – recognized as surely as a lost glove that matches its pair. This somehow puts more pressure on the process. It's the hardest and most consuming way to work: fascinating, frustrating and elusive, but the most rewarding. In the best productions there is no demarcation between direction and design. It is a complete collaboration, a seamless whole. These, I believe, are the best experiences for everyone concerned, including, ultimately, the audience.

It is the responsibility of the designer to tell the story in the best possible way. The design must evolve organically, and directly from the text. The physical space is defined by the action. The focus must be on the performers, who in turn must be 'held' by the space. Designing from the inside towards the outside, not creating a surrounding world and expecting a performance to live inside it; not just covering the brick walls of a theatre and decorating the surfaces. We must design plays, not scenery.

We need to be restrained and rigorous ourselves, even if it means being rigorous and restrained about a flamboyant gesture. I'm not talking about the puritanism of the chic single-bare-light-bulb-school, sometimes perceived as grim, bleak and austere. I'm talking about a kind of puritanism which at its core is enriched by a love of the particular, relishing the extra-ordinary, and embracing the idiosyncrasies of everyday life. All this is a central part of the work of Peter Gill and Mike Leigh. I am applauding an approach to design that allows the best of everything, and only just as much as you need, leaving not an over-egged pudding, but a tantalizing and fascinating sense for an audience, that they know what they feel and where they are; they understand the world of the play, and they themselves have taken part – the difference between obsessive naturalism and its poetic form.

Playwrights may be tempted to give overly naturalistic stage direc-tions, yet the total realization of a naturalistic world can make an audience feel over-secure. I don't believe in spoon-feeding, when the poetic form of naturalism can keep an audience on the edge of their seats. Designers need playwrights to write what they feel, and not to design the 'scenery' on the page; they don't need to worry about what it is and how it can be realized. We need them to be free and then we will also be free, to work from the text, to work with them, and design the play. This can liberate us from restrictive naturalism; we will be able to be expressive and poetic. Unlike film and television, a play is live, it is free – it can be 'anything'. It is about a story, ideas, performers and an audience.

One of the greatest influences on British theatre design recently has been the work of Philip Prowse at the Glasgow Citizens' Theatre – neither wedded to simple naturalism nor paralysed by limited financial resources. In the 1980s we saw his influence combined with that of continental Europe, in the work of what was known as the 'Ball's Pond Road School' – Tom Cairns, David Fielding, Antony McDonald – and then their influence everywhere in the 1990s. This work respects both text, and rich and beautiful design, and its approach is at the heart of exciting theatre.

Whilst looking around and deciding as designers which way to go next, most of us in the 1980s and '90s ricocheted from the white box to the black box, the haunted ballroom, the crashed chandelier, from bowler hats to balloons, toyed with expressionism, with the 'lift and tilt' school, and explored empty grey worlds with six chairs and a naked light bulb. All of us – both those associated with one style of design and those not easily pigeonholed, free spirits like Bob Crowley, Bill Dudley, Tobias Hoheisel, John Macfarlane and Ultz – have been and are exploring through our own and each other's work how best to support the performers and tell stories. With each production we are testing how far along the tightrope we can venture, towards an ultimate, refined, essential 'something' that is absolutely and exquisitely what we are looking for.

Funding is a great controlling factor in deciding which direction we take. Lack of money for the theatres and, more particularly, reduced budgets for productions has forced us all to be more ingenious, more economical, even more restrained. The results are often exciting, released and free, like the so-often elusive work in a sketchbook. This is particularly true on the fringe, where, because the overall budget is smaller, there is less pressure from producers with financial targets. This energy needs to feed back into our work in the large houses.

This is a complicated and paradoxical subject. As designers, it is our responsibility with the production managers to create physical things and we know we can't do our best without financial support; design is a time-consuming and expensive business. We are talking about fine art and fine craftsmanship, and each discipline requires its own time and care. The complexity is enormous – every skill combining to make the exquisite, elaborate whole, which needs to be served up on a daily basis, and the highest standards must be maintained. We make prototypes, not sausages! Yet in one sense, unfortunately, we are very good at surviving while being creative – the wartime spirit: make do and mend. The theatre thrives on this. Many of us love to work in the theatre; there is a committed body of workers who give their lives to the industry for little financial reward, an invisible form of funding that helps many organizations survive.

I don't make a case for underfunded, valiant and impoverished work; my point is that theatre will go on, regardless. It will continue to help us make sense of our lives, to enrich us, and to make a spiritually healthier nation. Theatre matters. Let's pay for it properly.

I am optimistic for theatre itself – as practitioners we have to be, it's in our nature. We need to be realistic, but optimistic. I can hope the same for design. Despite the appetite for simplistic naturalism in the past, I see audiences changed by the experience of astounding, striking and bold work. I see and hope for more and more colour returning to the stage, and I hope for a collision of all that is best that has gone before with what we are working at now. We should relish the quality of scene painting and our scenic artists, together with the expertise of our engineers, and embrace both the sculptural influence of Adolphe Appia, Gordon Craig and Ralph Koltai, and the restraint, honesty and respect for the text of the Royal Court school exemplified by the work of Jocelyn Herbert. I love to see writers like Sarah Kane take up where Brecht, Kantor and Beckett left off. Such work is vigorous, visual, poetic and often restrained. Free of obsessive naturalism, this work is not depressing, because it is not sentimental. It may seem bleak and desperate, grim and pessimistic, but for me it is entirely cathartic and reassuring.

The future for design looks positive. There is a never-ending stream of fascinating and talented applicants to the Motley Theatre Design Course from every field of the arts, the theatre profession and drama degree courses at the universities and, of course, the odd wild card. Even when reminded that this is a life-consuming and financially unrewarding profession, these aspiring designers stubbornly remain positive and optimistic. At Motley I am able to pursue my passion for teaching – straightforward and directly related to the profession. We are determined to make it possible to offer places to any mature students with obvious signs of talent, who are passionately interested in our profession, regardless of their formal qualifications. We survive on little or no money, not in any way a viable role model for the established theatre design schools. But, by being prepared to be poor and nomadic, we retain our independence and freedom to focus on the students.

Our priority at Motley is teaching. Educational establishments should have the responsibility to educate, and not have to spend all their time recording meticulously the fact that 'something' has or has not happened. We have a building open 24 hours a day and seven days a week. All the tutors are theatre practitioners. Basically we are concerned with teaching students to design plays. We help them develop a respect and love of the text, writers and performers. Students naturally develop as human beings over the year at Motley, but in addition they must learn how to study, to develop a work process, individually and in a group, and, most importantly, they must develop a personal philosophy and aesthetic. It is our intention that Motley graduates will leave after their incredibly intensive 11-month course better artists and thinkers, who can argue their ideas and express themselves clearly; better, more rounded people, with the potential to become great collaborators and designers whose work will be honest and pure, practical and brilliant, full of energy which supports the play and the performers.

There is the fascination of something so elusive and transitory about the theatre. It is tantalizing how easy and, at the same time, remarkably hard it can be to create something with a group of people. We try to work that out. The art and the fun is taking the text, our foundation, the ideas, the unformed matter and quite simply creating something together. Despite the frustrations in the search for the perfect process and the final product, we love it and carry on.

Designers need a personal philosophy and political stance, an ability to study and a vision, artistic flair and organization, flexibility and control, and an unlimited and passionate interest in every aspect of humanity and our world. There is a long tradition of great theatre design in Britain that is recognized around the world. Somehow or other, we are good at it. So, like Oliver, we keep asking for more – more money, more theatre. The inherent self-confidence and commitment in the profession no doubt help governments and funding authorities have fewer qualms about reducing their support, secure in the knowledge that new plays will be written that will add to the wealth of material that interprets our lives, and all of us will continue to struggle to make them happen.

More, please!

8

PAULE CONSTABLE

Light Silently Erupting

Paule Constable is a lighting designer and her work has taken her to the USA, Australia and New Zealand, as well as many countries in Europe, including Russia and Lithuania. Her designs for the theatre include The Street of Crocodiles, The Three Lives of Lucie Cabrol *and* The Caucasian Chalk Circle *with Theatre de Complicite;* OMMA, More Grimm Tales, Jungle Book, Haroun and the Sea of Stories *and* Tales from Ovid *for Tim Supple;* The Mysteries, Uncle Vanya, The Beckett Shorts *and* Don Giovanni *for Katie Mitchell; and* The Weir *for Ian Rickson at the Royal Court. She has designed operas for Welsh National Opera, Scottish Opera, Opera North and English National Opera. She was nominated for the Olivier Award for Best Lighting Designer in 1993 and 1999.*

I BECAME A LIGHTING DESIGNER BY ACCIDENT after studying Drama and English at university. Lighting interested me because it was intangible, unwritten, unexplained – an unexplored new territory, subliminal almost. As a lighting designer I could play and paint with colour, shape and shadow; using light opened up a huge potential language. There are now degree courses where one can learn to be a lighting designer but I am not sure how this can be taught as a particular area of study. I would suggest that anyone wanting to be a lighting designer should take a visual arts foundation course first, to learn about paint and colour and to learn how to look. As babies one of the first things we react to is light, but we soon forget this and lose our direct emotional response to the light around us. Learning to be a lighting designer is a process of learning to look and to see again.

Lighting design is a recent addition to the language of making theatre. Shows have always been illuminated in some way but until the latter part of the twentieth century this has tended to be seen as functional and interpretive: a role taken on by a technician not by a separate member of the creative team. There are still many practitioners who consider the lighting designer is present simply to illuminate and not to elaborate or collaborate. Equally, audience members are often as bemused by my job – often asking what a lighting designer actually does! The way a piece is lit is another way in which the narrative is told. As a set designer gives information using objects, scenery and space so a lighting designer uses light in the same way. Through my work I am trying to develop a language for light which is closely linked to the entire visual language of a production. By spending time in rehearsal, through reading a text and familiarizing myself with reference material and by involving myself in the design process I am making light another integral layer in the process of theatre as a whole.

Many people assume the job is highly technical. To me the technology is merely a means of expression; it is the tool which I work with. We are constantly being bombarded with new developments such as the introduction of computerized control systems and the development of moving light sources, colour changing systems and advanced technologies for light sources. The importance of these new tools is not what they do in their own right but that they allow greater creativity. The technology is not exciting but the appliance of it is. Almost anything is possible but the quality of ideas has to be the most important thing. Technology should not dominate. It should facilitate.

Essentially, I learnt on the job. I assisted lighting designers and toured a great deal as a chief electrician, recreating other people's designs on the road. I also served as a production electrician for lighting designers whose shows were transferring into the West End where I would have to solve many of their technical problems and communicate with the production crew on their behalf.

At first it was difficult being a woman in a man's domain. I was 25 and inexperienced. As soon as I walked into a meeting I felt that everyone else was thinking, 'What right have you got to be here?' I felt I was constantly required to prove myself. When I was asked to light my first production at the Royal National Theatre, *The Street of Crocodiles* in 1992, the director, Simon McBurney, wanted me to attend throughout the rehearsal period – I was going to be the production manager for its world tour as well as the lighting designer. The only way we could arrange for me to be present all the time was for me to be paid as an assistant stage manager. I remember that at every production meeting the National staff would not introduce me as the show's lighting designer but as the ASM. I am sure this would not have happened to me if I had been a man. Yet, as well as being the first woman to light a show at the National – remarkable in itself that it took until 1992 – I was also the only ASM to have been nominated for an Olivier Award. At that time there were only a few female lighting designers, such as Jenny Kane and Tina McHugh, in Britain. Now it is less unusual, and my new battle is to combine the demands of being a lighting designer with raising a family.

Lighting designers face a range of challenges from production to production, not only because of the different personalities one meets but also because lighting is difficult to discuss and is usually – and wrongly – one of the last things to be added in to a production. I try to develop a 'language' for each particular production with the director and designer, so I become involved in the process as early as I can in order to understand the aesthetic of the piece, what is carrying the narrative – is it an actor or is it an image? – and at what points. With devised work, many of these decisions have to wait until the last minute because the rehearsal process will not have produced solutions until later in the production process.

Generally I watch rehearsals in the first few weeks to see if what the director and designer have been discussing is actually happening with the actors present. At run-throughs I try to get an idea of how I am going to 'see' the show, but it is not until the technical period that one has the opportunity to put anything into practice. This is the most pressurized moment in the production process, moving out of the rehearsal room into the theatre, and the lighting designer has very little time in which to work. As a result a lot of what I do is like being a therapist. Many directors are terrified of light; they think they cannot control it and, until they see it, they cannot say what they want. Their frustrations during the technical period, in seeing what is not working or being realized properly on stage, are often taken out on the lighting designer, although often these problems will not have anything to do with the lighting.

There may also be a clash between what the director wants and the needs of the actors and audience. For example, some directors pursuing a realist aesthetic want ever lower lighting levels on the actors; they mistrust more light as being too lyrical and metaphorical. Yet I have to support the actors with light, and if the audience cannot see the actors they will not be able to hear them. The reality of the stage is, necessarily, at one level a metaphor, an artifice, so the lighting designer always has to create a conceit, even if it is to help to give the impression of the real – or of the dark.

When I did the lighting for *The Mysteries* at the Royal Shakespeare Company in Stratford-upon-Avon in the winter of 1996-97, the director Katie Mitchell gave the actors the power to make production decisions. The basic rule was that I and the other technical artists, such as the set designer, could not add anything externally that was not created by the cast. The Creation was the only moment when an effect was produced externally, because nothing preceded it; until God said 'Light' it did not exist. After that it was over to the actors. Eden was not created by a fantastic lighting plot but by the actors themselves. There was an open lighting state all the way through, which was very exposing for those on stage. When it came to God giving the humans a rainbow after the flood, the actors wanted a scenic effect but I refused, because this would have been breaking the production concept. Ironically, I think they felt I had let them down because they believed I could not – rather than I would not – find a way of making the effect.

Sometimes inspiration comes from other members of the artistic team. I was lighting a production of *Tartuffe* at the Royal Exchange, Manchester, and had no idea what to do. The set, designed by Simon Higlet, was beautiful and baroque, but I was stuck. The production's composer, Gary Yershon, told me the director, Robert Delamere, had said he wanted a score that was baroque and contemporary, and Gary had suggested using a double bass and trumpet to play baroque jazz. I picked up on this mix of the old and the new, and lit the show imitating the specific light of a seventeenth-century still life painting but using working lights and fans too, like something out of a Ridley Scott film. There is a strong link between light and music: both are emotional and abstract.

Each lighting designer is different and works differently. Many do not attend rehearsals as often as I do and, consequently, can undertake more work. However, they have to make many decisions in advance, particularly about the type of production it is going to be, and then have to live with the consequences. This can lead to lighting for its own sake, in which pretty pictures are created that need not have anything to do with what is happening on stage. I light what is on stage, and to do that I work in a team, with other technicians and with other artists. The more I understand about the process that has created the work that ends up on stage, the more I can bring to the final result without simply 'plonking' the lighting on top to define arbitrary or conventional external factors, such as day or night, interior or exterior, hot or cold.

Each lighting designer is also fascinated by different areas of the art; it might be colour, it might be technology or, my own obsession, resonance: what happens when light hits a surface and how one lighting state affects the next. For instance, if one is looking at very blue light that is then taken out and replaced by white, it looks yellow. Using light as a series of contrasts: an outdoor scene followed by an indoor, a private scene followed by a public one, a moment of tragedy followed by a moment of comedy.

As a practical necessity I come into contact with an unusually large number of productions in a year – often in the realm of fourteen or so – and I find myself working in collaboration with a wide selection of directors, designers, writers, actors and other practitioners. This is caused by the frustrating low pay of most lighting designers, who tend to be paid relatively less than other members of the creative team and therefore have to take on more shows. The one advantage is the constant turnover of influences and relationships, which means, I hope, never becoming stagnant or complacent, and constantly asking myself, or being asked, 'Why?'

My answer is not – and would not be – concerned solely or narrowly with lighting, but with a far wider concern for the 'how' of storytelling, the elaboration of a narrative and the piecing together of a language to communicate the whole, both on a literal and a metaphorical level. Whilst my involvement with these areas is obviously linked to the visual in particular, the visual language of any production must go through the same vigorous process of questioning as any other component part.

It is, therefore, now that I want to explore the state of theatre as a *whole*. This is not only because lighting cannot be considered in isolation but also because in this context I find theatre in a state of crisis, unclear as to its function or form. We are in the midst of a technological revolution, which is throwing up constant questions about every aspect of our lives: how do we work, how do we communicate, how do we play, how do we interact? At the same time audiences are staying away from many theatres. How do we compete with the Internet, with television and with the movies? Unfortunately this debate does not seem to be alive amongst theatre practitioners, and I fear we ignore it at our peril. Theatres can no longer assume popular appeal, either within the subsidized sector of the RSC or the Royal Court or within the commercial world of the West End musical. We have to redefine our purpose and encourage a new, younger audience to visit the theatre to experience something unique.

There are several alarming trends running through much current work that make me feel that practitioners are simply accepting their potential fate. By this I mean holding on to a nostalgic idea of what theatre was, a refusal to accept the notion or need for change. We become obsessed with recreating Shakespeare's Globe or watching productions of classic plays that smack of sentimentality but never really involve us. They are representational, showing us a neatly packaged idea of what the past might have been while forgetting that many classic texts, be they Greek tragedies, Shakespeare or Chekhov, were written with, and for, a social purpose: to celebrate, to explore, to question, to involve an audience.

Acknowledging this is not only the responsibility of the director but of all of us who are involved in making theatre. I am talking of a theatrical culture today where we have become more involved with an individual's portrayal of a role than the role itself; we may applaud one actor's interpretation of Lear or another's performance of Uncle Vanya, enjoy watching the actor make the journey. But the very fact that we are constantly aware of the actor's definition of the role means that there is a separation between our experience of watching and our emotional response. Theatre is failing to engage and, if this trend continues, theatre will no longer be live and alive but a museum, part of our great British heritage industry.

Separation between audience and stage is key to this trend. The more an audience are pushed back into their seats and encouraged to have an uninvolved and passive relationship with what they see in front of them, the greater the distance between the audience and the work. The experience is like looking through a telescope, or to take the heritage idea further, like looking at something presented in a glass case in a museum. Theatre will become a celebration of a craft of the past. Looking at a piece of cloth in the Victoria and Albert Museum, we may admire the workmanship, and may even have an emotional response to something that belongs to the past, but it does not reach out and touch us. We deny it the responsibility of communicating directly to our inner subconscious; it is forced away from art to being craft.

This trend is reinforced by the tendency to define our work in relation to other pieces of theatre rather than to open up a debate with the audience about the effect of the individual work. Practitioners are constantly comparing productions of the same plays, enjoying new plays in terms of how they relate to other already existing work, or looking forward to the day when a young director, designer or actor comes to be as accomplished as someone more established. If this becomes the primary reason and function behind the work, we come to a position where the audience is denied any involvement. If we deny an audience, we lose awareness of who they are or for whom we are making theatre. Once this dialogue becomes one-sided, it is hardly surprising if people no longer find theatre entertaining.

Theatre, I believe, is suffering the classic malaise of 'postmodernism', and one can see a similar crisis happening elsewhere. In much music and fashion culture we have already embraced the 1980s as being 'retro' and therefore worthy of pastiche and reinvention, and have reached a point where last year is almost 'retro' before it has happened. Surely the only logical conclusion to such constant repetition is that we reach a point of stasis. Why move on when the past and the present are so rapidly becoming one? Is there ever really such a thing as a new idea and should anyone be looking for one anyway? This is inward-looking in the extreme and lazy, a sickness that seems dominant in much of our culture. It is, perhaps, indicative of a general feeling as we approach the millennium. Maybe it is part of the same syndrome that leaves much of the population uninterested in the existence and function of the Millennium Dome?

This tendency to protect theatre by pushing it into the past or into its own ghetto is accompanied by a converse movement to redefine theatre in the language of television and film in an attempt to make it more immediate and accessible. Television and film may be the dominant forms of popular entertainment at present, aside from pop music, but meeting their challenge by absorbing their characteristics into our theatre work may sometimes prove to be as detrimental as choosing to ignore them. Film can strike one with a huge layering of images simultaneously; it can give visual information, aural gratification and pre-packed emotional response, and all at whatever pace is required. It is an emotional roller coaster ride but, rather like a roller coaster ride, the sensation is immediate, of the moment and short-lived; the emotional response is fixed and quickly passes. Good film directors can take one on huge journeys but they are telling one what, when and how to feel.

This can be highly successful in a medium like film, which is created in a format that is larger than life, yet when directly translated to the stage it has produced a trend of work which is very accomplished, often including massive sets and effects, but which seems to result in a dwarfing of the human element. There is still a considerable amount of highly acknowledged theatre work that owes much of its success to the way in which it imposes ideas and agendas upon an audience. One hears practitioners talking in terms of *coup de théâtre*. This usually means moments when the stage machinery takes over from the actor and the text to create an external and contrived moment. As in action-packed movies, we are given cheap thrills in a way that can excite and entertain but, just as film achieves greater technical excellence and extravagance, theatre can only compete on these terms by becoming more saturated. More and more is loaded onto plays, which often become crushed under the weight of the vision of the production team.

Productions of this size not only demand a scale of gesture that is far greater than anything we see in the everyday, they also belittle the human element by simply dominating it. This is an aesthetic that requires endless business because the simplicity of doing something subtle or the tension of being still cannot be sustained when it appears so small that it registers as almost nothing relative to the scale of the elements around it. The simple beauty of the most human of gestures is being ignored and replaced with a representation of an idea of what an emotional state may be. A similar confidence and boldness is demanded of every area – lighting, costume, performance – and, as a result, the imagination is denied a journey. There is a kind of dictatorial arrogance in the complete denial of any kind of search for a truth. We sit back and watch a representation of life while denying that it relates in any way to our actual lives, and to the 'size' of day-to-day life.

Perhaps this is where the future of theatre lies: a celebration of spectacle that has no purpose to reflect. However, if this were true then surely we would not be witnessing the demise of the huge West End musical as we are just now, for these are the ultimate celebration of style over content. Paradoxically, it is also within the West End that some of the more heartening movements in our current theatre can be seen. The resurgence of drama, particularly the success of the Royal Court in its temporary West End homes, has had a far-reaching effect on the whole of the commercial sector, with an unusual quantity of new plays produced and successful both here and on Broadway. The Royal Court has achieved this while not compromising its creative policies: it has continued to produce new work; it has kept ticket prices low, with very cheap deals available at least once a week; it has presented free student previews; it has maintained a youth theatre policy and seasons of new writing; and, most important, it has continued to take risks. The very success of this venture should be making us reassess who is going to the theatre and why. It should be telling us that there is a new, younger audience who are enjoying having their voice heard on the stage and that theatre can still be relevant to them.

Installation art and contemporary dance are also enjoying growing audiences, particularly amongst the young, and one only needs to see something like Circus of Horrors or the thrilling tightrope walk across the Thames that occurred in 1997 to be reminded that people still love a live event. The excitement of seeing two figures walk across the Thames on a thin wire suspended 100 feet up on a windy evening is unlike anything that could be achieved in the cinema. All these types of performance are linked by the fact that they are both live and collective; dangerous, smelly, real – and that they are human. I have to believe that we do want something else which can leave us exhausted – and exhilarated. The more technology pushes us into working and being entertained at home in a solitary situation, the more the existence of something as immediate and collective as a live event should become very important. We should be celebrating this aspect of theatre, the fact that it is a shared experience, which is constantly changing, and that it is a declaration and exploration of the human, with no pretence to make it into something else.

Within the theatre we may simply have to go back to first principles and redefine what we are doing. To be effective, this should involve the shedding of custom and tradition concerning how a piece is made and the language of theatre we use. It is vital that our work encompasses the opinions and voices of younger generations, and education and outreach work should be a central part of our process, as they were in the 1960s and '70s. We should take responsibility for *why* we make theatre and debate the issue of what its function is. And we should attempt to create an environment where we encourage ourselves and others to see our work in terms of a collective process rather than purely in terms of product. That, of course, is harder, given the 'free market' and the entertainment industry.

It is hardly surprising that we find ourselves in this current crisis. Theatre, like the whole of society, will take time to recover from that period when Thatcher was able to say 'there is no such thing as society'. What could theatre reflect if the very thing it should reflect was eroded and discarded? This, together with the resulting emphasis upon marketing and product, are very much to blame for where we are now. But the important thing is to move on, and not to accept this situation as our lot, or theatre will become an irrelevance. There is hope if we accept there is a challenge. Our greatest enemy is complacency.

9

PETER HALL

Theatre Under Threat

Sir Peter Hall has been Director of the Arts Theatre, London; Director of the Royal Shakespeare Company (which he founded in 1960); Artistic Director of Glyndebourne (1984–90); and Director of the Royal National Theatre (1973–88), successfully establishing it on London's South Bank. Since forming in 1988 his own company, The Peter Hall Company, he has directed over thirty productions including a landmark season of thirteen plays at the Old Vic in 1997. His publications include Peter Hall's Diaries, Making an Exhibition of Myself *and* The Necessary Theatre.

The following arose out of a conversation with the Editors in London on 20 March 1998.

AS I LOOK BACK OVER FORTY YEARS of British theatre, there is a definite turning point in the Seventies when two significant *political* factors began to affect the country, the arts in general, and theatre in particular. It was in the Seventies that the Labour Party completely lost its nerve. Then came Thatcher and the Thatcher years – still potent influences on our national thinking. I have a vivid memory of that moment of change: I was taken out to lunch by the then Minister for the Arts, Norman St John Stevas [7th November 1979, *Diaries*]. He told me that Prime Minister Thatcher had decreed that since we lived in a mixed economy, arts funding would have to get more mixed. The arts in future would have to get sponsorship from the private sector and were to be viewed as an 'enterprise'. New developments in an arts organization would have to be funded by private sponsorship. If it worked, it would be a good example of the power of free enterprise. New private money would lead directly to new developments – a perfect example of our mixed economy. At the same time, he assured me that this new philosophy would in no way threaten established subsidy – which was (and remains) the core funding of all arts organizations. I was fourteen when the Second World War ended, and although the late Forties and Fifties were austere and difficult years, they were also a time of hope – for education, for the National Health Service, and for the arts (who were given subsidy for the first time in their history). The sense of hope and of caring was extraordinary. I was being told over that lunch that those days were over.

It was from that point that I began to fight the whole idea of the market economy being rigidly applied to our culture. Art is not produced by market forces but by visionaries. The public do not need art produced by market research; they demand the new and the unexpected. After innovation, it is possible that art will provide the possibility of exploitation. But it has to be that way round.

I suspected that the sponsorship introduced by Thatcherism was the thin end of the wedge. It would be a means of reducing subsidy. And so it proved. We went into twenty years of funding that was never linked to inflation and, as a result, the Government was able to reduce subsidy to the arts, reduce the power of the Arts Council, and dismantle the whole ecology of theatre-making and music-making that had developed since the war.

This wasn't change; it was revolution. Some change was of course necessary; nothing can remain alive without development. And certainly our country needed some fundamental reforms. By the Seventies the Unions were running the country in an extremely undemocratic way. But Labour could not easily challenge the Unions. It took the Tories to do that. Equally, during the long twenty years of the Tories, it was clear that philosophically the party wanted to stop subsidizing the arts completely. But they didn't quite have the bottle to do it. It now sometimes seems that New Labour is tempted to do to the arts what the Tories always longed to do and never accomplished.

From 1979 we forgot what subsidy was for and with it forgot what supporting the arts was about. Subsidy is linked to education and makes accessibility and availability to all the country its mission. Subsidy is about keeping seat prices low and enabling a whole country to participate in a developing national culture provided not simply by those who want to make money but by those who have vision.

I was hoping that New Labour would champion the cause of subsidy and make it live again. They have done no such thing and in many respects have taken on the abusive vocabulary that Thatcherism developed towards the arts. There have been increases in funding, but they have nothing like made up for the decimations of the last twenty years.

One of the worst consequences of this has been the decline of the regional theatres. A rich regional theatre is essential not only to the profession and to new playwrights, but also for developing tomorrow's audiences. It can be argued that we are a small island and that everyone can get to large cities like London or Glasgow. But the sense of belonging to a community that the old Birmingham Rep had, or the Bristol Old Vic in its heyday, was quite different. When I started in the theatre in the Fifties there were reps everywhere – not always very good and sometimes relying on only a week's rehearsal, but they were nonetheless part of their community and a living reflection of it. They also provided a training ground (of audiences as well as actors) which is now lost. Twenty years ago the Bristol Old Vic had a Studio where the Assistant Director did many cheap productions of the classics. In those days the man assisting the Director of the theatre was Adrian Noble, who now runs the RSC. Now the Studio of the Bristol Old Vic is mostly closed and the Director of the company no longer has an assistant.

Without the rep system, young actors do not have the opportunity to learn from older generations, nor are they tested by a rapidly changing repertory. A crucial training ground for actors, directors, designers, technicians, stage managers and writers has all but disappeared. Tomorrow's audience is consequently diminishing.

Drama schools have also been diminished because they have become more and more commercial in their struggle to survive. One of the marks of the Nineties has been an increasing number of letters each week from young drama students to people like me: they ask for £20 a term to help them pay their tuition fees.

Are we taking care of our heritage?

We are also still suffering from a failure of nerve from the Arts Council in the Seventies. As the National Theatre opened, they had a *real* opportunity to make a truly 'national' future for the theatre in general. I was passionate that the National Theatre company should visit all the major repertories and that the major repertories should visit the South Bank. This did not happen because of the politics of the day. The Arts Council *knew* that there were insufficient resources. So instead of fighting for more, they, in a cowardly fashion, played the National off against the regions, and the regions off against the National. Each side was made responsible for the sufferings of the other. This produced a misconception that the existence of the subsidized theatre companies – the National, the RSC, the Royal Court – *ipso facto* drained money from the regions.

Margaret Thatcher also played politics with the Arts Council. She dismantled it by taking much of its power away and *seeming* to give that power to the regional arts associations. This, with the appointment in 1982 of William Rees-Mogg as Chairman of the Arts Council – who quickly made it plain that his brief was to reduce subsidy – meant that creativity and productivity in the performing arts markedly declined.

Now, in the late Nineties, whole communities have lost their local theatre, and the regional theatres that are left can rarely afford decent actors. A chain reaction has been set up: poor actors lead to poor box office and poor theatre. We cannot have a strong National Theatre, or Royal Shakespeare Company – or any strength in the theatre at all – without the regions. The repair of the regional theatre movement should be New Labour's prime objective. Instead, they seem to turn their eyes away and lecture us about outreach or education – all things that we tried to do in the Sixties. What we need is the replacement of reduced resources, not more management.

There was another critical watershed in 1979. The word went out from the Arts Council that ticket prices must go up and we must charge what the market would bear. Once that is accepted, you have forgotten what subsidy is *for* – namely to make sure that anybody who wants theatre can afford to go to it. I find it socially unacceptable that the Royal Opera House should take £15 million from our taxes and yet expect me to pay £200 for a seat. But make no mistake – this has been forced on them by successive governments.

All this is the background to the current muddle of British theatre. We are a very stupid country: we are extremely proud of our arts, and our prowess in the arts. Yet we suspect our artists and love to demean them. We created the greatest theatre culture in history at the time of Shakespeare. And thirty years later, we pulled it down in the name of Puritanism, utterly destroying it. Four hundred years later, after the great postwar renaissance in the arts, a whole Thatcherite vocabulary was developed to denigrate what had been achieved. Words like 'luvvies'; 'whingeing'; 'welfare state mentality'; 'begging bowl'. There is now a whole culture of denigration used by Arts Ministers and by both the popular and serious press. The Chairman of the Arts Council recently observed in a lecture that those who work in the subsidized arts needn't think they have a 'meal ticket for life'. This is the man who is supposed to be on our side. Recently the Arts Editor of *The Times*, writing about awards, blessed me with a special award as the 'chief whingeing luvvie'. Whose side is he on? Not the arts.

New Labour is obsessed by designer arts. 'Cool Britannia'! They are bedazzled by video, pop music, architecture, fashion. They do not seem to value the oldest and most primitive ways of knowing: music, drama, painting and drawing. These things are basic to our educational system and thus to our lives. They don't seem to understand that. For them, as for the Tories, the performing arts are 'product'; entertainment is an 'industry'. The theatre is thought to be old-fashioned when in fact it breeds talent for the next generation in film and television. Above all, it helps us know and understand, because it is a community's live debate with itself.

Small amounts of subsidy applied to the arts after the last war for the first time transformed the creative potential of Britain. It produced a rich musical culture, great opera companies and ballet companies and a roster of great composers. In the last fifty years we have had twenty or more dramatists of world rank. From 1979 the Tories starved the arts in a very covert way. One can understand that subsidy was diminished by Thatcher because it was absolutely contrary to her basic beliefs in market forces. On the other hand, the *economic* argument against subsidy is nonsense – the arts manifestly earn much much more than they spend. In a recent survey, the arts were shown to be one of the leading industries of the country and a high earner of foreign currency.

New Labour has been a terrible disappointment to the artistic community. After the Tories starved the arts for eighteen years, New Labour arrived and claimed that the arts were badly managed. *Crisis*-managed would be more just. Bad management is a charge that is just not true. The arts in Britain have been in crisis – and have managed remarkably. Admittedly, the mess of Covent Garden has not helped anybody. Their inefficiencies have done considerable damage to the cause of the subsidized arts in general. But it was inefficiency which was initially produced by underfunding. We seem to think that we can run an international opera house for half the cost of any other country. And because it is elitist (what art isn't? – it is special and unique) it has become a very useful stick with which New Labour can punish subsidy.

It is not surprising that the theatre of the Nineties reveals a failure to respond to society's actual needs. Resources have been reduced year on year. So there have been cuts in education programmes, school visits, training, all forms of outreach, and all forms of access. New Labour now lectures us because we don't do them. But we only don't do them because we can't. Give us the resources, give us some support and the fears will disappear.

And there is fear – a fear of taking risks, of losing money, even of being enthusiastic or passionate about belief in the arts. Bureaucracy has increased at all the big companies, while the number of artists employed has declined. It is always safer to have a feasibility study rather than a production. Authority will then excuse any losses. Although the number of theatres has been cut, the number of people having meetings with each other has increased.

I have a lifetime's experience as a producer and manager alongside being a director of plays. Years of running the subsidized companies – the RSC, the National – and limited artistic responsibilities at Covent Garden and at Glyndebourne have made my last ten years in the commercial sector something I was well prepared for. The process is the same: choose the people with vision and with obsession to do the plays, then provide them with a management that gets the very best out of the resources.

The commercial sector faces a very fragile future. Most medium-sized theatres requiring plays can now very rarely get them on a commercial basis. They usually come from the subsidized sector. The subsidized sector has also developed talent for the commercial side and audiences too. I wouldn't now be able to do serious plays in the West End if I had not spent twenty-five years in the subsidized theatre. I have an audience that supports me, as well as a wonderful band of actors. So in working terms, it is a false distinction. The commercial theatre depends on investors; the big companies depend on subsidy. The need to be commercial – to manage well and to attract huge audiences – is the same in both sectors.

A realistic appraisal of the current commercial theatre is very telling. There are fifteen or twenty medium-sized theatres in London's West End, many of them rather beautiful and worthy of preservation. But they are not large enough for musicals, not big enough for the popular plastic theatre that has attracted the tourist trade for many years. Essentially, they need plays, but they are not getting the product – plays are not done by most West End managers because it is impossible to make enough money out of them. No play is viable in the West End now without an expensive star who will bring in the audience. The star is an insurance. But he or she will not play eight times a week for more than two or three months. The eight-performance week is a nineteenth-century habit and a nineteenth-century working practice. It is tantamount to a prison sentence after two or three months. Most people now work a five-day week. Not the theatre actor. So the star will resentfully do eight performances but only for three or four months and on very high wages. So the producer cannot recoup costs and decides that the best thing is not to do a play. Productions for an eight- or nine-hundred seat theatre become increasingly difficult to mount. Only the subsidized sector can launch them and then exploit them on the commercial stages.

I still believe that London needs several theatres, each of which has a policy and a personality. I tried to do this at the Old Vic for a year. And now I have had a year at the Piccadilly Theatre – trying to do repertory. This of course can never be commercial. The backer would be much better off doing one successful play than running a repertory. The costs are much less. Changing over the sets costs money. Rehearsing and maintaining two or three plays rather than one costs money. But the benefits in the working practices of the actors, their standards and above all the choices that the audience can make, prove that it is the only way to run a proper theatre.

The problems are not radically different in the subsidized houses. There is a tendency to think that subsidized theatres are cushioned and can lose money without worrying. This is not true. I created the RSC and ran it for ten years. I ran the National for fifteen years. Every morning, at both houses, the first thing I did when I came to the office was look at the returns from the night before. Unless the figures showed a very high percentage I was quickly worried. And that has not changed.

Because of the constant cutbacks in the subsidized sector, most serious theatre in this country has to exist on an absurdly high budget figure. When I went to Stratford at the end of the Fifties, we would budget on 95 per cent box office. The question was whether we would get 97 per cent or 98 per cent. It was a kind of audience support which I also had in the early years at the National Theatre – which made it possible to do dangerous things like Tony Harrison and Harrison Birtwistle's *Oresteia*.

During my time at the National the productions that did consistently the liveliest business were the new plays. My year at the Old Vic with my own company in 1997 enabled me to do half a dozen new plays on Sundays and Mondays as special events. I found that audiences would come for new plays, particularly on Sundays. They liked impulse buying – going to the theatre as they go to the cinema. That is how to harness a young audience. But it is a risk. In 1998 I was back in the West End and in spite of Bill Kenwright's generous backing I could not do new plays. And I could not open the theatre on Sundays: it was too expensive. Innovation is risky.

We are now so frightened of elitism or of standards that we start approving 'dumbing down' as a democratic activity. We look suspiciously on Shakespeare – perhaps he is too elitist, too difficult, too European. The classical theatre tradition is constantly attacked and I don't think that this Government, for all its cries of 'Education, education, education!' is doing nearly enough. Managements have been set impossible tasks by governments playing to a populist gallery and apparently are only too willing to look warily at artistic challenges. There is no point in education if it has no opportunity to expand the cultural and creative strengths of our people.

We live in a non-verbal society with an active distrust of speech – a distrust, indeed, of any form of decorative language or rhetorical form. Everything is brought down to the easiest common denominator. The politician of today wants to appear on television as a bloke – and be immediate and talk unpretentiously on a one-to-one basis with the man in the street. Rhetoric is out. Major areas of debate, complicated ideas are reduced to soundbites. The old rhetorical concepts are an announcement of the argument, followed by the putting of the case, followed by a discussion, followed by a summation. These are forgotten. Shakespeare learnt the energy of debate at school. And he turned that into drama.

Public speech, public debate, public rhetoric seem to be more and more important in an increasingly passive society that gets its drama from just looking – not participating. Shakespeare will obviously decline as his language becomes more and more difficult. But I believe the importance of public speech and the *live* communication between audience and actor will be seen as more and more precious.

In the long term, far from declining, I think theatre will become more highly valued. Whether or how it will exist, I don't know. I get angry that we have been so wasteful – partly because we have been lucky enough to live through a golden age during the last fifty years. We have had great actors, great productions and a really *live* theatre. So why do we not value it now? Partly, it is the British prejudice against the intellectual. We are the only country that uses the word 'intellectual' as a form of abuse. We have a puritan suspicion of creativity. And a conservative fear of anything radical. Certainly part of the Thatcher campaign against the arts was a belief that art produced 'lefties', looking for a revolution. We are a mad people. We are eccentric and passionate, but also cold and conformist. Perhaps that is why we are so good at theatre.

I am afraid I believe that for social reasons the Government would probably like to privatize Covent Garden. This will be the beginning of the end. It will then be possible to privatize the RSC and the National Theatre and the Royal Court. Possible and desirable. That is my real fear for the arts after the millennium. Our Government points at the Metropolitan Opera of New York because it is entirely privately subsidized. The donors, however, get tax breaks. The loss to the American exchequer is almost precisely the same amount as the subsidy that is given to Covent Garden. Subsidy allows the artist to walk tall and do new works from Berio to

Birtwistle. The Met can only do a conventional programme because it must not displease its sponsors.

As with education or with the Health Service, you cannot quantify the arts in terms of profit and loss. It is a matter of the cost of cultural health. In that sense, theatre is unique. It may take fifty years for a book to be fully appreciated, or a poem. But the act of theatre means public contribution, public support and public judgement *now*. If there is nobody in the audience, you are not creating theatre – and that is only the beginning of the experience. And quantity is not the basis for judgement. A 90 per cent audience does not mean that it is good – or a 30 per cent audience that it is bad. But unless the actor meets an audience, there is no theatre.

This is the ancient strength of theatre. It is live – a living dialogue. And that is where encouragement is needed. When the Arts Council was originally set up, it was an 'enabling body' – it was about actively encouraging what had already been created. It did not try to plan art into existence. It encouraged the creativity that was visible. You cannot plan art. You can only tend it, nurture it, give it care. And then make *absolutely sure* that it is accessible to everyone who has an appetite for it. And that is a factor of price. The arts *must* be cheap, cheap, cheap. Once you say (as Thatcher did) 'The arts must charge what the market can bear,' you have made the arts elitist and unresponsive.

If I were asked what I would do if I could influence the arts policy of this country, I would say we need a National Arts Trust to take care of the arts as the National Trust takes care of our heritage. It should be supported by the public who should be a mighty pressure group watching the antics of Government and what they do to our arts.

We can only save the theatre by concentrating on the regional theatres. They breed the next generation of artists – and above all the next genera-tion of audiences.

I think that the RSC and the National are much too big and I know why they have to be. In order to get proper conditions of work they have had to grow and grow and grow over the years (I was there, doing it). But it does not help creativity. Possibly both of them should be split into small component companies and have less bureaucracy, less marketing, less sponsorship. There is a danger that the peripheral activities, because they keep the ship afloat, are more important than the central activities of putting a play on the stage. We need to start again – bare boards and a passion, and some actors and a good script.

I am sometimes asked whether I envy Peter Brook for leaving England and finding a context in France where he could work without a daily fight for existence. I do envy him, of course. When he told me he was going to Paris he was still with me at the RSC. I begged him not to go and said that somehow I would find the resources for him to do his research programme with the RSC. He didn't doubt that I would try, but he was sceptical: 'You might even succeed. But you must remember that people are not subsidized in England. Only institutions.' So that is how we lost Peter Brook. And Joan Littlewood.

So where are the arts as we reach the millennium? Certainly not enshrined in the Millennium Dome. It is the only great building in history built with absolutely no idea of its purpose. It is a bit like building a cathedral without having found God. I think the only honest thing is to leave it empty. It is a political act, and a desire to show off built it. And I suppose it will be a political act when they get round to putting things inside it. I don't see British arts figuring: certainly the theatre won't be there. There is no theatre space inside it.

My hope is that the integrity of live and lively theatre will be maintained. Three actors can walk on to a bare stage and say to an audience 'This is Rome'. If they have the right text and real talent we believe them. The audience imagines with the actors. The bare stage becomes Rome. But put a camera on them and film the three actors walking on to the bare stage and it will not be Rome. It will be a shot of a place where Rome is absent. The imaginative contract between actor and audience only happens in the live theatre – never in the cinema. And that will never change. The live event will never die since it is as old as human beings – as basic as a group of children making up a story in their play.

The theatre is a place for play. A debating place. A place for fun. A place for understanding.

Ultimately, I am optimistic. I think the creative madness of the British will ensure that the theatre continues in some shape or form. But this will only be after huge convulsions. The theatre in America is virtually dead. There are flickers of hope in the regions, but almost none on Broadway.

Most of their dramatists – Mamet, Sam Shepard – are off in films. Film is the art of our century. But it can never be a live experience, trading in that dangerous chemistry of interaction, imagination and make-believe. It must be different each performance. And at each performance it will elevate the imagination. That is its essence.

10

Venu Dhupa

Creative Producing

Venu Dhupa has worked in the arts for a number of years, initially as a performer and now as a manager. She has experience as a freelancer and in small and middle-scale companies. As well as producing theatre she has produced in radio and video. She is currently Executive Director at Nottingham Playhouse.

I AM WRITING THIS CHAPTER at a critical stage in the arts world when we are hoping for change that will inspire us into the next millennium. I will, however, be addressing problems that face producers, managers and directors today. Although the issues will remain, perhaps with foresight and luck the problems will vanish in the near future, and we will all be relieved to 'surf' through history. That is my hope.

At the Nottingham Playhouse, a producing theatre where I am the Executive Director, we have a senior management structure that, in my view, aims to nurture vision in our artists. We have a triangle, at the two base points of which are the Artistic Director and the Administrative Director, and at the peak is the Executive Director. Our roles are quite distinct: the Artistic Director is responsible for making and developing the art and the artists; the Administrative Director is responsible for the day-to-day running of the theatre, and the Executive Director works with both to maintain a balance between the business and the art, and to develop and maintain an overall strategic vision for the organization. My job, as the Executive Director, is a combination of 'producer' and 'manager' but with the emphasis on creative production.

This is not a common structure in British theatres, and many artistic directors find it threatening to remove the art from the peak of the hierarchy. I feel that the Nottingham Theatre Trust Board has been courageous in instituting this structure – the Board has realized that the supportive role of the 'creative producer' is becoming increasingly important. It has also acknowledged that theatre has to be involved in the life and concerns of the community it serves. Surviving the rapids of the endless flow of reports and paperwork, and the onerous task of running the organization, cannot be achieved by an artist alone. There is also the need for someone to be an advocate for the organization, not only in the region but also in the national forum. However, in my view, it is essential that the person who is responsible for the strategy is also creative, in order to enable the art to breathe life in what is currently a tough financial climate.

If the above structure offers a model that is workable for the future, then where do we find those producers within the subsidized sector who have the skills and the concern for art, business and the community?

In my own case, after graduating from university, I obtained a discretionary grant to go to drama school in London. After some years as a performer in theatre, cabaret, film, television, video and radio, I took a different route, into producing and management. My interest in this area initially grew from working as producer for a company at the Edinburgh Fringe Festival, then from doing various casting jobs, and subsequently gaining an Arts Council Training Bursary for Producers. Throughout, I was balancing this with a continuing and thriving acting career, and I became used to managing and maximizing my time and resources, as all artists and creative producers need to do. If one were to ask a hundred arts administrators how they arrived at their jobs one would no doubt get a hundred different answers about their career paths. The fact that there is still not an effective method for training arts managers *or* producers is worrying for the future. Although the situation with discretionary grants has been eased by New Labour, Arts Council Bursaries have decreased. The drama schools are now peopled by an increasing number of entrants from the privileged classes. Without adequate funding, one needs a job to pay one's way through drama school but the reality of holding down a job and at the same time working one's way through the course is at best formidable and at worst impossible. In addition, the ongoing day-to-day grind that faces the majority of arts administrators makes it impossible for them to offer placements, nurture trainees, or give young people work experience. This means that virtually all doors are closed to the creation of the kind of individual who would otherwise be equipped to face the challenges confronting the arts in the future. This is now left to chance.

At the Nottingham Playhouse we are, therefore, constantly inventing ways of enabling such training: we are trying to take advantage of programmes – such as the Labour government's New Deal – and to form partnerships with the Quality Training Initiative; the Vocational Training Agency; the Training and Enterprise Council, and various European training initiatives – such as through the European Social Fund (ESF). This is time-consuming and we work hard to reassure such funders that our organization can, in today's terminology, 'deliver the outputs'. For example, a recent programme, part-funded by the ESF, had to deliver 10,000 [sic] hours of training to young people between the ages of 16 and 24. Every session had to be monitored and the information processed. We were delighted to deliver the programme – but were living under a tyranny of paperwork. Most of these programmes only contribute a percentage of a wage, so we need to secure support from other sponsors *and* a level of participation from the community.

As producers we sit in our offices and wonder why the national strategists, the funding bodies, the lobbyists, and the advocates are not representing our interests more effectively in Europe. We also question why they are not networking with other national bodies on our behalf – either to obtain information which could be disseminated or to bid strategically for nationally run programmes which could be delivered by local arts institutions, instead of the free-market struggle of countless organizations all operating alone and against the odds. To offer just two examples: there are a number of theatres that are unable to afford proper support for Information Technology. Why is it not possible for the Regional Arts Boards (RABs) to employ a full-time specialist who could be on call for all the organizations in the region? – a much more cost-effective approach that oddly has not been suggested until recently. Even if this required a subscription from each theatre for such a service, this would still be cheaper for any one theatre than a full-time wage. We have to buy in Information Technology services at the rate of £250 per day;

we only need to pay for two days yet we are virtually paying a weekly wage. To take another example: arts organizations have to supply endless facts and figures in endless different formats. Why can't RABs engage a finance officer to create a template or software for their clients that would enable the standardization of all necessary information – instead of the current wasteful situation in which individual theatres have to pay different finance managers to come up with different systems? In the long term, a single finance officer could be situated within an RAB, and access all facts and figures in the required format for all theatres in the area, thus leaving time for the arts administrators, many of whom have no formal training in accountancy, to tackle the other aspects of their demanding and multifaceted job.

Another urgent strategic issue for the creative producer is the relationship between theatre and the new technology. This goes much further than the issue of Information Technology mentioned earlier, because here is a potential tool to enable development of new forms, growth in access to theatre, and innovation in theatre education, if used imaginatively. For example, an interview with an actor in a current show could appear on the Internet, or an extract from the show itself could be seen on a website. Yet this kind of development is inhibited by several key difficulties: theatre practitioners are frightened of new technology; they are resistant to the innovations it could bring, and only a few understand how it could be utilized to greater effect. The chances are that those running our leading theatres are mostly inexperienced in the use of this technology and fail to see it as a complement to the theatre – only as a threat. So the practicalities that need to be negotiated before we can see its impact are not being addressed. For example, how would actors be realistically remunerated for giving an interview on the Internet, or for an extract of a play transmitted on a website? If technicians were to be filmed during a technical fit-up, what pay rate should apply? Managers need to sit down with the relevant unions, such as Equity and BECTU (Broadcasting, Entertainment, Cinematograph and Theatre Union), to discuss such issues, and then undertake an experimental format to obtain measurable results. If parties are unwilling to work together, then progress will be slow and patchy, not only in relation to these examples of partnership between the arts and other sectors, but also in many other areas where the potential for innovation – and thus access – is enormous.

Many regional theatres also face the issue of the pay scales they can offer or might be able to offer in the foreseeable future. At Nottingham Playhouse only six out of more than sixty full-time jobs pay more than the national average – a poor reward for unsocial working hours, a short-term contract and extreme dedication. There is little hope that our artists or other staff would be able to invest in pensions, mortgages, private health care, or any other 'dreams' urged on us – particularly in the eighteen years of Conservative government, and now with the Labour government. For the majority of theatre workers the most they can aspire to is simply keeping their heads above water.

In all the years I was a performer, and in my first years in administration, I was only out of work for a total of six months. Nonetheless, I could barely afford the rent on a small flat, a 'third-hand' car, and a small private pension contribution. The result is either burn out – or get out! The highest number of better paid jobs in the theatre are to be found in areas of transferable skills, such as marketing or consultancy. For many other employees, even senior administrators, the daily tasks required to fulfil the job leave little time – or money – for self-development. Cross-training is a low priority for most theatres and, although staff may be successful in their specialisms, there is little opportunity to transfer these skills in order, for example, to become a better executive director who can develop and maintain a long-term vision. At Nottingham we often feel we are training people only for them to leave our profession which, in turn, reduces the number of possible inspirational role models.

As we approach the new millennium there is, and should be, a growing emphasis on access, since going to the theatre is a practice enjoyed only by the minority. Access is being targeted at young people, those who are socially excluded and the culturally diverse. For the first time there has been state funding in the 1990s for groups who perform in a non-European language; for all its faults, the National Lottery has enabled funding to go directly to small groups through the Arts For Everyone Express Scheme.

But while regional theatres up and down the country are being advised to target new audiences, nobody can tell us where to find such groups or, if they are found, how we are supposed to entice them into the theatre. Why should anyone expect to come to your home without knowing you? Yet our funders expect results. What we are trying to do in Nottingham is to work with the City and County funders to set realistic targets both in terms of numbers and geographical areas, and this often involves outreach work. In this way we are partners with our funders, and we are not chasing imaginary audiences or competing with other arts ventures for the same clientele. Thus funders could assist us with our access policy and plan their own more strategically.

When it comes to finding an approach to attracting an ethnic audience, it may help if one believes that one does need to give in order to receive. The first question for those of us who run arts institutions is the question of values and of quality. We tend to judge art by our own values and standards. Recently I went to the Hackney Empire in London's East End and saw a comedy from Jamaica. The subject matter was not to my taste but the place was packed and everyone was enjoying it immensely. I had to acknowledge that there was a thriving market for this kind of theatre. If we genuinely want to welcome people into our buildings we have to welcome them on their terms and not on ours. Sometimes one needs to listen to what people want – and not give them what we want them to have or what we perceive will be good for them.

What draws people to an event is something that touches their lives – a factor that works better than all the subsidized tickets in the world. Once people have an awareness they can build their knowledge of the aesthetic and even become creators themselves. People want to participate in activities they perceive as being valuable. With changes in industry, in the ways we make money, and the increasing emphasis on the management of human resources, I believe that the arts are well placed to nourish the skills that will be in demand. I produced an arts project for young Asian women at the Royal National Theatre, called NADYA (from the Hindi for 'river' or 'link'). At first I stressed the performance skills element of the programme – a stress that was not valued by the majority in the community I was targeting. As soon as I made the participants aware of other skills that would be enhanced – such as lateral thinking, team work, problem-solving, assertiveness and presentation – the participants realized those skills would be of value to them in the workplace or for getting a job, and they supported the project wholeheartedly. They had recognized the wider value of the artistic activity. Imagine what could be achieved if the value of the arts were reinforced for everyone in our society from nursery education upwards.

If we want to improve the quality of ethnic work we have to empower and nurture both the audiences and the artists. Empowerment is the bridge into the arts. Role models from ethnic minority groups often disappear without trace, yet they are invaluable sources of information and encouragement. If the information could be accessed from renowned artists such as Carmen Munroe or Rudolf Walker it would save the younger generation reinventing the wheel. For many minorities it would help us break through psychological barriers. One doesn't feel so alone if someone has done it before. It would offer real encouragement and there are times when one needs it. For example, I often have to give talks about the theatre in which I work, and I usually take a trainee with me. Several times it has happened that on our arrival the host would head straight for the – white – trainee with hand outstretched in welcome. They had assumed the trainee was the person giving the talk – while I was in tow as the trainee. The hosts were always extremely apologetic, and never intended any harm, but it taught me a great deal about people's expectations.

Another instance of these kinds of assumptions took place when I was once leading a post-production talk with the audience in the main auditorium of a theatre near London. I had done several such talks with the cast of that particular show. A member of the audience thought nothing of commenting on how good my English was, and then proceeded to talk about *Bhaji on the Beach*, a film I had not seen and which was in any case completely irrelevant to the discussion. One learns to handle this, of course, but it can and does affect other people's perception – one is almost forced into a minority position whether or not minority issues are being addressed.

Funding bodies could or even should consider projects that contain an element of disseminating experience in order to overcome both the lack of role models and other people's assumptions and expectations, particularly in relation to minorities. We also need people who understand the work, and can discern the potential of an artist or a company – yet producers, managers or administrators from ethnic groups are rare. Once such work has been identified, then those artists need the space to develop and cement their original promise. The experience of British minorities is complex, and so much hope is invested in every piece of work which, inevitably, cannot please everybody. When a piece of work is criticized, senior administrators of some institutions often feel unable to support their artistic choices, and retreat into platitudes of political correctness. Such bad experiences are costly, especially in terms of morale, and then a new work by the same artist remains unproduced for years.

Another common mistake is the funding of minorities to explore their experiences only as minorities. If funding bodies enabled artists to work as artists first and minorities second, it would open up a host of experiences that would enable people to compete for prime opportunities. Institutions and venues should be funded and required to produce and host a range of work, including work exploring minority issues, because such work should be perceived as necessary. This should apply irrespective of where they are geographically located. Managers should not be put in the position of saying to a 'minority' company: 'Oh, sorry, I can't include your work in my season because I've already got a black company.' If I heard this, my heart would sink: if my work were rejected, then I would want it to be because of the quality of the art, not the colour of the company.

One of the things I did when I started at my post in Nottingham was to go out and see what else was on offer and to meet as many people as I could who were sampling various forms of entertainment: this took me to pubs, clubs, bingo, the dog track, football, the cinema, the races, cricket, the ice stadium, and so on. But more importantly, it gave me a feel for what was influencing people to buy tickets. At least I now have a chance of attracting them into the theatre even if it is not initially to buy a theatre ticket. It may be for a drink, to see a late night comedy act or some other forms of light entertainment such as bands, ventriloquists, cabaret shows, karaoke. If people can relax in the theatre and feel they have ownership of it then they will see it as part of their community and they will have a stake in its success. The arts should be promoted as a conviviality against a landscape of industrial toil – or unemployment. If an enjoyable shared experience is reduced below a certain level, no amount of profit can effectively satisfy society's 'soul'. For many minority groups, cultural conviviality is the norm – so the funding bodies must ensure that they are enabled to access their own riches.

There is a growing attitude in Britain that art has to prove itself. I am not sure how far this is rooted historically in the British psyche. In many other cultures, art is considered organic to people's lives. It may not be the kind of art we are used to seeing in our theatres in Britain, but it can allow for access, education and celebration, and may be a potent force for change here. It can also be remarkably effective in building social cohesion and empowering people. There have been some wonderful examples in Britain that have empowered whole groups as well as individuals: for instance, Mind the Gap is a national performing arts organization that works with people who have little access to mainstream arts. It has run programmes in Bradford to enable people with learning difficulties to release their potential through theatre techniques such as improvisation, music, dance and devised work. I do believe that creativity is inherent within human beings, and I agree that art may be a tool for creative education, but it should not be a tool for implementing a politically motivated hidden agenda – social work in the guise of access. Equally, it is the case that creative potential requires the right circumstances in which to flourish. We do not need a 'luvvie' culture in which it is the 'who' making the art that provides the valuation for whether it is good or not – such cultural valuations strangle some genuine and diverse talents. We need to open networks to all kinds of groups so that they are equally able to aim for artistic heights, and not be marginalized or hidden.

It is ironic that while many theatres pride themselves on their access policies, and regard the large sale of concessionary tickets as an indicator of how well they are doing, there is nonetheless greater and greater pressure to earn box-office income. To balance this demand with providing genuine access is a major pressure for any organization. It was disappointing when I recently heard of a publicly funded scheme to nurture new audiences – only to find out that the application for such funding was by invitation only. Many arts organizations read about money allocated only in the press. I must make it quite clear that I am not blaming our RAB, which had made the effort to invite the application. They themselves are working under enormous pressures, and are having to deal with rapidly changing central policies. If organizations are to be accountable then there must be a level playing field, including the Royal Opera House. If our sponsors or funders wish us to produce new models for access instead of just staggering incoherently into the future, then they should have the courage to fund more creatively and more equally – and then examine the results.

Many theatres, including the Nottingham Playhouse, perform well and responsibly year after year. When it is evident that the best value for the artistic health of our region would be delivered by increasing the funding of our theatre, considerable political courage would be required in the current social, economic and cultural climate to implement such a policy. It would seem that everybody concerned with the arts needs to alter the prevailing national ethos that does not consider art a priority because – according to those who oppose subsidy of the arts – we have not yet devised a means of quantifying its value. And that is exactly what one cannot do with culture any more than one can quantify the value of education. Yet the Labour government has put education at the top of the list for investment. Perhaps one day education in the creative arts will be valued, and then it may be that audiences drawn from a wider spectrum of society will increase justification for proper subsidy. 'Art for art's sake – but money for God's sake.' Why, though, does the funding system penalize those institutions that are performing well? And where is the forum for genuine debate of such issues? Such genuine debate is now needed more than ever if politicians are to be persuaded, attitudes changed, and people enlightened.

These are some of the difficulties and pressures faced daily by a creative producer. If one were to ask people currently working in the arts sector where they would least like to work at the present time, I expect they would respond by saying 'running a regional repertory theatre'. Yet I feel privileged and excited to have the position of custodian of a community resource, and would not want to work anywhere else.

With such issues of vital importance for the future of theatre – from training and pay scales to the use of new technology and access – I hope I have made it clear that the role of the producer (and indeed, manager) has changed enormously in recent times. To conclude with perhaps an unusual angle: it is not only playwrights, performers, directors, designers and musicians who must exercise their creativity to make theatre. Increasingly the focus will be on creative producers and managers. Whether managing the most modest local arts project or the most wide-reaching national arts strategies, to be successful, future producers will be acknowledged as visionary strategists as well as artists in their own right.

11

GENISTA MCINTOSH

The Price of Change

Genista McIntosh is Executive Director of the Royal National Theatre. She is also a Board member of the Young Vic, Sheffield Theatres Trust, Sadler's Wells and the Theatre Museum, a member of the British Council Drama and Dance Advisory Committee, and Chair of South London Common Purpose. She was created a Life Peer in 1999.

ALTHOUGH MY PROFESSIONAL LIFE in the theatre has always been associated with large national companies, except for an initial spell with, and subsequent brief return to, an agency, my interests and the sources of my theatrical knowledge have always had a much wider focus.

The formative stage in my career coincided with the explosive growth of the fringe in the late 1960s and early '70s. It was the fringe, along with some of the regional theatres, that was then providing the networks which allowed actors, directors and writers to develop; and that development was what interested me when I was working for the Royal Shakespeare Company, first as Casting Director at the outset of my career and subsequently as Planning Controller, Senior Administrator and Associate Producer – and it still does interest me now I am at the Royal National Theatre as Executive Director.

The running down of these networks since the 1980s, mostly as a result of funding decisions, has meant a progressive reduction of the opportunities they offered for training and development. This represents a real material loss not just to audiences who have been denied their work but to the theatrical profession as a whole. There is no longer the variation, strength and depth there once was.

Having worked on both sides of the employment fence – at the RSC and the Royal National Theatre as a provider and, from the time when I went into partnership with an agent, as a seeker on behalf of others – I have been able to observe these changes in opportunity across the spectrum of activity, from those at the top who are able to command a high salary and choose their own projects to those coming straight out of drama school.

In parallel with this, my work has also involved me in managing the changes in funding. The RSC got involved in sponsorship and private funding quite early on and had a well-established set of relationships by the time I returned in 1986 as Senior Administrator. In those early days of arts sponsorship, corporations were willing to become involved, using their marketing or sponsorship budgets, with productions that would have happened anyway. A theatre company could say: 'We are going to do this production of *Hamlet*. If you put your name to it, we can offer you publicity and facilities to entertain your clients and the money you give us will go into our general revenue kitty, which will support the production as well as our other core activity.'

Government encouraged the search for private sponsorship, claiming that this was not replacing funding for core activity. Gradually, however, private funders became less and less willing to support activities that would have occurred regardless of their support, or to back whole companies. They wanted to be identified with activity that was specifically theirs, that would not happen without their money. This led to a proliferation of extra activity that was driven by the requirements of sponsors. They were not dictating what that activity should be, let alone its content, but simply that, in order to earn the sponsorship, theatre companies produce work that they would not otherwise have done.

Much important work, in touring and education in particular, grew out of this situation, which created new opportunities for employment and helped companies to diversify. But at the same time, funding from the public purse was generally held at a standstill or cut. The consequence was an increase in output that had to be supported without an increase in resource. The defining core of work, for which companies received public funds, struggled to survive.

In the case of the RSC, the company, in a seeming paradox, had to expand to stay afloat. It redefined its core activity as it increased the number of theatres it ran from two in the early 1970s when I joined, to five when the Swan was opened in 1986. There were terrific benefits, not just because the 'risk base' was spread but because of the much greater range of work on offer. But there comes a point in any arts organization's life when it reaches an optimum size. This is as true of a very small as of a very large company – once it grows beyond that size it becomes increasingly difficult to retain a clear identity.

In the 1980s there was much of this kind of expansionism, driven by the requirement placed on companies to attract private as well as public funding. Integral to this trend was the need to demonstrate 'value for money'. Theatre, widely seen as a lame duck industry, spent a lot of energy on arguing the economic points – job creation, contribution to the exchequer through National Insurance, income from tourism, prestige abroad, etc. There was great pressure on theatre companies to demonstrate that they were making maximum use of the money they received; annual reports would emphasize the number of productions created, the number of performances given, the number of people who had attended them and, if possible, a diminishing subsidy per seat.

The argument was so well made in certain quarters that it sometimes became the *only* argument. This was counter-productive. Vital as it was, the 'value for money' case left out the importance of the art itself – and why audiences respond to it. These days the economistic justification for public funding is still heard but has lost its centrality. There is an increasing recognition that mere quantity of activity is not the point. The expansionist tendency has burnt itself out; it simply could not be sustained. Whilst there is a democratic requirement for subsidy to be properly accounted for – the arts are not a separate world in the universe and do not need to be, nor should be, protected from wider social reality – there is, nonetheless, a growing realization of the necessity to keep reinforcing the spiritual values that should be at the heart of all human activity of any worth, and especially of arts activity.

Interestingly, even before the election of a Labour government in 1997, questions about the direction and balance of arts policy had begun to be asked by people in the private sector. The Arts Council of Great

Britain, as it was then, was following a political agenda set by the previous Conservative administrations, which had abandoned the arm's length principle of the postwar consensus; the values of public subsidy and private sponsorship were converging, and the Arts Council was trying to broker a more or less satisfactory arrangement between the recipients of funding and the providers. Yet leading figures in the commercial sponsorship sector were concerned that their role as funders was becoming too central, and added their voices to the chorus that was reminding Government that willingness to fund the arts was an important indication of the political and social health of the nation.

Unlike some, I don't think the introduction of private sector funding was a pollutant. It is possible to argue that the great amount of time, effort and resource required to generate the extra that the private sector has provided could have been better spent on creating art but you cannot prove a negative. I believe the contact the theatre has made with commercial organizations has been stimulating and useful: it has brought to bear different perspectives and expertise. Creative energy has not been stopped in its tracks by the sponsorship culture – Theatre de Complicite, for example, was originally funded by the private sector before achieving public funding and its international reputation – but I think it is now much more difficult for people to find ways of getting started.

Fund-raising has changed enormously in the last decade or so, both in terms of its sources and how theatre companies now have to approach those sources. The early National Lottery projects, for example, have hugely affected the availability of funds from the private sector. The emphasis on capital support has significantly influenced the ability and willingness of private funders to provide money for revenue, where it is really needed. All of this has tended to breed caution and apprehension, even in young people who should be our innovators and risk-takers.

It is easy, however, to sentimentalize or glorify the past and to imagine that the big institutions used to experiment more and constantly do risky things, unlike today. Nostalgia for what genuinely was remarkable then should not obscure the fact that creativity and innovation nearly always come up from below. Raw talent is rarely first encouraged by big companies; it usually takes root in the undergrowth and by the time it emerges into the established theatre world it is quite robust. To take a recent example: Stephen Daldry's 1992 production of J. B. Priestley's *An Inspector Calls* made a tremendous impact and was ground-breaking for the National, yet neither his creative formation nor the genesis of this production originated there. As with the fringe, when a theatre in a basement or above a pub becomes part of the theatrical mainstream and another springs up to take its place, so it is with individuals. A new play by a young playwright might be received with more generosity at the Royal Court Theatre Upstairs or at the Bush than if it were produced at the Cottesloe or The Pit because of the different expectations that operate when the big companies are involved. True risk-taking tends to happen away from the large institutions, but innovative artists are facing increasing difficulties in raising funds for experiment, especially at the beginning of their careers. That kind of project funding from the public purse has been reduced and reduced.

As the revenue base of companies shrinks – Arts Council or regional arts funding, funding from the private sector, and funding through ticket sales – so, if quality is to be sustained, artistic activity will tend to reduce and that in turn leads to questions about the defining characteristics of a company. The Royal National Theatre is a three-theatre operation and each of those three theatres should present a mixed repertoire so that in any given two-week period there could be nine productions on offer. This is an extremely expensive system because it is labour-intensive; large numbers of actors are required for the type of repertoire presented and a large number of support staff are also needed in administration, in marketing and press, front of house and backstage, to manage the complexity of the system. But this repertoire programming is what makes the National distinctively itself.

'What is the National Theatre?' is a question that never goes away but is particularly urgent now, as the value and meaning of big artistic institutions is under such scrutiny. Increasing emphasis has been laid recently on the importance of good financial management, leading to the implicit (sometimes explicit) suggestion that 'artistic' ambition should if necessary be held back. It is symptomatic that the Royal Opera House was briefly run by a Chief Executive seconded from the accountancy partnership Coopers & Lybrand. In my view you cannot separate managing such institutions from their artistic philosophy, which in turn cannot be separated from their economic support system. An artistic director cannot just be responsible for the art and let someone else worry about the money and the management, nor can I, as Executive Director, be solely responsible for managing and let someone else worry about the art. Every artistic judgement has an economic impact and every change in the economy of such organizations has an impact on the art. Management, therefore, requires flexibility and new skills, which have to be developed almost on the hoof.

We need to have a sense of what is likely to work now, artistically and financially, rather than what worked five years ago, which means keeping up to date with what is happening elsewhere and what funders are likely to be willing to support now and in the near future. We must have the ability to assess the potential of any piece of work, or any combination of pieces of work, before they have been produced and be able to understand the implications for the whole enterprise if any one piece does not perform as expected – and we need to have strategies for adjustment if our projections turn out to be wrong.

These are testing times. There is little popular support for the arts, no strong consensus to sustain continued public funding. The disastrous unfolding of the Royal Opera House story has given ammunition to those who see the 'high' arts as the province of a small, socially exclusive and excluding group, whose private pleasures are being massively subsidized by a population who can get no benefit from their contribution. This situation was exacerbated by early decisions concerning the distribution of Lottery funds (widely characterized as 'the people's money'). The allocation of £78 million to the Royal Opera House in 1995 (and their reaction to it) was probably the single most damaging event in the recent history of the arts in the UK. It gave licence to the latent hostility to art and artists that has been evident in this country for a long time.

Although we are on the edge of a new millennium, and political leaders of various persuasions have confidently predicted the imminence of the 'classless' or 'inclusive' society, we are still riven by social divisions and conflict that survive pretty much unchanged from the nineteenth century. The political status of artists (and therefore of art) has always been ambiguous – they appear to be outside the accepted social structures (barely respectable and liable to hold dangerously radical opinions) whether viewed from 'above' or 'below' and are consequently regarded with deep suspicion from every angle. The 'luvvie' stereotype, together with the wide-spread scorn for 'modern' art (look at the language used in the tabloid press whenever the Turner Prize is about to be awarded), reinforce the perception of an unbridgeable gap between high art and popular culture, which, incidentally, is assumed to include a number of pleasures, horse racing for example, that are predominately the province of the rich. I do not believe this gap needs to exist, but our collective eagerness to keep it going seems ineradicable.

However, I don't think our philistinism is all bad. It has engendered a tremendously lively, pragmatic kind of creativity and although there is a lot of serious work going on we tend to approach it with a lightness of touch that is admired elsewhere. It is ironic that this creative quickness, and our realization that not everything has to be deeply significant, is part of that anti-intellectualism to which the Lottery has given such sharp focus.

We need to harness new technologies, but we need also to remind people of the importance of live performance. There is a current demand for live performing arts organizations to make more and more of their work available through broadcast or recorded media in order to justify public funding. There is a simplicity in the argument that is appealing and hard to resist; people who do not have direct access to the live performance can have access by these other means. But there is also a danger; if the recorded artefact diminishes the value of the original source, either because it is modified beyond what is possible in live performance or because its quality is so poor that nobody could be encouraged to try the live experience, then there will be no more live performance and, hence, no more artefacts.

The transitional period we are in is, I believe, a time of much more profound political change than we have yet allowed ourselves to acknowledge. If we take advantage of it, and if we are rigorous, we can answer the core questions: what are we doing and who are we doing it for? We can remind ourselves and society at large that there is an activity which can only be done one way; it requires people to be performing in front of other people who are watching, live, at the same moment in the same space. If we do not make our case well, live performance will become a rarity and skills will be lost forever.

I am not optimistic about the short-term future. Things are going to get worse before they get better. But we live in exciting times and must take the opportunities as they present themselves. The arts community has recently been put on the back foot and needs to regroup, to find new allies and to build up support differently on the basis of a much more deeply rooted argument about why it is necessary to sustain artistic activity. Given that there are only a few arenas left for serious public debate, this will have to happen to some extent in private. It may seem on the surface that everything is in decline and is fragmenting, but if we can survive, which is a crude, visceral kind of activity, and use this time to rebuild politically as well as physically, something that the Lottery has made possible, then we might be able to find a subtler, more sophisticated argument for our existence than either the quantitative 'value for money' economic case or the aesthetic elitist assertion of right. This is a big intellectual and political challenge and has an analogy in the political field. The goal of creating a society that operates on egalitarian values remains the same even in New Labour's philosophy but the methods have had to change and will continue to change. We have to find a language that allows us to move forward and that isn't stuck in regret for the past. We have ourselves been guilty of sloppy thinking as well as having it imposed on us by others. If we don't take up the challenge, we will lose the battle to survive.

LEILA JANCOVICH

Reinventing Ourselves

Leila Jancovich formed the company Bhathena-Jancovich with Chenine Bhathena in 1993, following a combined eleven years' experience in arts administration. Since then they have focused on supporting the development of new live performance in the UK and have become one of the leading producers for contemporary arts, particularly physical theatre and visual performance. They act as consultants to new and established companies as well as providing a tour management, fund-raising and marketing service for UK and international work. They also undertake festival and event coordination and produce the 'Total Theatre Awards' in Edinburgh.

THE LATE 1990s: a new millennium approaching, a new Labour government, and London voted the coolest international city. The arts should be blooming. But after twenty years of cutbacks in theatre, during which, according to the Independent Theatre Council, more than a hundred touring companies folded in the early Nineties alone, you won't find many people working in the industry who are celebrating.

Even the money the arts receives from the National Lottery is not secure. Since the Lottery began in 1995 when its first organizers, Camelot, were awarded a five-year contract, they have distributed funds to support five 'good causes' – the arts, sport, heritage, charities and the Millennium Fund. As the Millennium Fund was only ever intended to operate until the year 2000 a sixth 'good cause' was proposed in 1998. Distributed via what is called the New Opportunities Fund, this embraces schemes designed to improve health, education and the environment, and it has already reduced the percentage share available to the arts. When the Lottery contract comes up for renewal there is no guarantee that Camelot, or their successors, will continue to allocate the money in the same way. As the only new area of money that has come into theatre for many years, allowing ambitious projects to be dreamed of again, its loss or reduction raises a real concern. The Lottery must not be used to replace statutory funding and help keep taxes falsely low.

In 1998 the Labour government began a major review of the Arts Council's structure and functions. This has already resulted in a new, slimmed-down Council and devolution of some of its grant-giving powers. If theatre is to survive and flourish in the twenty-first century this continuing review must be total, to include not only how we manage funding but also how we manage our theatres.

Since the late 1980s the Arts Council has practised a policy of 'equal misery to all' – keeping established companies on standstill funding and reducing funds for projects and new developments. This policy has made life easier for the Government. It is so much harder to mobilize opposition when a new company is not awarded funding than when a known and established organization has its funding cut. The public perception is of a whingeing theatre industry that constantly cries bankruptcy but never actually closes.

In 1996-97 the Arts Council Drama Department spread limited money between new projects (under £2 million) and long-term revenue funding arrangements (over £25 million). Similar percentages can be seen across other art forms, and the beneficiaries of long-term funding would need to make a serious mistake to lose their funding. These revenue clients, however, are frustrated because, with real costs increasing through inflation, standstill funding means their money has to be spread thinner each year, and project applicants become disillusioned as decisions are increasingly predetermined. The same companies receive project funds year after year, leaving no space for genuinely new talent to compete.

If money is scarce, and it will continue to be so, we have to be willing to cut the revenue portfolio to free up more money for new emerging work and we need to develop the role of theatre buildings. Instead of repertory theatres churning out ever safer and more conservative product, they should transform into laboratories. With companies and artists resident in them, they would offer a more varied programme. Touring companies, instead of aiming to progress from project to revenue status, should be encouraged to abandon their separate offices and administrators and to reduce their overhead costs by sharing resources with other companies.

Charles Handy, Visiting Professor at the London Business School and author of a number of best-selling management books, uses theatre as a model that business will follow in the twenty-first century. The multi-skilled worker on short-term contracts is already replacing the single-skill worker with a job for life. Our actors, stage crew, directors, designers and writers have always had to be adept at balancing a portfolio of work. As managers we have held on to our own security and created a myth, perpetuated by the funding structures, that every theatre company needs a full-time office and a full-time administrator for the work to develop.

In 1993 my business partner and I gave up our jobs as arts administrators to set up a management company offering arts administration, marketing, event and tour management on a consultancy basis. What we began to offer was a cost-effective way for a number of companies to share administrative resources, whilst still retaining and developing the administrative expertise required to support the work the companies wanted to create. Where previously we managed one company each, we now have a portfolio that covers ten or more companies a year, currently including five overseas companies and five UK-based companies. Their focus is on new work and they generally tour once a year, mainly on the arts centres/studio theatres network. Each company pays the equivalent of one day's consultancy per week rather than the cost of a full-time administrator and office. This reduction in the administrative cost in turn increases the amount spent on creating the art. Such is the popularity of this way of working that we now hold a database of people doing similar work to us.

In contrast, the workforce based in theatre buildings has grown as marketing, sponsorship and fund-raising departments have become vital for the survival of the theatres concerned. Many artists decry the constant struggle for increased income generation, but it is a reality we will continue to face. Yet these building-based institutions, which take up such a large proportion of available funding, surely have a responsibility to share their expertise with the wider theatre community, and should do so.

The more imaginative theatres put 'bums on seats', not by compromising the artistic process to the white, middle-aged, middle-class traditional theatregoers, but by collaborating with a new generation of artists. They have looked for new, younger and culturally diverse audiences, and have taken on the challenge of creating work for them.

As well as the need to find new audiences, the need to find new money from commercial sponsorship, social funds and economic regeneration budgets has given theatre a sense of itself within a wider context, making it less isolated as a business and therefore less vulnerable.

Cultural trends are now showing that audiences for theatre are on the increase. In 1994, according to statistics provided by the Independent Theatre Council and the Theatrical Management Association, 23 million people attended nearly 70,000 theatre performances. The projected changing work patterns brought about by new technology and home-based working offer the possibility of more control over both our work and leisure time than was on offer in the 1980s. If theatre is going to compete for people's leisure time, it needs to go on supporting work at the research and development stage, where the latest innovations are explored. For this to happen we must fund the newest work that is emerging and not tie up all support on historically based funding. The funding bodies must adapt to cultural changes instead of opting for safe traditional work. Even if funding levels were increased, a system of continuous funding to the already established companies and rewarding successful new companies by bringing them into the mainstream is unsustainable. As new companies form each year, levels of subsidy would also have to increase each year in order to accommodate the new whilst maintaining the old.

When the Arts Council was formed in 1945 it had revenue commitments to thirty companies, and its main objective was to support a repertory system that had a local theatre in every town. These 'reps' provided a programme of work for a local audience and also acted as a training ground for actors and directors. By 1984 the Arts Council revenue commitment had increased to eighty organizations, with the 'reps' having developed a reputation for conservative programming as well as an ageing population of theatregoers.

Many young artists were frustrated by the formal and hierarchical nature of this repertory training and began to devise work themselves in their own companies. The work of these companies provided an alternative programme of touring work, which was less literary and more theatrical, incorporating the physical theatre influences of Europe and reflecting the cultural diversity of Britain. Companies such as Theatre de Complicite, the David Glass Ensemble and Trestle Theatre redefined what had been seen as 'fringe', building new audiences for experimental work and feeding this into mainstream theatre production. Others, like Black Mime Theatre, Tara Arts, Talawa and Graeae, developed culturally specific audiences whilst also educating mainstream theatregoers in a broader world perspective, which again influenced mainstream theatre's casting policies. Such companies became the inspiration to many hundreds of small companies who provide work for a touring circuit that includes arts centres, community venues, schools and colleges. Yet despite the growth in project and touring work, it was this most vulnerable but also most experimental sector that bore the brunt of each new cut in funding.

The Arts Council's original brief was to respond to artists rather than direct policy. It existed without a review of policy until 1984 when, in *The Glory of the Garden*, 'in recognition of the financial constraints inside which government is working' it made its first response to the forthcoming cutbacks. The report gave priority to repertory theatres over the emerging touring companies, but urged venues to use their funding to support the wider theatre community by setting up education departments and housing touring companies. The *institutions* of theatre were preserved but told to modernize by recognizing the cultural diversity and education needs of their wider constituency rather than relying exclusively on the traditional theatregoing audience.

In 1991 a further review was undertaken. The Council's Arts and Media strategy acknowledged that the 'reps' were not taking on their supportive role. Far from developing audiences the 'reps' had, in fact, experienced a 13 per cent drop in attendance between the mid-1980s and mid-1990s. By 1996 the Arts Council's Drama White Paper was showing that the provision in studios, which the Council had hoped would house the touring work, had reduced by 25 per cent (against only a 7 per cent reduction on in-house shows). Venues that were still programming a healthy season of touring work were offering reduced fees or box-office splits. The thriving touring market was under serious threat. The Arts and Media strategy changed priorities from buildings to companies, and project funds received a 22 per cent boost. But within two years this commitment had been completely overturned, with project funding sinking to three quarters the level it had been in 1986-87. The Arts Council did not have the courage of its own convictions. Increased funding to projects meant making radical cuts to revenue-funded organizations. Decision-making panels made up of revenue clients were not willing to do this.

In spite of the disproportionate assault on new projects, figures from the Independent Theatre Council and Theatrical Management Association show that touring companies still offered 31,700 performances in 1994 compared with 37,500 performances by the larger, established building-based companies. The Independent Theatre Council, the membership body for touring theatre in the UK, still boasts 450 members, many of whom find their own ways of creating innovative work that crosses art forms and of operating as lean, efficient businesses without traditional funding.

In today's climate, following the overhaul of the Arts Council under New Labour, there need to be new priorities. We must hope that rather than maintaining a failing status quo, and repeating the historical mistakes of the last twenty years, the new Council finds a vision for the management of theatre that allows work to be created rather than institutions to be formed. In order to do this I see no option but to reduce revenue funding and the support for small institutions that become reliant on subsidy for evermore (or until they fall out of favour with their funders). Instead, money should be freed and given to the artist, specifically for research and development. Bursaries to individual artists, directors and writers should be expanded so that they can develop ideas and programmes of work. These can then be created in collaboration with other artists and theatres already possessing the administrative resources to support them.

While investment in research and development should be the centre of our arts policy, there will still be a need to support theatre buildings for the presentation of work, despite the poor track record of many of them as creative centres. Their funding should, however, be dependent on an expanded role, as recommended in *The Glory of the Garden* – to support touring work as well as creating in-house productions. Rather than just urging theatres to collaborate with other artists, such cooperation should be a condition of their funding. The level of subsidy would be determined by the range and quality of the artists whom those running the buildings could attract to be in residence. Just as a theatre commissions a writer to write a script, a theatre would commission a company to develop a piece of work. Just as the commissioned writer has no guarantee that the play will be performed but is able at least to develop his/her craft regardless, so a company would not be guaranteed a slot to perform each year but would be given the time, space and resources for research and development.

Alongside this strand of funding, project funds should be significantly increased and made genuinely available to both established and new companies. The money should not be distributed simply according to the company's track record but because of the company's capacity and ability to be innovative.

The costs of this would be covered by reducing the number of revenue-funded companies, reducing the theatres' own programmes and hopefully generating more local financial support by involving more local artists. If we imagine a company of four to six artists resident in a theatre for a whole year, the cost of bursaries would be around £100,000, all of which would go to the artists. This is equivalent to the lowest levels of Arts Council revenue support, of which most goes in administration and overheads. Furthermore, this structure would allow a creative dynamic to form. Directors of theatre buildings could not remain insular but would have to inform themselves of the talent that existed outside of the venues they were running. The resident artists would have the spaces to develop their own work whilst engaging with other resident artists from different disciplines, thus breaking down traditional barriers between art forms. The theatre buildings would also offer an administrative and marketing base for the companies associated with them, supporting touring through networks.

Out of necessity, reduced subsidy has created an environment in which such models are already being tested. The Coventry Theatre Network, for example, was awarded £500,000 from the Arts Council's Arts For Everyone scheme in 1998 to support local artists in association with the city's Belgrade Theatre. The aim is for the companies to develop the arts scene there over three years without losing their own individual identity. A project coordinator, the resources of the Belgrade, and a planned new complex to house the companies and provide rehearsal space, are all envisaged.

For such a model to work we need artistic directors who are not only interested in what production they are going to direct next, but have the vision to support and develop new work across many art forms. They must also recognize that research and development is as much about failure as it is about success. If we do not explore the process without having to guarantee the finished product, the product neither changes nor develops.

By offering time-limited investment rather than ongoing subsidy, funders encourage as well as create boundaries for ambitious ideas. Wise public investment in the early days of the dance company Adventures in Motion Pictures helped it become commercially independent later when it attracted huge audiences for its innovative production of *Swan Lake* in the West End in 1996–97. Theatre de Complicite has co-produced with the Royal National Theatre and has appeared in the West End, and newer companies such as The Right Size have transferred work from small venues to the commercial sector.

Not all companies and styles of work have a commercial potential, nor should they be expected to, but neither should we continue the meaningless funding distinctions between that which is art and that which is commercial. If we talked more of investment in art and less of subsidizing institutions, the Arts Council might find itself funding work that does make a return on its investment. Current practice creates waste as companies will spend the last of their grant simply to avoid having to return any surplus and thereby reduce the amount they can ask for in the next round of applications. Too many companies produce a show each year because the funders say they have to rather than because of an artistic impetus.

Nevertheless, for all Britain's problems, when I visit festivals overseas and import international work here, I am proud of the variety of work we are able to offer. Despite being primarily known for our great literary tradition, theatre in this country also boasts advanced work in cultural diversity, an active and progressive participatory scene and exciting cross-art form collaborations. Britain has always underfunded and undervalued its art. The belief in France that theatre is central to the intellectual, creative and social expression of our times has long meant a drain of talent there from Britain, with notables such as Peter Brook and Footsbarn preferring not to create work here any more. We fail miserably to celebrate our work and yet well-supported overseas companies have taken our audiences by storm, proving that theatre can be as popular over here as elsewhere. In Quebec, for example, recognition of the value of theatre as a cultural ambassador overseas led to investment in a small street act ten years ago. The circus that developed, crossing cultural and language barriers, is now the multimillion pound, multinational, Cirque du Soleil. Despite this company selling out the Royal Albert Hall for three weeks a year, the Arts Council has proved unable to resolve whether circus is art and, if so, which art form department should assess it for funding. The country that is the birthplace of modern circus does not fund a national circus company.

To sum up: the Government needs to increase funding to our sector in recognition of the role theatre plays in society and the benefit of investing in it. But this money should be spent on the artist and on research and development, not on long-term revenue commitments. We should encourage collaborations, and the sharing of resources and projects, instead of encouraging more permanent companies. Many companies will argue that without revenue funding there is no incentive to develop. I would assert that time-limited programmes of work encourage more imaginative thinking. After the allotted time, a company may build a different relationship with a venue, or even take on the leadership of the venue itself.

The time is right to make these changes, whilst the National Lottery still provides an opportunity to reverse the crisis in theatre, or we risk losing this opportunity in the new millennium. If Government continues to fail in its responsibility to invest through subsidy, if Lottery money is steered away from the arts to education and health and if the Arts Council once again shies away from major change, our desperately beleaguered sector will not have the energy left to reinvent itself. Our theatre will become more tired and conservative and we will lose the new audiences that are beginning to develop. If this happens I fear theatre in this country will look back even on these hard times as the best of times.

13

IRVING WARDLE

Waiting for Dionysus

Irving Wardle was Theatre Critic for The Times *from 1963–89 and Theatre Critic for the* Independent on Sunday *from 1989–95. He is the author of* The Theatres of George Devine *and* Theatre Criticism. *His play* The Houseboy *was staged at The Open Space, London, in 1973.*

I MADE MY START as a theatre reviewer in 1955 and dropped out in 1995: that is to say, from the launch of the English Stage Company to around the end of Richard Eyre's regime at the Royal National Theatre, with various other things happening in between. It was a great stroke of luck to coincide with this period, which enabled me to see the giants of the 1930s, some still at the height of their powers, as well as everything that poured out of postwar Pandora's Box. If, like me, you were in your twenties at the time, it felt as though the theatre was being reborn. But by the early Sixties, George Devine, the man who had got the whole thing going, was wearily shrugging off 'this great revolution that everybody talks about'. And now, forty years on, I sometimes find myself looking at the repertory, the quality of production, the audience, and wondering whether anything has changed at all, apart from the fact that Ralph Richardson, Edith Evans, Michael Redgrave, Peggy Ashcroft and Laurence Olivier have dropped out of the party.

In expressing that doubt I am myself succumbing to the mood of the 1990s, which has shown a violent change against the theatre from the very people who in the past would have been among the first to spring to its

defence. Take that word 'luvvies', a term of playground abuse that has
somehow crept into the vocabulary of opinion-formers who would never
think of labelling novelists as 'scribblers' or painters as 'daubers'.

Towards the end of my time in the reviewing trade I came to realize
that I was working for arts editors who only approved of anything I wrote
when I put the boot into some sacred thespian cow. Outside newspapers
you find the same dismissive attitude in television and radio arts debate.
The feeling seems to be that theatre people have had things nicely sewn up
all these years, and now it is time to call their bluff. And simultaneously,
revisionists have started appearing on the scene, pleading that what
happened in the Fifties (*1956 and All That*, to quote one recent title) didn't
really happen, and anyway things were in quite good shape before the
arrival of John Osborne.

I would not deny that the theatre has lost the position it once held at
the centre of British cultural life. Whatever the dream of any ambitious
newcomer, it is no longer to get a play accepted by the Royal Court or
to create some directorial powerhouse in a Soho basement. It's hard to
think of any cause that sets today's pulses skipping – beyond the perennial
complaints over shrinking subsidies and closing buildings. In the days
when the new writers were going off like rockets, with German agents
coming to blows over the latest Peter Shaffer, it used to be said that money
follows ideas. Nowadays the argument is rather that without some benevolent patron or a private income no fresh ideas or talent have a chance of
breaking through. Both propositions are equally true: in the sense that the
first refers to exceptional times, and the second to normal times. If there
are geniuses around, money is no problem. If there are no geniuses, money
is all that counts.

For most of its life, in any country and at any time, theatre is a
conveyor-belt industry, run by minor artists and superlative craftsmen
who depend on the cultural resources of the past. The pattern goes back
to the ancient world: first the good plays were written, then the stone
theatres were built. Twenty years ago the Royal Court slogan, 'the writer
leads', was accepted as a truism, but you seldom hear it nowadays. Perhaps
it will return. What we have now, as in the early 1950s, is a conveyor belt
– governed by rational calculation and planning, formidable talents, and
seldom disrupted by unscheduled outbreaks of creative madness. It is, of

course, the existence of the conveyor belt that safeguards such occasional visitations from Dionysus, which otherwise would just go up in flames. There is no more necessary theatrical job than minding the shop.

To state the obvious: the British theatre of the 1990s is a very different place from what it was in the 1950s. As you read that statement, perhaps a blurred picture of the past forty years flashes before your eyes as through the mind of a drowning man. A glimpse of Jimmy Porter war-dancing round the ironing board; a labyrinthine apartment block with Pinter characters in every room guarding their space; Peter Hall facing a strangely silent multitude as he proclaims the Government's obligation to pay every bill he submits; a classroom full of eminent playwrights, each one staring hopelessly at a blank sheet of paper; a tank rolling down Shaftesbury Avenue with Andrew Lloyd Webber and the Baroness Thatcher in the turret.

Typically for someone of my generation, these are images of combat. They also suggest a trajectory, from an energetic and hopeful take-off through to a pancake landing. Every item on the list relates to something that has survived to form part of the current scene. But they do nothing to define the difference between the 1950s and the 1990s; nor do they cast any light on what kind of theatre we have now. To grasp that, and sense its future direction, it is useless simply to survey what is presently on offer and award marks out of ten. Think of Peter Hall's Piccadilly Theatre venture: he opened with a recast revival of *Waiting for Godot*, Elaine Page's classical debut in *Le Misanthrope*, and a production of Shaw's *Major Barbara*. All that tells you is that someone is trying to promote serious repertory in the West End. The event only takes on meaning and implications for the future when you connect it to the rest of Hall's career. What is the principal architect of subsidy doing in this commercial set-up? Is it a terrible mistake or is it the completion of a pattern dating back to Hall's International Playwrights' Theatre of forty years ago? Ask that question and you begin to sense how things have moved on, and to remember what has been lost as well as what has survived. The fact, for instance, that, after all the upheavals and alternative stages of the past half-century, the West End remains the theatre's central territory. The fact that it has its own audience, which is markedly different from that of the National and the Royal Shakespeare Company. Recognizing that was crucial to the success of Hall's latest gamble even if it had not run on to the rocks of boardroom politics.

Theatre history is of limited use, but at least it shows certain recurring patterns of how things change and offers some consolation against gloom and cynicism. Take the often abused West End audience, a phenomenon dating back to the Edwardian carriage trade and beyond, signifying the moneyed entertainment seekers who from age to age drag the stage down to their own trivial level. For ten years and more that audience has been riding high. Formerly there were all manner of attempts to create new audiences, to carry theatre to the darkest corners of the land, and to incriminate the commercial public at every opportunity. What developed from this was ghetto theatre – companies playing to any number of minority groups. What never emerged was that ever-retreating ideal: the broad working-class audience. And with the arrival of Essex man in the Thatcher years, it became clear that the aspirations of TUC members included neither trips to the RSC nor any plans for a stage of their own. Ariane Mnouchkine in France and Peter Stein in West Germany likewise discovered that their beloved target audience wanted nothing to do with the theatre. The lesson was obvious. European theatre is a middle-class elitist phenomenon, and should settle for pleasing its loyal customers and waste no more time whoring after the mass audience. Granville Barker dismissed his own attempt to reform the Edwardian West End as 'ploughing the sands'; and generations of disappointed would-be reformers have come to the same conclusion.

But once you look at what Granville Barker, Peter Hall or other crusaders actually did, the conclusion becomes far from obvious. England by common consent is a philistine country that happens to be good at making theatre. It is also a country where those who are best at making theatre often end up as philistines. Witness the case of Granville Barker himself, the Crown Prince of the modern stage who made a rich marriage and wound up as a sterile snob in a morning suit. In our history there is a fairy-tale division between the vagabond performers and the respectable public: as in the story of Rose Trelawny, who lost her talent by making a genteel marriage – as recounted by that most genteel of playwrights, Granville Barker's contemporary, A. W. Pinero. Yes: English theatre then as now was there to serve the middle-class public. But it has only succeeded in doing so through recruiting artists whose dearest wish has often been to blow the middle class sky-high. Thus you find

Granville Barker prospering by staging plays by Shaw and himself whose main purpose was to incriminate their well-to-do spectators. And what does Hall do as soon as a profitable middle-brow institution – as the Shakespeare Memorial Theatre then was – falls into his hands? He tears the outfit to bits, squanders the financial reserves, and launches the RSC, which then becomes a far greater middle-brow hit than its forerunner.

The point I'm making is obvious, but is often misunderstood even by those whose livelihoods depend on it. I once sought an interview with the veteran manager Donald Albery on the topic of pleasing the public. Albery deplored the avalanche of new writing that had hit the stage since 1956 – not because it was bad work, but because it came from unknown writers, and that confused the public. The old West End, he said, did good business because it stocked trusted brands. It functioned like a traditional grocery shop where the customers knew their taste and could be relied on to choose the latest Noel Coward and Terence Rattigan like Frank Cooper's Oxford marmalade and Arbroath smokies. Things were in such a mess nowadays because there was all this new stuff on the shelves and nobody knew what to choose. Then almost in the same breath Albery began talking about his greatest success, 'the once-in-a-lifetime thing you get down on your prayer mat for' – namely the unstoppable run of *Oliver!* by Lionel Bart, one of the uncouth unknowns who were supposedly wrecking the business.

I suppose it is natural for managers to dream of a trouble-free set-up with docile authors laying golden eggs as required and public and practitioners hitting it off like members of the same exclusive club. Happy the theatre that has no need of artists, as Brecht might have said if he had been running the Haymarket. Such a harmony did indeed prevail in the days of Binkie Beaumont's West End after the Second World War, and that was precisely what was wrong with it. You couldn't breathe in that perfumed atmosphere, from which I developed a homespun but service-able rule: the ritzier the dresses, the worse the show. The mood was ripe for a barbarian invasion. Which, indeed, is the process by which the English theatre – including the theatre of Binkie Beaumont – has renewed itself. Even without looking for any higher aims, it is only through perpetual invasion by outsiders that the clubland audience has been satisfied and kept the conveyor belt turning. Over the past two centuries our greatest dramatists turn out to be Irish who can beat the Brits at their own game; and our actors turn out to be working-class children who can make royals look ill-bred. Not to mention Beaumont himself, who started off in a cinema box office in the depths of Wales.

So there is nothing new in the continuation of this process over the past forty years; apart from the sheer number of barbarians on the scene, and the speed of their transformation into institutional figureheads – aided by the arrival of subsidized stages. Just as the Victorian gentrification of the theatre cast a lingering blight over the subsequent age of Gerald du Maurier and Noel Coward, so respectability took on an organizational form in the National Theatre and the RSC – where job-consciousness, office politics and the other ills of bureaucratic and corporation life finally took root in the theatre. These institutions, of course, were new, and the most obvious way of showing how the theatre has reached its present state is to examine the convulsions the profession underwent in accommodating this alien monster. I have mentioned one of its negative attributes. But it does not take much experience of continental civil service theatre to make you grateful for what we have got.

Predating subsidy, what was new in the late 1950s was the sense that it was time for the theatre to 'restate its milieu'. The phrase is Devine's but it could equally well have been coined by Joan Littlewood, Peter Hall, Peter Brook, John Osborne and other reigning or emerging talents who viewed the existing set-up as moribund. It was like a once fertile and diverse farm that now grew only one diminishing crop. It was controlled by blinkered people who were at once greedy and who asked for too little. They were offering 'entertainment'. What a thin-blooded and superfluous product – compared with joy, awe, exultation, laughter, lust, and the self-transcendence of experiencing these emotions communally. I don't know of anyone who has tried to catalogue the different forms taken by this impulse to reclaim the theatre's lost heritage. But I can testify to its existence as a pervasively intoxicating force of the time, and for which there is no avoiding the word 'vision'. It was the vision of an inclusive event, where individual differences would be burnt away by the shared experience, and instead of belonging to a club you would come out feeling glad to be a member of the human race.

Such was the driving energy that kept Joan Littlewood going at her tumbledown East End pleasure palace; that drew the wagon-trains of new authors to the Royal Court's Sunday night shows; which mobilized the resources for new theatre buildings throughout the land. There is no forgetting the buildings because they stay there even after the life has gone out of them – like the desolate reps of Farnham and Leatherhead. Whereas other theatrical initiatives have been lost without even leaving an empty shell behind.

I wonder how many of today's policy-makers remember Ed Berman, founder of London's Almost Free Theatre, whose work formed a spectrum from avant-garde writing (including Tom Stoppard) to running a city farm for children in Camden Town. The same question goes for Naftali Yavin, who took experimental shows into prisons; Jim Haynes, who ran his Drury Lane Arts Lab as a round-the-clock party, everybody welcome; Charles Marowitz, who pioneered Shakespearean collage and the work of Artaud from his Tottenham Court Road basement; or Keith Johnstone, who launched the comic improvisation movement from the springboard of the Royal Court Writers' Group.

All these people were outsiders – many from America – in one sense or another, who were drawn to the London of the 1960s as a place where theatre was spreading out into the community at large; and where there was the freedom for them to strike their own deal between art and society. All the above names, and others I haven't mentioned, were obsessed with redefining the spectator/performer relationship, and with making the theatre (in the name of Marowitz's basement) an Open Space. Yavin dropped a staff job at the Israeli Habimah Theatre to work for nothing in what was then the theatrical new world. These people have now gone. Either dead, like Yavin, or dispersed – Marowitz to California, Keith Johnstone to running his comic empire from the west of Canada, and Jim Haynes to hosting Sunday night dinners to anyone who turns up at his house in Paris. For him the party is still going on. But not for the rest of us.

If this sounds like a childish hankering for the Sixties, I have to agree. To the extent that theatre was reborn then, it was a childish period, with accompanying delusions of omnipotence and temper tantrums. It then started growing up and shedding these follies in favour of self-discipline and hardening institutionalism, and before long we are into the mean world of Thatcherite politics and the pharisaical ser-monizing of the 'state of the nation' dramatists; with entertainment sliding back in the form of bank-vault musicals. Even without those monster events that reduced theatre criticism to toothless impotence, I should still feel homesick for the hopeful decade before we started building ourselves new prisons.

Looking round the 1990s scene, one can imagine some Minister for the Arts pronouncing an official verdict on the theatre's past half-century before the sounding of the millennial bell. A period of unmatched variety and energy; it was often bewildering then, but now the dust has settled and we can see the lasting achievements of the time – world-class play-wrights like Harold Pinter and Tom Stoppard; a generation of actors equally at home in Shakespeare and on the musical stage; and two great national institutions that not only serve their own public but service the now flourishing commercial sector. Now that the dross has subsided it is clear the theatre has much to be proud of.

I would not even disagree with that, except to say that it is not only politicians who have short memories. Theatre itself is notorious for its forgetfulness and ingratitude, which is my pretext for dwelling on what is now the distant past. For long-term theatregoers the experience is like watching a slowly changing cloudscape with one shape melting into another until there is nothing left of what you first saw. As a rule you simply adjust to what is there, taking the current level of work – however brilliant or mediocre – as normal. But occasionally the shadow of the past falls across the picture, and you see what is in the perspective of what was and what might be.

So, returning to the bustling 1990s scene, it is cheering to compare the West End of today's producers, Bill Kenwright and Cameron Mackin-tosh, with the snobbish, greedy, philistine place it was under Prince Littler and Beaumont. The wicked 'bricks-and-mortar man' has vanished like a thwarted demon king, while commerce is manifestly thriving, the more so since the subsidized sector has become a tryout venue (for musicals and readily comprehensible new plays) rather than a rival. The theatre is always in crisis but there is nothing along the length and breadth of Shaftesbury Avenue and St Martin's Lane to set the alarm bells ringing. It feels, in fact, as safe and snug as Donald Albery's grocery shop, with Alan Ayckbourn and Hugh Whitemore taking their place with Oscar Wilde and Noel Coward among the trusted jams and jellies.

It may be the result of having been around for too long, but my theatregoing over the past decade has begun to feel like a self-indulgence. In subsidized houses as well as the West End the sensation has become more like gorging a luxury than breaking bread with one's fellow man. One small example: I saw three productions of *Hamlet* in 1997. Two of these were from the former Soviet bloc, in which the Ghost variously embodied the still active Communist past, and the spirit of historical justice who dissolves into anguished lamentation when Claudius, like so many modern tyrants, escapes to die in his bed. These shows had something urgent to say to their audiences in Moldavia and Lithuania. The third show was Matthew Warchus's politically emasculated Stratford version, described by its director as 'a family story people could relate to'. Not all our Shakespeare is as trivialized as that but what productions of the past five years have added anything to our lives like *The Wars of the Roses* (1963) or Brook's *A Midsummer Night's Dream* (1970)? The very word 'relevance' now strikes the Shakespearean high command as a long-discarded cliché.

That is one shadow from the past, to which one can add the disappearance of permanent companies, the loss of autonomy by artistic directors in the age of sponsorship, the narrowing mainstage classical repertory, the decline of original work in the surviving regional reps, the shortage of heroic actors (particularly women) under the age of forty, and the absence of experiment on any stage involving serious money. Less tangibly, but more important, the lack of theatrical causes apart from those of special interest groups. 'New Writing' is no longer a compelling slogan, and where once even the smallest stages had the resonance of sounding boards, now the work they put on is strictly the concern of the few people who see it. You can understand the argument of some arts editors for shifting all fringe coverage to the Internet.

That this has not happened is thanks partly to the periodic arrival of new authors like Mark Ravenhill and Sarah Kane, who manage to kick up a stink on the news pages, as in the good old days. Perhaps I underestimate them. Significant development is often more visible at long range than it is in close-up, and I note that the 1998 Berlin Festwochen featured Ravenhill and Kane as representatives of an emerging radical group, 'Thatcher's Heirs', along with Conor McPherson who (like Martin McDonagh) has shown that West End audiences will now welcome not only Irish playwrights but the kind of rural Irish play that used to spell death at the British box office. These, be it noted, are all Royal Court writers, and when you add Ayub Khan-Din, author of our first-ever British Asian smash hit *East is East*, the Court emerges as no less a changer of public taste than it was forty years ago. Without question, the West End has opened up to a new generation of outsiders. The price of acceptance is that their work has to be naturalistic, which is not cripplingly high if it admits talents like these, along with the TV white hopes Ben Elton and Patrick Marber, who have vastly enlarged their range by writing for the stage.

Taking a rosy view of the future, I can imagine a commercial sector in which theatre does succeed in regaining its carrying power, and which welcomes multi-ethnic work to the extent of truly reflecting the life of the country. I can imagine the artistically buoyant continuation of the National under Trevor Nunn, as Richard Eyre has shown it can be done. And maybe the Germans are right, and a band of ferocious young writers is even now preparing to take over the fringe and sweep David Hare and the rest of yesterday's radicals into oblivion.

Whether any of this comes to pass depends, as ever, on the continuing arrival of the obsessed, hungry, ego-driven unauthorized aspirants I have lumped together as 'outsiders'. The outlook for them is not good. For just as public taste is expanding to accept them, the sources from which they are more likely to appear are being dammed up. Every stage practitioner, even the writer, needs a training, a jumping-off point. Notoriously, only a few are going to get it: those with private means. The upper-middle class. Farewell to the future Pinters, Osbornes, Finneys and Billie Whitelaws; hello to the nascent Oxbridge tribes – which means, in effect, a future theatre of directors. When I mentioned this prospect to the director of one of our subsidized houses, he said it would be better for these dinosaur institutions to perish forthwith, leaving the theatre of tomorrow to be reinvented by children.

14

JOYCE MCMILLAN

Critics Under Siege

Joyce McMillan is the theatre critic of the Scotsman, *and also writes a political/social commentary for the paper. She has been a political and arts columnist for the* Herald, Glasgow, *political commentator and theatre critic for* Scotland on Sunday, *and Scottish theatre critic of the* Guardian. *Her history of the Traverse Theatre, Edinburgh was published in 1988. She is involved in Scottish and European campaigns for democracy and human rights, and lives in Edinburgh, from where she broadcasts frequently on Radio Scotland and Radio 4.*

IN 1992 I WAS COMMISSIONED by the Scottish Arts Council to write *Arts for a New Century*, the Scottish section of the Conservative government's Charter for the Arts exercise. It was a fascinating project, involving the gathering of views from people in the arts and from the general public on every aspect of cultural life, from ticket prices and the importance of public transport to the role of Scotland's ongoing debate about national identity – or Glasgow's attempts to re-define itself as the essential post-industrial city – in shaping artistic work and providing it with a sense of context.

But there was one aspect of the Charter process that particularly caught my interest, as a critic with a passion for the art of reviewing; and that was the tremendous ambivalence expressed by many artists about the role of artistic criteria – or 'artistic value-judgements' – in the funding process. On the one hand, there was widespread expression of unease at the way in which artistic values seemed increasingly marginalized in the decision-making process. But on the other hand, there was also an immense resistance to the whole idea of artistic judgement or evaluation. Time and again, during the Charter process – as at other moments of crisis in arts funding – people would express indignation and even shock at the idea of the Scottish Arts Council making artistic distinctions and evaluations. 'No one has the right to judge,' said one contributor to the Charter process, categorically. Others suggested that peer-group assessment was the only acceptable approach, as if the arts, so far from seeking relationship with an audience, were somehow a closed system that only other artists could properly understand or evaluate.

It is clear that the bitterness of the debate over funding decisions, and the criteria behind them, reflects the particular power of bodies like the Scottish Arts Council to force companies out of existence and to exert a drastic influence on the livelihood and prospects of individual artists. In Britain at least, the activity of critics, as judgement-givers, rarely if ever acquires this kind of life-or-death importance. But we should take note, nonetheless, of the deep antipathy to the whole idea of authoritative evaluation and criticism that has become entrenched in our culture. As many commentators have observed, the 'cultural revolution' of the 1960s, and the massive questioning of traditional canons of excellence and value which began at that time, not only changed the view of what excellence in the arts might be – and certainly in terms of class, race, and gender, such a revolutionary reassessment was long overdue – but has also led, more problematically, to a wholesale rejection of the idea that 'quality' or 'truth' even exists as any more than a subjective impression. The baby of purposeful critical debate, of shared experience, of the common pursuit of excellence, has largely been thrown out with the bathwater of an oppressive old cultural establishment that gave a bad name to the very concepts of excellence and truth. It is within that climate of intense individualism that critics now have to work. 'Well, it's just one person's opinion, isn't it?' is the standard lay response to the whole activity of arts criticism in the 1990s, the assumption being that the opinions of an individual are an arbitrary phenomenon, unconnected to the reactions and experience of other people, to the life of society as a whole, or to any objective reality at all.

It goes without saying, therefore, that theatre criticism in the 1990s is an embattled business. It not only deals with an art form that is perceived by many editors and media producers as stuffy, old-fashioned and unpopular, it deals with it in a way to which our culture, by and large, is strongly antipathetic. Indeed, under the circumstances, we should perhaps be wondering not why the space given to serious arts criticism is declining, or why reviews are having to fight their way into arts pages and programmes increasingly dominated by preview features and listings, but why arts criticism in the media has survived at all, and in such a resolutely hostile ideological climate. For, if critics are to carry out their work with any passion or commitment, they can never fully accept the individualistic and relativistic attitude that has become *de rigueur* in the media, as elsewhere. As critics we could not work at all, or find the language in which to work, if we did not believe that our perceptions have at least some representative quality; we draw our whole energy as writers and speakers from the impulse to generalize from our own experience, to make others feel what we have felt, and accept our arguments about why it matters. And it is perhaps worth noting that, despite the strong cultural prejudice of the age against the idea of authoritative criticism, editors and media producers still recognize, up to a point, the sheer vigour of writing and speaking that the effort often produces. They may not care to analyse why so many critics write well, punchily, amusingly, with precision. But criticism survives, even in many parts of the popular press. It is an embattled form of discourse, no question, but it is also proving strangely resilient, unwilling simply to roll over and die.

When the radical iconoclasts of the 1960s and '70s began to hammer away at the structure of old ideas about duty, patriotism, service, hierarchy, religion and morality that had dominated our social structures since the High Victorian age, they perhaps imagined that once their work was done there would be a thoughtful pause, to consider what new world would be built on the ruins. But instead, what rushed into the vacuum created was something much simpler and cruder; it was the idea of the market, the model of commerce, the conviction that when the chips are down, almost everything can best be understood as a commercial transaction between customer and provider. And at the beginning of the 1990s there came a moment in Britain when we all suddenly found ourselves being called 'customers' in situations where the term seemed unfamiliar at best and at worst downright tasteless. Hospitals, trains, unemployment offices – they all seemed to have received a simultaneous message from the *Zeitgeist* that the only way to signal a proper respect for their public was to talk to them as if they were purchasers of some tangible piece of goods. Many people felt uneasy with this wholesale transference of marketplace terminology to places where we had been used to thinking of ourselves differently, perhaps as citizens enjoying a freely available public service, or as vulnerable human beings receiving the care we needed at the hands of a compassionate community. But, as his strange series of Citizens' Charters showed, for John Major the words 'citizen' and 'consumer' were largely indistinguishable; and in that, he was at one with the spirit of the age.

The key consequence of this belief for our society is the gradual disappearance, in both the physical and the psychological sense, of our public or 'civic' space. In the last two decades, what used to be the teeming public spaces of our cities and towns have gradually become segregated by function, gated off, designated as motorways, shopping precincts, pedestrian zones or upmarket housing developments. As both political campaigners and the Salvation Army have discovered to their cost, we do not enjoy the same civic freedoms in new meeting-places like malls and supermarkets as we did in the High Street or town square. This dwindling of public space has a profound effect on theatre, which, at its best, is a kind of extension of the bustling street life of a busy town or city, a place where people come together at the end of a hard day's work or shopping to see something that will take them out of themselves, make them laugh or cry, help them to see themselves differently, or to get a new perspective on life. Physically, it makes it more difficult for theatres to have an inclusive, 'open-to-the-street' atmosphere; like everywhere else, they need locks, doors, security, entrance policies and well-guarded car parks for their better-off customers. But for critics, the really important factor is the loss of psychological public space; the sense – hard to quantify, but nonetheless very powerful – of big commercial interests crowding in on the zone of free-flowing performance, free comment, and free debate about that comment where theatre ideally takes place.

There are, I think, three main ways in which commercial pressure impinges on the work of critics. The first involves straightforward conflicts of interest caused by the fact that most critics now work for large media groups with wide-ranging interests in the entertainment and media industry. To an extent, of course, the sheer unimportance of theatre, in the minds of most of today's big commercial players, protects it from their interference and their interest. Theatre critics are rarely in a position to suffer the kind of ribaldry regularly directed at media critics in papers owned by Rupert Murdoch whenever they write anything favourable about their proprietor's satellite channels.

Nonetheless it is not unusual for critics to discover, in this age of pervasive business sponsorship, that the marketing department of their newspaper has entered into sponsorship deals with theatre promoters or venues, or even with the producer of a particular show, without even asking them whether they thought this was a good idea, or could in conscience recommend the show to readers. Theatre criticism remains relatively free – so long as people consider it unimportant. But if it ever, by chance, acquired the power seriously to damage a 'product' in which the proprietor had a major investment, then I suspect that such freedom would evaporate overnight.

The second pressure is a more subtle one, involving the increasingly aggressive marketing of theatre and the impact of that marketing activity on the climate in which critics work. Most theatre marketing is fairly unsuccessful, and is treated with contempt – sometimes more than it deserves – by everyone connected with the media. But from time to time the world of theatre produces something that becomes a 'hot ticket' even in advance of opening – a show with some quality of media 'sexiness' that has everyone cheer-leading for it and predicting great things.

Once that kind of bandwagon begins to roll – carrying with it the smell of money to be made, and the emotional and professional investment of all those who have predicted its success – it becomes extremely difficult for a critic to go to the first night and puncture the bubble, to point out that the Emperor has no clothes and tell the world the show is no good. One of the key tricks of modern consumer capitalism is to create an enthusiastic feel-good factor around a particular brand or product even when the product itself is rubbish. It is a brave critic who stands up in the middle of the post-production celebrations and not only trashes the product itself but, by implication, throws into question the whole process by which the rubbish has been sold to the public. One might think that in the competitive world of big business a media boss would be quite happy to see his or her theatre critic blowing the whistle on someone else's marketing efforts. But there is something about the public denunciation of a huge, expensive and apparently successful marketing operation that makes the whole Anglo-American corporate culture extremely uncomfortable. Being an independently-minded theatre critic is an activity closely akin to protecting the consumer from the powerful corporation, and it is more radical than it seems. Indeed, I sometimes wonder whether the legal category of 'fair comment', which currently protects arts and media critics, would be able to survive any serious corporate lobbying against critical activity that can seriously damage the reputation of carefully nurtured commodities.

The third and by far the most important effect of the commercial ethos on the work of critics concerns its impact on the texture of theatre work itself, on the selection, the style, and the inner rhythm, of the productions we see. In essence, many people involved in the practical running of theatres now simply assume, explicitly or implicitly, that the survival of the art form depends on the professional marketing of it as an upmarket, aspirational 'lifestyle' product – the kind of attractive leisure activity that people at a certain level of disposable income will enjoy doing, or will feel good about having done, and for which they will be prepared to pay a substantial ticket price. Naturally, theatre that is to be marketed in this way requires clear, attractive 'selling points' of a fixed and reliable kind, i.e. attributes that will be present at every performance and will leave audiences feeling, at least on a superficial or quantifiable level, that they have had their money's worth. Among the most popular and successful of these 'fixed' attributes are star casting, spectacular sets, exceptional 'special effects' of one kind or another, and the attributes 'musical' and 'comedy' used separately or in tandem.

But what is clear about all of these key 'selling points' is that none of them tells us anything about the actual quality or 'enjoyability' of the show. They are designed, for reasons of risk reduction, to minimize the link between a show's artistic quality and its box-office success. Worse, some of these attractive attributes – notably the vogue for big sets and special effects – militate against creative live performance, in that they tend to dictate the movement of the performers and drastically limit their ability to take charge of the event and build a living relationship with the audience.

Theatre, in other words, is profoundly resistant to these kinds of marketing strategies, because the one unique 'selling point' it actually possesses is the one that cannot be standardized or guaranteed in any way, namely the moment – often a moment of silence or non-action – when an actor is free to reach out for real emotional contact with an audience, and the audience is free to accept or reject that offer. It is because of this unpredictable element of freedom in live performance – the fact that it cannot be censored, edited, canned or cut during performance – that makes theatre unsuitable as an infrequent 'luxury purchase', and, as it happens, often gives it an exceptional importance in countries with oppressive political regimes. Theatre works best, as Peter Brook observes in his book *The Empty Space*, when it is poor, rough and holy – an unpretentious, easily accessible and yet magical part of everyday life. Yet what seems to be evolving, in response to the demand for 'theatre-as-product' is a type of performance that is none of these things; it is one that fulfils all the external criteria of a successful, prestigious and perhaps even demanding theatre event, but during which, in terms of real communication, nothing actually happens at all. Actors run around the stage, of course; musicians play; impressive things happen to the set and lighting; the script is usually jocular to a fault, full of witty or bitter one-liners. But all this activity seems more like an attempt to distract the audience from the emotions that might be unleashed by the play than to offer the experience of them; there's no stillness, no silence, no beauty, no confidence, and no living sense of connection.

There is no doubt that productions like this present severe problems for reviewers. At the level of what one critic used to call 'trades descriptions', they do exactly what they say they will do, and often do it well. To criticize them is to talk about an absence rather than a presence; it is to insist that theatre, if it is to be worth having, has to retain at its centre that moment of freedom and fluidity that well-trained modern urban audiences, used to impervious canned entertainment, tend to find disconcerting. It is once again to run counter to the psychological ethos of a consumer society that depends on sustaining demand through high levels of restlessness, dissatisfaction, and anticipation, constantly catered to but never satisfied. Of course, there are still 'big' directors – Peter Brook, Peter Stein and Robert Lepage, for example – who have the authority to insist on naked silence, the slow rhythm of natural breath, the creation of some space in which to think and feel. (Lepage's *The Seven Streams of the River Ota* was certainly the boldest and most theatrically articulate challenge to modern western assumptions about pace and action that I have experienced.) But our theatre is under increasing pressure to provide a laugh or a gasp a minute – if only to protect audiences from the dangerous possibility of having to feel or to think.

Yet that, I think, is enough of pessimism; for to list the difficulties and pressures facing theatre and theatre critics in the 1990s is also to sketch the outline of the kind of survival strategy – or strategy for something better than survival – that theatre criticism will need in the twenty-first century. It should be said right away that such a survival strategy must involve a substantial and serious engagement with social issues that go far beyond the world of theatre and the arts. The media for which we critics review, the funding and management structures of the theatres we attend, the working conditions of the artists, the attitudes of the audience, and even their very presence or absence in the theatre, are all part of a dense web of social and economic interactions. If we fail to understand and address those wider trends we are likely to find the ivory tower in which we conduct our reviewing lives suddenly swept away by a flood of indifference or hostility that we barely noticed was rising, far less tried to avert.

Thus, in the first place, it seems to me that theatre critics must become warriors for the preservation and extension of that civic and public space in our society where good theatre, and good theatre criticism, can take place. As I suggested above, theatre critics can barely function unless they believe that a successful society is based on some common perceptions and values; that theatre is one of the key arenas for the free assertion, negotiation and celebration of that shared experience; and that theatre criticism has a role to play in publicizing, elucidating and continuing the process of public debate that is begun by a successful theatre event. We are faced with a political and social ethos which constantly denies the existence of powerful and effective shared values, which prefers the dead 'consumer' model of theatre to the live 'civic' model, and which treats critical comment as at best a sensational soundbite and at worst a complete irrelevance, rather than a serious reflection on the collective dreaming and storytelling of our society. We therefore have some obligation to take up the cudgels in defence of the kind of experience that gives meaning, and sometimes even joy, to our professional lives. We should be clear that in doing so we challenge one of the big lies of our age: that the differences between individuals are somehow decisively more important, and more powerful, than the things they hold in common. We should also recognize that in describing the possibility of powerful shared experience, as distinct from the exaggerated 'punk individualism' of the time, we are often offering a glimpse of warmth, colour, connectedness, openness to change and even real eroticism – as opposed to commercialized smut – of which our culture is starved. Hence the strange survival of theatre criticism in a cold climate. Unfashionable or not, at its best it takes us to a place where human beings need, and yearn, to go.

Secondly, and in order to sharpen our ability to defend civic life and space, I think we need to strengthen our sense, as critics, of working for and within a community that we try to serve. This is perhaps a relatively simple matter for me, as a critic working in Scotland. Scotland is a small nation, with a powerful and evolving sense of cultural identity, a long-running and absorbing public debate on its political future which provides rich and highly topical material for artists and writers, and a strong civil society, in which the arts play a substantial and acknowledged part. Under those circumstances – fairly typical of small European countries in a nation-building phase – envisaging the community to which criticism and debate is addressed becomes almost deceptively easy. In the end, asking the question about what community we serve is more important than finding a definitive answer. Once a critic accepts that responsibility, and begins to work with that question in mind, answers begin to suggest themselves and to shift and evolve in ways that are never less than interesting.

Thirdly, I think we need to stand up for theatre that is 'poor' and 'rough', in an age when so many pressures are driving the art form in the opposite direction. It is very easy for any professional critic to become locked into a circuit of comfortable upmarket theatres, which present large and important-looking productions and run effective press offices. But it is often more rewarding, in artistic terms, to go off the beaten track, to places where people are making theatre out of passion and despair, rather than out of a routine obligation to make up a season. In *The Empty Space*, Peter Brook suggests that one of the prime tasks of the critic is to 'hound out incompetence'. But today, I think hounding out the glib, the deadly proficient, the skilful but shallow, the fluently facetious, is at least as important; and at the very least, time spent in poor and rough theatres tends to cast a sharp and unflattering light on that other kind of work.

Finally, we need to defend the 'civic space' within our own industry, the media, constantly torn as it is between its vital and universally acknowledged responsibility as a mediator of society to society and the ever more strident and hysterical demands of a colossally competitive marketplace. In that respect, theatre critics are little different from other journalists: trying to write copy that will thrill and entertain, and still be true to the event; trying to uphold a few concepts of truth and integrity against the imperatives of corporate competition; trying to clear a space where we can do some service to society, while still being published and paid by Mammon. But it sometimes seems to me that theatre critics have a special source of strength in trying to resolve these near-impossible contradictions. It is the strength that comes from the art and the artists themselves; the strength of the true shared experience, of which the whey-faced men in our offices know little; the strength of live theatre, which is the subject of this book, and which we are privileged to draw on, every day of our working lives.

ELLA WILDRIDGE

New Plays – We Need Them

Ella Wildridge's theatre work began with new playwriting programmes, such as 'Words Beyond Words' and 'Off the Wall' at the Royal Lyceum Theatre, Edinburgh, where she also originated the newsletter 'New Playwriting Scotland'. In 1991 she moved to the Traverse Theatre, where she initiated 'Windows on the World' – regular programmes of international playwriting and innovative theatre encounters – and created 'The Monday Lizard', a monthly playwrights' platform. In 1998 she was responsible for setting up 'Colours of the Chameleon', a programme for emerging European playwrights. As a writer/translator she has worked on the texts of dramatists such as Tankred Dorst, Oliver Bukowski, Lutz Hübner and Serge Kribus.

IN TRYING TO PROJECT into Utopian futures we must establish what our values are, what it is we want to take forward and why. Yes, plays, we need them. It follows that we need playwrights too.

'New Theatre' is a phrase that can have many different meanings, depending on who is using it. My own outlook is mainly based upon my experience working in the theatre in Scotland, as dramaturg at the Traverse Theatre, which is dedicated to presenting contemporary work, particularly new plays.

In May 1999, Scotland, where I am based, set up its own parliamentary assembly, devolved from Westminster. There are changes imminent in this country in relation to which playwriting might have an important significance. I hope that when considering 'the way forward', however, what I have to say might be of some use anywhere that playwriting is, or could be, active.

My work as a translator – primarily from German – and my present position as Literary Associate at the Traverse have also brought me into contact with contemporary plays on a worldwide basis and enabled me to study different approaches used in different countries with regard to playwrights and new plays. I make no apology for my interests. To me the dialogue-based play, with characters, storyline, and all that other old-fashioned paraphernalia, is invaluable and irreplaceable, particularly when presented live. Those who write plays have simultaneously to be deep-sea divers into individual/social depths, composers creating scores to be inter-preted, and variously disguised clowns showing different faces to the world.

I don't like to think of playwrights as lame ducks, or precious artists whose every wish must be obeyed, but I do see them as a particular type of writer with particular needs in pursuing their performance-orientated craft and a need to be supported and sustained in their endeavours. There are many different kinds of playwrights, of course, and some of the most famous have become rich and poor several times over. I am thinking, however, of a wide spread of playwrights from many different social and personal locales, a diversity which gives contemporary playwriting its relevance and strength.

If, in spelling out my commitment to the play, the script and the individual playwright, I seem to be stating the obvious, my defence is that it has become far from obvious in recent years when 'devising' plays, with or without the involvement of a writer, has become so popular, and words improvised by actors have come to be regarded, by some, as every bit as good as words put down by a writer as a unified text on a page. There are many possibilities and the devised and improvised are an integral part of theatre but the written play lays down on the page the marks of a particular sensibility in action. Theatre will be much impoverished if it ever cuts itself off from this source.

Another rejection of the written play has come from the zones of 'visual theatre' where words are regarded as suspect, and text, if it exists, is supposed to hang somewhere in the air above the image. Characterization and acting are likewise rejected and any idea of straightforward narrative is apt to be met with a yawn. I generalize and there are doubtless plenty of examples to contradict me, but the move to regard the visual as superior to the enacted drama has become a strong trend. Whilst I love paintings, even on the stage, I am not willing to accept them as a substitute for or step beyond drama. Drama is not abstract. It is human and personal. This is of fundamental importance. As in *Waiting for Godot*, any tendency to get too lofty is answered by a fart.

Hopefully in the future there will not be such divisions between verbal and visual modes in the theatre. It was, after all, Antonin Artaud who exerted such a strong influence towards giving the different elements of theatre an equal force. Though he was both a writer and a director, he wanted theatre released from its wordbound restrictions and to make everything 'the word', whether visual, sonic or gestural. In the early Sixties his work was a direct influence on, among others, Peter Brook and Jerzy Grotowski. But that is another story. The idea of the play that I pursue is generally quieter than what Artaud had in mind, quieter even than Brecht, with his extolling of a noisy cigar-smoking boxing ring auditorium. I believe it is important for the audience to hear the words. Though theatre can be sensation and full of vaudeville and fun, the theatre of contemporary drama, as I understand it, is primarily a theatre in which the individual continues to have a voice and in which all 'truth' is debatable.

What is playwriting for anyway? The director of a repertory theatre located in tourist Scotland will give you one answer, a cultural nationalist (or anyone else with a cause) will give you another. Whereas one is looking for something attractive and entertaining – an evening's diversion – the other is looking for a fervent vehicle in a particular tongue. When young people ventured into theatres to see *Trainspotting* they went in search of the latest thing. Cool. Whether it was a play or not didn't come into it.

For the nova politicians emerging from a day's hard jaw at the new Scottish Assembly, I expect theatre will be just an adjunct to a civic occasion, on a par with a good meal. The last thing they'll want will be for it to have teeth. So it goes. Community plays, gay plays, hetero classics, actors looking for plays with parts, educational plays, plays for kids, plays to warn against the dangers of smoking, or celebrate a famous football club. All kinds of plays for all kinds of purposes. Occasionally you might find a genuine play in among them but by and large it's all disposable fare.

A genuine play? It's a dangerous phrase. What do I mean? For me, in a play there must always be risk. If it is stuck within the one point of view or set of values it will not be absorbing. It has to have dialogue in it of one sort of another – between ideas, attitudes, characters' fears, desires and – most vitally – between the play and the audience. A playwright must have an urge, a 'something to say', a need to show off, shock or lament; but always there is space in a good play, room for interpretation, both by the actors and the audience. There is freedom of thought. There is conversation. Plays are public rituals from which the priests have been debarred – re-enactments without censorship. The world needs them.

In order to begin to think about a different kind of future we must imagine that something central in the present has been changed. For playwriting this would be the current practice of the play commission. The foundation of playwriting for the stage in Scotland is the Scottish Arts Council commissioning scheme. Through this, theatres and companies can apply for money to commission plays. The overall amount involved is around £5000, paid out to the playwright in stages related to the progress of the script and its likely production. The SAC receives many more requests for commissioning money than it can hope to satisfy. New writing development money, for workshop schemes and the like, is also in high demand.

The amount paid as a commission fee has crept up over the years, from around £1300 in the early Sixties to £5300 in the mid-Nineties. Ask most of the established Scottish playwrights, such as Iain Heggie, John Clifford, Sue Glover or Liz Lochhead, and – apart from perhaps complaining that the money is not enough – they will praise the scheme. For some it was the basic precondition for them to write a play at all, enabling them to give the process time and care, and to work in a defined and active relationship with professional theatre. For a new writing theatre such as the Traverse the commissioning scheme is the mainstay of its activity, allowing it to engage some writers (though not nearly enough) in writing plays in the course of a year. For any company or theatre active in Scotland the existence of the commissioning scheme has meant that in pursuit of new plays at least one problem was taken care of – the basic payment to the writer. Yet in thinking about the future, it is the commissioning scheme I would like to remove, or at least consider removing.

Primarily this is because the scheme tends to prevent us from thinking about other ways of supporting writers. It becomes a stereotype, a cliché, like always feeding the kids with pizza. It satisfies immediate needs, but what does it provide by way of nourishment for the future? It locks the playwright into the same hectic patterns as everyone else: three weeks rehearsal, get the play on, try to get someone with a TV reputation to play the lead. Will the press find it interesting? Does it make for good copy? The theatre is a bit more hard up than usual at that particular time of year so would it be possible to double up on some of the parts, or would cross-casting with another show be possible? And so on. This is not meant to disparage the many brave efforts to cope with reality which are made year after year within the world of Scottish theatre but simply to question whether the scheme is the best vehicle for playwriting.

Then there is the issue of the 'touring show'. In Scotland most companies which don't operate through their own theatres have to take productions out on tour if they hope to get backing from the SAC and other sources. This is not to say that good plays cannot be written with touring outlets in mind. It could well be argued that facing up to a wide range of audiences in different communities and locales is a healthy challenge for a writer. But in practice that is not the case. The tendency is to tailor the show to comply with the audiences. It's perfectly under-standable but it's far from ideal for creating new plays.

The commissioning system also gives the artistic directors an inordinate influence over the kinds of plays that are written and produced. We are so used to this we think it natural. Many directors are strongly committed to helping playwrights create new plays, and are well able to do it. It is also often the case that the needs of the director and the writer might coincide. Ideas for new plays can arise from one or other. But there are also careerist directors who latch on to new writing as a means of helping them to move up the directorial ladder. Or there are established theatre directors for whom new plays become a ploy in an overall cultural politics game. In other cases it is a matter of convenience and often new plays yield their place to new adaptations. The commissioning scheme can be officially used this way, to support new adaptations, and no one dare complain because a writer is being employed.

Other weaknesses of the scheme are more to do with the frequency/infrequency with which a writer is commissioned. If a writer comes out with one successful play, a shower of offers will follow. It is extraordinary how one or two names can dominate the scene for two or three years (for example Iain Heggie and Chris Hannan in the Eighties and David Greig in the Nineties); it can seem like everyone you talk to is planning a

project with the same writers. At the same time, because the commissioning money is only a relatively small amount, the writers succumb all too
easily to the offers and a period of being over-commissioned follows. Meanwhile someone else has gone out of fashion and is wondering why the
phone's not ringing.

There is an Internet site called 'Scottish Playwrights' that gives
biographical details and playlists for a number of writers, mostly of
the older generation, such as Tom Gallacher, Hector MacMillan and
Donald Campbell. Few of them are still actively involved in writing for
the theatre. At some point in the past their work played to large audiences,
or they were closely involved with a particular company or rep. Now,
though their past triumphs become the subject for academic books and
studies, it feels as if nobody wants to know. Discouragement, disappointment, sometimes bitterness set in.

This neglect of older writers is partly a reflection of the cult of
youth. Again it is understandable. Theatres need new audiences, need
to keep in touch with the young, and it has seemed in recent times that
theatres might soon be sunk by ultra-violent films and acid-house
spectacles. It is good, however, to see new young writers emerging: new
energy – a sense of continuity – the baton is passed on – democracy –
everyone can write – creative education. Nothing wrong with all that,
is there?

It may be partly as a result of this obsession with youth that some
of the youngest playwrights around have had to take a novel type of strain:
they find themselves being commissioned almost before they have written
a play. Not quite true. They will have written something that proves
they have some ability, but haven't yet written for the fully professional
stage. Nonetheless, somehow they've got the image. Before they know
it they have taken on an agent and a couple of commissions from big
organizations too. It takes a few months before they start to show signs of
stress and strain, but inevitably they do. Only some of what is being offered
to them, or asked of them, is genuine: the rest is due to a competitive quest
for novelty.

Nevertheless, for each point I make critical of present practice,
several examples come up in my mind to contradict me, or a voice tells me
I am being too harsh, too cynical, too pessimistic. Yet I feel it is necessary,
if we have any real belief in the worth of playwrights, to challenge a

situation that on the one hand seeks to exploit them too soon while on the other abandons them when they get ill or go out of fashion.

As for plays, it might be interesting (if anyone could be bothered doing it) to inquire into the fate of plays produced under the commissioning scheme over the past ten years. It is obvious at a glance that the wastage factor is very high. Examine those plays that have made an impact, however – *Life of Stuff* by Simon Donald, *The Steamie* by Tony Roper, *The Cut* by Mike Cullen or *Perfect Days* by Liz Lochhead to name but a few – and it is abundantly clear that their authors already had an active relationship with the theatre and were already in collaboration with others working in the theatre. They were not creating at a distance.

We should try to ensure that writers have ample opportunity to be in the theatres, and that free-flowing spontaneous interactions between writers and actors are taking place each and every day. Setting aside a space for this purpose should be given high priority. There should be ample opportunity for trying out ideas, without it being any big deal, and any plans to commission or produce should be left till later. On the other hand, the writer is of no use to the theatre if he/she is always present in the theatre. Every playwright has to be a two-headed monster, one part in the theatre and the other 'at home', taking 'at home' to be not just a physical location but also whatever is the playwright's 'source' outside the theatre – that which the playwright draws upon, the inspiration and meat for the plays.

Playwrights need to be funded in two ways, to enable them to be 'at home' and to enable them to be in the theatre. This funding needs to be sustained, not just confined to specific periods of writing or rehearsing plays. To achieve this I would initiate a funding scheme that would offer playwrights financial support over a number of years, during which time they might or might not write plays. I would make sure, however, that each writer supported in this way was involved in a theatre somewhere, not sunk down reading other people's scripts, but active as themselves, as writers – theatre writers.

The amount of financial support offered to the playwright would be enough to ensure continuing survival without having to resort to other 'more commercial' forms of earning income. Writers might have to agree to concentrate efforts in a theatrical direction, but should never be called to account with regard to how much or how little 'work' they write for theatres within the time period receiving the financial support. Can anything be more detrimental to creativity than the current stress on 'accountability'? Let no one in the future be forced to make a five-year plan.

At the same time, subsidiary programmes would operate – such as can be found at places like the Banff Centre in Canada – where writers can go to write, meet other writers, or work with actors on scenes from their new plays. Grant schemes might underpin that. Playwrights' centres would help everyone develop a clearer sense of the reality of playwriting and enable at least some of the new plays to develop outwith the theatres – the National Studio reinvented as regional resource centres.

There would also be provision for travel and exchange, with writers living and working abroad for a while in theatres in other countries and writers from those countries coming here. This would be accompanied by an exchange of repertoire. Whilst the 'home' writer would be hopefully opening up a new outlet 'abroad', the incoming writer would be offering a different perspective to audiences here. The audience would become privy to something those of us working in theatre literary departments already know – the strength and excitement of modern playwriting when considered internationally. In this way a 'self-evolving' playwriting could begin to develop. Instead of being tied to the latest short-term objectives of survivalist directors, playwrights would be free to discover what their next play should be.

Along with the dismantling of the commissioning scheme, other things need to change. The power of the directors needs to be modified. They must come to realize that some essential creative processes between people in the theatre will only work if they are not interfered with or 'directed'. This is not to dismiss the director's role in relation to productions, nor to attempt to exclude directors from the creative process/generating end of things. It is simply to create equality where it is needed – all in it together, rather than one being up on a platform telling everyone else what to do.

Writers would have to change their attitudes in the opposite direction. After years of being the one brought into the theatre situation – not part of but introduced to the company, the lovable eccentric – the writer finds himself/herself already in the situation. After years of being expected to keep one's mouth shut in the face of others' theatrical expertise, the writer is now expected to speak, to have more than just opinions, to be an agent provocateur for the meaning of the play. Some writers might become directors but the main point is that they are accepted as writers and that their role and outlook is valued in and for itself. Instead of moaning on the sidelines, the writer is confronted with the challenge of 'Well, what do *you* think?' and has to take responsibility within the community of people working in the theatre.

What kind of theatre am I imagining in the future? Obviously it is more than slightly different from the theatre we have now. Considering the Utopian – the fantastic – future, my imagination seems to be projecting situations where there are something resembling standing companies in which the playwrights can be constantly working with actors, actors working with each other, musicians initiating things, designers returning to being artists, and so on. How has this miraculous situation come about? By closing the reps.

At some point in the next ten years the decision is taken not to wait until headlines appear in *The Stage* about yet another big theatre building getting into trouble, but to close them forthwith. This is part of a New Deal for Theatre. The big buildings, with all their economic problems, their frantic 'bums-on-seats' mentality, their boards of directors primarily selected to ensure the confidence of the funding sources – these are done away with, with the exception of one or two left standing for the whole of the UK. In their place we construct black boxes everywhere. Almost end-of-the-pier stuff. Theatre returns to having an active life. Productions no longer need to have soap opera superstars in lead parts to ensure someone will come to see the darned things. Theatre becomes more exciting than TV, because it's free – free perhaps in more ways than one, because the New Deal has pledged support for Theatre Everywhere under the new Direct Funding policy.

With Direct Funding, middleman bureaucratic activity is reduced to a minimum, thus saving on a lot of funds. If there is to be an Arts Council it will not be called that any more. It's simply the office through which the distribution of the Direct Funding takes place. Everything is made as straightforward as possible. No one need fill up another Lottery application form because all of that kind of thing has already been agreed and taken care of under the New Deal pledge which will stand (with small revisions along the way) for the next twenty-five years.

It will be considered risible that in the last decade of the twentieth century creative minds allowed themselves to droop alongside flip-charts whilst the latest management consultant lectured the company on the best use of time. Under the New Deal business methods are banned. Artistic directors are no longer expected even to pretend to have managerial skills. The new black boxes are as simple to run as possible. The people who make theatre are trusted. Instead of having to work out mission statements and cringe in the face of drama committee criticisms, they are left to get on with things at last – accountable to themselves and their audiences.

There is no education policy either. It has finally been recognized that to make theatre subject to education is to smother theatre. Theatre must be free to be badly behaved. That's what makes it relevant and exciting. Of course the theatre-makers will want to be reaching out to young people, and education officers will still be employed, but they won't be called that any more. They will simply be enthusiastic individuals who work for the company, linking it up with young people. The New Deal would also guarantee Travel Pass money to help the new theatre to get around. Any new plays created would be premiered not once but several times in different parts of the country. It would be expected that a play would change and develop over a period of time.

And the audience? Who are the audience for this amazing new endeavour? The important thing would be to get the energy flowing. In small spaces. It's similar to music. Suddenly a place gets going where the music is good. People flock to it. There isn't the same need for a brochure. The audience support the place. They are involved and active, no longer 'bums on seats'. They don't need to be sold the show. The programme can change from week to week. Unexpectedly. The return of spontaneity! Imagine it!

Coming back to earth, I wake from my fantasies into a world where the Government has announced a compulsory reading hour in schools, with the books to be read prescribed by them, and I have to admit the prospects for my 'funded freedom' seem dim indeed. Yet I am still working at the Traverse Theatre where much of what I've been discussing is already in place, and it feels as if there might be something negotiable between the fantasized Utopian future and the realities of now.

I meet up with a scientist in the cafe and discover he's just written a book, not a scientific treatise but a work of fiction. He is obsessed by the urge to write a play. Whatever you plan, you can never be sure. The best things seem to happen by accident. The next real play might come from anywhere.

COLIN CHAMBERS

That's Entertainment!

Colin Chambers is a theatre historian and writer. He was a journalist and theatre critic before becoming Literary Manager of the Royal Shakespeare Company (1981–97). He is Senior Research Fellow in Performing Arts at De Montfort University. Among his books are Other Spaces: New Theatre and the RSC, Playwrights' Progress: Patterns of Postwar British Drama *(co-written with Mike Prior),* The Story of Unity Theatre, Peggy: The Life of Margaret Ramsay, Play Agent, *which in 1998 won the inaugural theatre book prize awarded by the Society for Theatre Research, and* Kenneth's First Play *(co-written with Richard Nelson).*

A HUNDRED YEARS AGO a book like this, written by theatrical practitioners as a new century is almost upon us, would not have contained contributions from the world of literary management: in Britain the literary manager simply did not exist. As with much else in British theatre, the culture had not by then developed to the stage where such a function had become distinct, a job – if not an occupation – in its own right.

Even halfway through the century the situation would have changed little. Producers hired script readers and play doctors as necessary and, as in the century before, there were isolated cases of individuals informally carrying out tasks that were later to fall within the literary manager's orbit. But it was not until the advent of significant public subsidy that British theatre companies, borrowing pragmatically from the example of the mighty ensembles in mainlaind Europe, made this kind of backroom activity a recognizable feature of the British theatrical landscape.

When Laurence Olivier appointed the rakish critic Kenneth Tynan to the post of Literary Manager of the new National Theatre in 1963 he ensured that the job would at least be noticed. Since those intoxicating days the role has spread further afield but during that process it has become the domain of low-profile, hard-working specialists scattered throughout the land. They labour quietly and diligently in the national companies, in Britain's new play network (e.g. the Bush, Traverse, Hampstead, Soho or Paines Plough) and in regional theatres that are committed to presenting new work, such as the Birmingham Rep and the West Yorkshire Playhouse.

Despite this advance, during the eighteen years that I held the post at the Royal Shakespeare Company the position never acquired the status enjoyed in mainland Europe, where it was – and still is – common for even small municipal theatres to employ a larger dramaturgical staff than the RSC. There are signs, however, that, as is the case with translators in the theatre, the stock of the literary manager has been slowly rising. It is now even possible to study some of the skills required, although not on the scale nor with the career prospects offered either in the US or elsewhere in Europe.

It is not just an issue of having available funding; the appointment of a literary figure to the staff of a theatre is a cultural statement, an acknowledgement not only of the importance of the text in the kind of drama that theatre is presenting but, furthermore, a signal to anyone who cares to look that this kind of drama *matters*. The position and role of such a figure in any given theatre depends on the contending needs and personalities of those particular theatres and where in the hierarchy of power and concern playwrights and their plays fit in. (Is a literary manager's job, for example, to represent the interests of the playwright to the management or the other way round, and, when it is expected to be both and the two sets of interests clash, where does the allegiance of the literary manager lie?) Practice varies from theatre to theatre to accommodate this shifting matrix and, in deference to inevitable ambiguities, the title as well as the job description remains a little hazy. Peter Hall preferred the term Literary Adviser to Literary Manager, which, however, was the term favoured by the Royal Court, the National Theatre and subsequently the Royal Shakespeare Company after Hall left, as well as by most of the other theatres willing and able to employ a representative of this peculiar species.

British theatre companies have mostly avoided using the term 'dramaturg', unless applying it to an involvement in a specific production, where it signifies a person attending rehearsals with a recognized authority in matters of the text. The derivation of the word captures the uncertainty surrounding the function. With an 'e' on the end, the word comes from the French and means 'creator of drama', but it can also be traced back to the Greek 'dramatourgos', which literally means 'drama worker'. With a hard 'g' at the end, the word descends from the German, where in the eighteenth century the playwright and critic Gotthold Lessing started this particular ball rolling. As mentioned above, the title 'dramaturg' implies a closer association with the notion of playmaking than the term literary manager – a connection underscored in Britain, notably at theatres like the Royal Court, by the number of playwrights who have in the past taken on the role, however temporarily.

The tasks of the literary manager usually cover textual work (with the writer if alive), response to submitted scripts, play research and repertoire advice – or, in some instances, even helping the artistic director to plan a season. None of this activity is especially literary, however, as the whole point of the job is to make judgements related to performance: should the company stage such-and-such a play, or can this new play be improved, and if so, how and why? The literary manager, who acts as a private critic for and artistic conscience of directors and writers alike, might be pressed into service in other ways too, by writing programme notes, giving public talks about a play being performed or, if suitably equipped, occasionally translating or adapting a play from another time or culture.

Such theatrical muscle as the job can boast would not have been developed, and certainly would have withered quickly, without the rumbling explosion of playwriting talent in the years after the Second World War, an extraordinary mushrooming of creativity that coincided with the arrival and brief consolidation of publicly subsidized theatre. This was an historic period when theatre pushed its way back to centre stage in the national cultural consciousness and became the natural home of the Ardens, the Pinters and the Bonds, a many-faceted forum of infectious energy, provocative ideas and urgent debate.

Its dismantling since the 1980s within a sustained political strategy of devastating sabotage leaves many who lived through the ascendancy of the subsidized theatre feeling unusually pessimistic about the current predicament. Naturally, in the world of the theatre, the present is always in crisis; anxiety is endemic in a creative activity, the production and reception of which is intimately bound up with taste, fashion and experiment. Nonetheless, recognizing this cannot soothe the sharp ache of loss and of lost opportunities, living, as we do, in the rubble of such a major cultural achievement which was not made by writers alone but which saw them at its heart, as prime artistic intermediaries between the theatre and its society.

That historical moment has moved on; the economic, political, social and ideological contexts have been transformed. National unease at the loss of empire combined with a new-found commitment that fed into the theatre of the mid-1950s, or the political upsurges of the late 1960s that challenged the hegemony of the US and of the consumer capitalism it represented, have been replaced by a new national and international framework for our theatre and its playwrights: in Britain we are embarking upon new constitutional settlements (for Scotland, Wales, England and Ireland, in their political structures and in the nature of political represen-tation); we look awkwardly both west towards the US and at the same time east towards the rest of Europe; identities are evasive and fluid, and there is widespread loss of faith and ideological confusion. The middle classes are being squeezed, the rich still grow richer and the poor poorer as we face technological change of unprecedented rapidity and suffer the ravages of an uncontrolled 'globalizing' economy.

Thatcherism, led by the battle-cry of its Commander-in-Chief – 'There is no such thing as society' – promoted the mores of the individual in a way that nevertheless rendered the individual totally vulnerable. The virtues of the so-called Anglo-Saxon model – low direct taxation, unfettered movement of capital, extensive privatization and flexible labour markets – produced deep and widespread insecurity and the splintering of society. New Labour, whilst trying to square the circle on welfare and other social concerns with Third Way politics, have embraced the model with open arms, and seem happy to embrace its populism and crassness on the cultural front too.

Yet, despite this assault, the British did not lose, and have not lost, their knack for making theatre – a richly mongrel art form which, by its very nature and existence, makes a statement that society *does* exist. Theatre did not and would not die. This survival drew sustenance from other supposed Anglo-Saxon qualities trumpeted by Thatcher, such as robustness and pragmatism; and they, ironically, bring in their train the very Anglo-Saxon mistrust of intellectuals and artists that has been successfully directed against the theatre and, with the aid of government economic hostility, has helped push it to the margins.

The nation resisted the establishment of a National Theatre for an age, and ever since its relatively late formation it has been a national pastime to attack it. The two major postwar directors, Joan Littlewood and Peter Brook, have been lost, the former altogether, the latter to Paris, which is where you now have to go if you wish to catch up with the latest play by Edward Bond. And when one of the enduring aspirations of modern theatre was finally realized in the founding of the Royal Shakespeare Company as an ensemble – an ensemble, moreover, which quickly gained an international reputation – our national funding policy could not sustain this achievement, and it degenerated into a commercial art factory with consequent damage not only to the interpretation of Shakespeare but also to the production of new plays.

Renewal and redefinition of theatre, however, are distinctly possible, even in the current beleaguered situation. There are, for instance, new opportunities to advance the slow and uneven process of overcoming the division of the theatre in the nineteenth century into high and low forms (which does not mean, however, the end of distinctions, either artistically or in terms of social practice, as new ones will inexorably emerge). This historic split between the 'legitimate' drama for the well off and music hall for the poor endowed theatre with a fixed social position that broadly related to the social standing and economic power of its audiences and imprisoned pioneering playwrights in a middle-class enclave. As society changed, so did theatre's status and function, and the impulse to connect with new audiences drawn from an ever wider social base has been central to the development of theatre throughout the century.

The new energy that was coursing through the theatre from the mid-1950s for a couple of decades gave theatre a new social role, although some of the old hierarchies remained and were consolidated by government and funding body policy (e.g. the notion of the ladder of excellence, with work in the regional theatres being seen as an apprenticeship for greater achievements a few rungs up in the capital). The alternative theatre movement challenged this situation in the 1970s but did not have sufficient economic or political clout to achieve the desired changes. Yet groups within this movement, like 7:84, Red Ladder or Monstrous

Regiment, as well as mainstream playwrights, such as John Osborne in *The Entertainer* or Peter Nichols in *Poppy*, moved far beyond the reach of T.S. Eliot's panegyric to the working-class virtues of music-hall singer Marie Lloyd to draw extensively on and overlap with popular theatre forms and traditions: the spirit of Joan Littlewood lived on.

Within this process of realignment the private theatre sector has come to rely increasingly on productions from the publicly subsidized sector, which in turn has increasingly been pushed into the arms of the private business world; commercial producer Cameron Mackintosh launches *Les Misérables* with the RSC (to some public reproach, it must be said) and the National Theatre presents musicals like *Guys and Dolls*, *Carousel* and *Oklahoma!* (not always without adverse criticism too). Such interpenetration of the public and the private has meant a blurring of old distinctions – the boundaries between the art space and the commercial space have collapsed. In this context, a proper debate needs to be launched to rescue the current buzzword 'access' from the so-called 'dumbing down' that is too readily accompanying it. The whole paraphernalia of theatre needs examining, from marketing, ticket pricing and choice of space to how theatre is made, in order to explore the democratic component of access and to answer the related questions 'What is access?' and 'Who is theatre for?' as well as 'Why is theatre important?' and 'Access to what?'

Unsurprisingly, just as the role of theatre has changed, so too has the work of the playwright and what is meant by a play. The play has come out of the study, where it was judged as literature, and a few select examples were canonized as art – Shakespeare, 'the world's greatest poet', however, has little to do with theatre. Paradoxically, the play was returned to the study just after the Second World War with the founding of the Drama Department at Bristol University, but now it was to be judged part of a living process of making theatre. (Oxbridge, it should be noted, still refuses to regard theatre as a proper subject of academic scrutiny.)

Dramaturgically, from the first appearance of Alfred Jarry's *King Ubu* in 1896, the twentieth century has seen a multitude of upheavals. In the early 1950s the distance between contemporaries Terence Rattigan and Samuel Beckett was enormous. Thirty years later the very notion of creating a play had been upended and the fine art discipline of performance art had been gathered in under the umbrella of experimental theatre, with directors and performers the new auteurs. A discernible trend towards a new emphasis on performance gathered speed after the social and political convulsions of the late 1960s and early '70s. The international and radical politics of gender, race and identity, especially in the industrialized white world, caused a profound slippage; a questioning of this western world merged with an exploration of theatre practices and forms from the east. All aspects of conventional theatre practice were challenged, from the single authorial voice to the primacy of linear narrative. Fundamental issues – how meanings are made, communicated, received and interpreted – were seen in a new light. This gave rise to new ideas of the relationship between the elements that combine in theatrical performance, not just between actor and audience but between word, sound, light and space. New notions of intention recast the text as a notation for performance created by all these elements rather than as the embodiment of a pre-exisiting truth that had to be revealed by them.

The renegotiation of the balance of creative power between all the participants in the theatrical process changed the way writers would work and collaborate. In Britain the dance and the so-called performance art strand remained relatively isolated from those who were operating within traditional theatre practice in order to change it. Groups such as Monstrous Regiment, however, worked in an avant-garde as well as a populist mode, developing a high-energy athleticism supported by contemporary music in cabaret-type shows. Both tendencies have fed back into the mainstream through companies often described as 'physical', like Theatre de Complicite, and through writers like Caryl Churchill, Martin Crimp, Sarah Kane and Phyllis Nagy.

Many of these shifts followed the onset of a crisis in the subsidized sector, which saw the decline of the epic public play and the rise of confessional, subjective drama alongside the domination of the mega-musical. Symptomatic of this crisis for the playwright was the closure of many studio spaces, which mostly had been opened in order to accommodate the expansion of new writing but which at the same time had also cordoned off new plays in a ghetto.

In this crisis the position of the playwright came under threat. Playwrights had gained an elevated status in the British theatre with the advent of substantial public subsidy, a process in which the theatre in general as well as the playwright had been 'professionalized'. Allied to technological advance in certain areas, this led to increased specialization – the emergence of the lighting designer, the sound designer, the administrator, the marketing manager, the research and development (i.e. sponsorship) director as well as the literary manager – and even to the possibility of a career in these new roles.

Increased unionization among playwrights in the 1970s won them minimum contractual terms and conditions in the subsidized theatre, though the commissioning system remained fraught. Theatres created a production line system: they would 'hoover up' fashionable new writers and yet only be able to offer them what was still very little money for the length of time it takes to write a play. Most or all of the money would be spent before the play was written and, inevitably, there was pressure on a writer to accept more than one commission at a time, or to turn to television or film to earn a living. It was hard to sustain a sound relationship with a theatre or to devote the time required to develop the enormously demanding craft of theatre writing.

Playwrights campaigned to improve their lot on other fronts too. They argued for more second productions, and more extensive publication of playtexts, a levy on television to repay some of its massive debt to the theatre for producing so many of its writers, and a levy on theatres in order to create a fund to support new writing. This new play levy, now called the New Writing Fund, was being neogtiated at the end of the 1990s by writers' representatives, funders and theatre managers. It is a scheme under which a theatre would pay a royalty every time it produces a play, whether in or out of copyright. This money would be topped up by Regional Arts Board money ring-fenced for new writing and by additional National Lottery money. It would be used to allow any theatre to stage a new play.

Writers have also fought back in the most important arena of all: the plays they write. The Royal Court has been the main, though not exclusive, focus in the 1990s, as it was in the 1950s and, just as then, energy has become the new currency, though the plays have tended to acquire a higher gloss finish. The poetic puritanism of the Royal Court under artistic directors from George Devine to Max Stafford-Clark was replaced by the playful, extrovert touch of the Artful Dodger, Stephen Daldry, who helped revitalize the West End when the Royal Court vacated its Sloane Square home in 1996 for refurbishment. Indeed, commentators mooted that the West End was becoming more progressive than the subsidized sector. They remarked on the fact that at one point in 1998 Patrick Marber's *Closer*, Mark Ravenhill's *Shopping and Fucking*, and Ben Elton's *Popcorn* – all sexually explicit new plays that attracted a young audience – were playing next to each other in Shaftesbury Avenue. David Hare reported that the average age of the audience for his play *Amy's View* dropped by twenty or thirty years when it transferred from the National to the Aldwych Theatre. Yet of the four new plays listed above, only one – *Popcorn*, written by a very successful TV celebrity – originated in the commercial sector; the other three began life in publicly subsidized theatres.

Writers have survived, and the play has survived. As ever, some writers have quit while some have journeyed from the margins to the mainstream. (David Hare has travelled from the iconoclastic Portable Theatre to a knighthood as he turned himself into the new Shaw, although G.B.S. turned down a proffered gong.) Some have rejected the very notion of mainstream and margin and have chosen to work in the theatrical world that the media frequently ignore, producing theatre by or for a particular and subaltern group, whether it be the young, the old, the disabled, or a community. This is a world of new audiences and of much experiment with form and playmaking, inspired by a political tradition that has moved on from Bertolt Brecht to Augusto Boal.

Writers continue to reinvent theatrical language, fed by an ever-widening set of influences, and to find new ways of dealing with and relating the political and the personal. We have volume as well as much crossover from one medium to the next, and not just out of necessity but also because of the shift in notions of performance. As writers have taken new aesthetics on board, so too must literary managers and dramaturgs. They must help refine and promote the role of text in creating and animating perform-ance, to find new ways of exploring meanings and values within the unity of form and content. But it is hard to find the right conditions in which to be creative, to be formally daring and speak one's mind. Actors and direc-tors are ill-prepared and ill-equipped, though often eager, and theatres are rarely able to provide adequate rehearsal time; the marketplace demands entertainment, and entertainment now. This pressure for entertainment turns emotion into sentiment, energy into frenetic activity and meanings of words into mere noise.

If playwriting is to flourish again, then by definition theatre has to flourish again – and it is not alone in facing such a challenge today. The professionalization of sport in a TV-dominated market has thrown up similar issues for the future direction of individual games or, to take another example, the powerful music industry is having to face the challenge of songs being down-loaded cheaply at home through the Internet instead of being bought expensively in the shops. Such developments are happening at a time of extreme change, as the nature of work and the role of 'leisure' time are undergoing revolutions. People have more highly differentiated social patterns to their lives, in which theatregoing has become not only an attraction alongside similar forms, such as dance, but also alongside younger art forms, such as pop music or film, and other collective social activities as well, like sport. The appeal of theatre can be as strong as ever but it has to be placed, and communicated, in this new context.

Theatre may have lost its privileged position but, for the most part, it is still imbued with the ideology of that privilege. For instance, though we live in a multicultural society and our popular music is multicultural, our theatre is not. To take a prominent example: Ayub Khan-Din's comedy *East is East* stands out not only because it is very funny but because it is a rarity, a play by a British Asian writer telling a story about a British Asian family. We are still at the stage where this has to be pointed out, where a black writer who wants to be just a writer – or a gay or female writer with similar aspiration – still has to operate in a culture which at present makes that ambition virtually impossible to achieve.

If theatre and its playwrights are to contribute forcefully and fruitfully to building our multicultural society then they must embody cultural diversity and the many productive interactions of tradition, significance and practice that flow from it. This will require political support and appropriate funding – the funding of individuals such as playwrights and not obsessively the funding of institutions. At present, though, it seems unlikely that either will be forthcoming.

Our post-postmodern world tells itself that the problems of sexual and racial discrimination are history and, moreover, that history is history because history has come to a full stop. But a dynamic role can surely be found for theatre if only it can renew itself, is able to experiment, and aims to reflect the variegated realities of the contemporary world to ever more variegated audiences. The infrastructure has to be rebuilt and, along with facing the artistic problems, theatres need to tackle a range of non-artistic issues, from child care to genuine equal opportunity, underpinned by a decentralized, pluralistic perspective, in order to allow a richer, more complex drama to unfold that once again speaks to a multifarious audience about the truth of their lives – not with a single voice but with many.

17

ANDREW LAVENDER

Turns and Transformations

Andrew Lavender is a Lecturer in Drama at Goldsmiths College, University of London, where he specializes in multimedia performance and the work of contemporary European and American theatre companies and directors. His own productions as director include Acts Without Words *and* The Singularity (*both for the London International Mime Festival*) *and* The Shift, *a mixed-media drama presented at the Young Vic Studio, London. He was formerly editor of* City Limits *magazine and writes regularly on theatre and performance for* The Times.

I F I WERE WRITING THIS CHAPTER a hundred years ago, would I have known where to look for the experiments that would shape the future? Would I have turned to Paris where, a few days before the end of 1898, Marie and Pierre Curie announced the discovery of radium? Would I have looked towards Moscow where, a couple of months previously, audiences had witnessed the first production by Stanislavsky's Moscow Art Theatre? Radioactivity and realism – what would the twentieth century have been without these equivocal giants?

I might not have made it to the lumber room at the School of Physics, nor even to the Hermitage Theatre on Carriage Row. But I ought to have discovered that there were pressing interests in the science of radiation and the art of realist representation, and that these were being vigorously pursued in many different places. Nobody then could have predicted the effects of their experiments on the impending century, and I am not about to attempt such a thing in relation to today's explorations in theatre-making. Instead I shall describe those developments that seem new and urgent and whose course is yet to run. In any case, the dominant forms of tomorrow are surely taking shape today.

The major explorations in British theatre in the 1990s have been aesthetic in nature. They are manifested in three distinct areas: an evolution in the nature of 'writing' for the theatre, the increasing presence of multi-media performance and the re-imagining of theatre space. They concern, then, the way in which theatre is created, the materials with which it is made and the place in which it is presented. To these developments we must add an alteration to funding systems, which means that different kinds of people are getting money for different kinds of ideas. Each trend applies across the country, and across the demographics of theatre. In other words, it is not uniquely the domain of the mainstream subsidized theatre, nor of the London 'fringe', nor of the various performance groups based in provincial cities, nor of educational or youth theatres. Yet it embraces them all, and in some instances extends into the commercial theatre as well.

To start with the means by which theatre is created. For a long time, and certainly since the early days of the Wooster Group and the activities of directors like Peter Brook and Ariane Mnouchkine, it has been evident that a playwright is not an indispensable cog in the wheels of theatre. You don't have to be a writer to 'write' performance – a view exemplified by an array of newer companies that favour methods of devising or the some-times drastic adaptation of existing texts. These shifting practices are now widespread in the realm of experimental performance (one thinks of com-panies like Forced Entertainment, Volcano, Scarlet Theatre Company and Primitive Science), and now feature with increased frequency on more mainstream stages.

Theatre de Complicite, most notably in the shows directed by Simon McBurney, provides an obvious case in point. After devising its own mordant slapsticks between 1983 and 1990 the company turned to texts by writers. Even here, however, it was evident that the productions were primarily crafted in the rehearsal room rather than the study of the author or translator. Thus, for instance, *The Street of Crocodiles*, adapted from Bruno Schulz's short stories, or *Out of a House Walked a Man*, derived from the writings of the Russian surrealist Daniil Kharms. Both shows were developed (in 1992 and 1994 respectively) under the aegis of the Royal National Theatre, whose director at the time, Richard Eyre, had been excited not by the writings of Schulz and Kharms but by the particular theatrical style of the company. The continued association of Complicite with the nation's leading subsidized theatre, then, marked the legitimation not of the work of the author but of a process of theatre-making that has its roots in the workshop rather than the written text.

'Writing' – or more specifically, here, the *creation* of a piece of theatre – takes place on the actor's body and the scenic space, not on the play-wright's computer screen. This attitude is energetically expounded by the French-Canadian director Robert Lepage, probably the most influential theatre artist to have staged work in Britain in the 1980s and '90s. Lepage has redefined the nature of contemporary theatre authorship through a range of devised productions and a series of auteur-like one-man shows. He describes the devising of material as an extended group endeavour, which nonetheless gives each participant a firm stake in the project:

> A lot of actors want to change their way of acting through writing . . . You don't act the same way when you perform your own lines than somebody else's, and it's the same thing for directing . . . We say, 'Okay, after three weeks of exploring we have to do an hour and a half of show.' We force ourselves to perform, and that's where the real writing process starts because, for us, per-formance is writing . . . What determines [the performance] is not just the material with which we come up, but the characters who appear in the picture. At first they're all principal charac-ters, but then they find their way through the hierarchy of the project. That's why it's interesting to write with actors, because actors incarnate what they write immediately through these characters.
>
> [*Unpublished interview with the author, 26 August 1996.*]

Creative authority, then, is no longer vested in the playwright but established on the rehearsal room floor as a group gains ownership of a project by jointly creating it. Admittedly this ownership is partial, and Lepage's hand is very evident in shows which bear his name. The conventions of authorship are observed in that respect – in fact they are crucial to the shows' marketability in an international arena. Audiences come because the production bears the (single) signature of its director. But Lepage's working process is far from singular. In a range of new British work the director has emerged – albeit less spectacularly – as the arbiter within a collective of 'primary' creators, as is evident, for instance, in the pre-eminence of Tim Etchells within Forced Entertainment and Phelim McDermott within Improbable Theatre.

In general terms the *playwright's* status is diminished, and this humbling of the figure who used to be seen as the mainspring of theatre is not without consequence for the medium. A form of creativity grounded in the rehearsal room is likely to be medium-sensitive and medium-specific. The pleasures that it offers are, in a word, *theatrical*. They revolve around the textures of space and movement and the purveyance of live performance skills. Experimental work of the period is less evidently concerned with social, political and ethical issues, the stuff of a tradition of playwriting that reaches from Ibsen, through Shaw, Osborne and Bond to David Hare. Instead the issue is about exploring – if not to say guaranteeing and extending – the dynamics of *live* performance in an age dominated by television, video, computer and cinema screens, and accompanied by the soundtracks of rock music and advertising jingles. This explains the significance of practitioners like Lepage and McBurney (and we could add British companies like DV8, Gloria and Improbable). Their shows are generated from the ground up, theatrically, by a group of collaborators in a three-dimensional space. The medium – in its reliance on bodies, on movement, on textures of live performance – is made to matter.

This particular avant-garde might therefore appear, paradoxically, to be fighting a rearguard action, defending the ground of 'theatre' in an age more preoccupied with other media. In fact, inevitably, a number of practitioners are busy raiding these other media, as is evident in the proliferation of mixed-media work. Shows of this nature are not necessarily an *alternative* to the theatre (which in any case has incorporated elements from new circus, contemporary dance and alternative cabaret in recent years), but they do throw down a gauntlet. Audiences are used to dealing with the rapid juxtapositions and layerings of information presented by video and film. Mixed-media performance offers a swifter route to the perceptual and representational languages of contemporary culture than older theatre strategies. We may have before us a genuinely avant-garde development, set to influence mainstream theatre in years to come.

The allure of multimedia work, as far as theatre is concerned, lies in the conjunction of the live and the mediated. The rhetorics of TV and film, of video and computer games, become a resource that can freshen up our stagings of modern experience, whilst remaining subject to the three-dimensionality and the liveness of theatre. There are broadly political implications to this development. Mixed-media performance offers audiences a chance to look differently, *critically*, at the image, in an age that has witnessed a sophisticated prepackaging of images by the print and broadcast media and, in particular, the advertising industry. The relationship between the human figure on stage and on screen allows us to dwell on the *presence* of the body, in the wake of the objectification of our bodies within a consumer culture. The point is that the theatre can *stage* the screened image – thereby effecting a form of Brechtian estrangement – in a way that television or cinema cannot.

The work of Lepage and his company, again, provides a good example of the new interface between theatre and the electronic media, although the productions are Brechtian more for certain formal effects rather than for any stinging view of social realities. *The Seven Streams of the River Ota*, a seven-hour touring show presented at the National in 1996, featured a set of sliding screens as part of the set design – perfect for the show's various forms of video, slide and shadow projection. In every instance, the projection was part of a live context, rather than simply a video excerpt which you could just as easily watch at home (as is the case in a number of productions that claim a 'mixed-media' provenance).

At the end of the first section of *The Seven Streams*, for instance, a series of projections shows images relating to the US military presence in Japan in the aftermath of the bombing of Hiroshima: a plane, with a woman painted on its fuselage, and pictures of reconnaissance trips over the Japanese countryside. These are not instantly revealed to the audience. Instead the projection is firstly a block of vivid green colour. A performer wearing a soldier's uniform appears, shown in silhouette, behind the screen. He is carrying a paint pot and a brush. He dips his brush into the pot and moves as though he is 'painting' the screen in sweeping moves. As he does so, the block of green is erased, in accordance with his strokes, to reveal the images (plane, countryside). In themselves the images are rather bland. But the interest for the audience lies in witnessing the nature of their revelation: a neat conjunction of the live performance and the pre-recorded image. The effect can only be achieved, of course, by the actor rehearsing in order to become precisely familiar with the video material, so the means of composition (actor is cued by video image) is exactly the reverse of the impression given by the staging.

In another sequence, a performer playing a Japanese woman comes in front of the screen and opens a charred photo album. As she does so, a still image appears on the screen – clearly the photo to which she has turned. The image then begins to move (the video plays, rather than pauses). It shows participants at a ceremony – perhaps a wedding. The woman turns and caresses the man who is central to the procession. She bows, in unison with the couple on the screen. She caresses the image of the man again. The image then diminishes in size until it forms a small square on the black screen. The woman gives two cries. Then she reaches up and the image slides down the screen as if she has grasped the photo and put it back into the album.

The melt from still to moving image has the effect of suggesting that the scene is 'remembered' by the woman. The most obvious reading is that she is grieving for her husband, now dead. Again the content is not particularly complex, but the pleasure it offers the audience lies in the mesh between the theatrical performance and the video projection. Neither element could exist independently. The projected image would lack its personal context (the wife attempting to touch the memory of her husband), while the woman's actions would remain private and abstract without the projection's amplified detail.

Lepage's shows can seem soft-edged, a result of their attempted fusion of the experiences of characters living in different continents and even at different periods. The work lacks a sharper sense of social and political definition. Indeed, the very nature of Lepage's devising process, which depends upon 'writer-actors' used to dealing with ideas and emotions, means that the 'voices' which emerge are often very similar. There is nothing blue-collar about the characters here. But I suggest that this work is valuable precisely for its formal experimentation. One aspect of this is that elements from different media are combined in order to produce a new kind of spectatorship: one where the viewer reads the screen *in conjunction with* the stage, where the screen only finally 'makes sense' in the living moment.

One of the problems for aspiring – and indeed established – multimedia practitioners is the cost of digital and electronic equipment. Access to computer and video technologies needs to be ensured at grass-roots level – in schools and colleges, especially, but also by facilitating the cheap hire of equipment for individuals and small groups. It would hardly be difficult for the Regional Arts Boards (RABs) to equip a number of resource centres specifically for the cheap hire of equipment. It might also be a condition that hardware purchased with grant allocations is made available to others, at peppercorn rates, when not otherwise in use.

The demand already exists. A number of colleges offer dedicated multimedia courses. Mixed-media practice features in the syllabi of a number of university drama departments nationwide (which also include courses on devising and adaptation). In future, perhaps, acting schools might also teach multimedia performance – a rather subtle art, I suspect. A new generation of practitioners, skilled in a virgin combination of disciplines, is about to come of age. The work which will emerge, because in some respects technologically driven, will be conceived in ways not previously imaginable.

I hope these developments continue apace, and in a deliberately enhanced manner. This by no means marks the card of the playwright (who in any case is unlikely to go meekly), but it does mean that the 'scripting' of theatre could usefully relate yet more closely to the creative work of a range of practitioners. Which is why I find only slight solace in the continuance of new writing schemes by the likes of the Royal Court, Paines Plough and the Bush in London and the Traverse in Edinburgh. A good number of plays written in the mid- to late-1990s demonstrate that 'new writing' is not that far from 'old naturalism', which positions theatre as a training ground for television and cinema rather than as a medium with its own special pleasures. If 'new writing' is still cherished, I would like to see 'new directing' and 'new acting' pursued in a similarly organized way, by means of developmental programmes with a scheduled range of outcomes. We have spent too long in thrall to a culture of the writer at the expense of a culture of intelligent theatricality.

Developments onstage have been accompanied by questions about the nature of the stage itself. When Stephen Daldry directed Arnold Wesker's *The Kitchen* at the Royal Court in 1994, the stage was built out into the auditorium, with seating arranged around the back of the original playing area. The show was memorable less for its brash hyper-naturalism than the panache of its architectural reorganization. Deborah Warner's production of Samuel Beckett's *Footfalls*, in the same year, was staged on one of the balconies of the Garrick Theatre, whose foyer and auditorium were swathed in something akin to Beckettian rags. In 1997 the National's main auditorium, the Olivier – a cavernous space modelled on the Greek theatre at Epidaurus – was turned (not quite perfectly) into a theatre in the round for a mini-season featuring Brecht's *The Caucasian Chalk Circle* and Weiss's *Marat/Sade*.

These ventures, and others like them, suggest an impatience with the apparent orthodoxies of fixed architectures. They accompany a theme sounding more loudly in the realms of experimental and community-based performance, where the theatre venue itself was renounced in favour of a range of preferable sites and spaces. The cachet that site-specific work has acquired in Britain in the 1990s is best exemplified by the activities of Artangel, a production company energized in 1991 by the appointment of James Lingwood and Michael Morris as artistic directors. Artangel both commissions and produces new work by contemporary artists, which means that the initial creative impulse is that of the 'executives' rather than the artists themselves. Its projects include Rachel Whiteread's Turner Prize-winning *House*, a concrete cast of a Victorian terraced house located in London's East End in 1993, and Robert Wilson's *HG*, an installation made in 1995 within a series of underground rooms at the Clink Street Vaults, near London's Tower Bridge. Other hands, then, helped the artists affix their distinctive stamp.

Such eye-catching endeavours change our understanding of the usual requirements for a performance venue. Unorthodox spaces are seen to be colonizable – once funding and assent from appropriate sources has been secured. The nature of the artist's engagement with the public does not have to fit into criteria established by years of custom and practice. The best of this work generates a relationship with its 'audience' that runs deeper than the allure of a faddish postmodernity, for there is, in the sense of uniqueness that site-specific work entails, a reverberation of the theatre's longstanding contract with its spectators, based on the choice to place yourself, in person, in live relationship to an event.

In the case of Artangel's projects, established demarcations between the inception (artistic) and the promotion (managerial) of the event are eroded. A creative producer is more akin to a commissioning editor in print journalism or in television, media which have themselves undergone extensive transformation over the last two decades of the twentieth century. One of the results of the 1990 Broadcasting Act has been the proliferation of independent television producers, responsible for generating concepts and seeing these through to completion. Meanwhile the expansion of newspapers into multi-sectioned monsters in the 1980s called for a new raft of section editors. Within different media, commissioning power has been disseminated across a number of semi-autonomous producers, responsible for both generating ideas and finding the right people to execute them. The entrepreneurial spirit of the 1980s manifests itself inside the very creation of cultural products in our *fin de siècle*.

The results cannot easily be summarized. The particular 'avant-garde' represented by Artangel is managed, produced, commodified. Its irruptions into the public sphere are oblique rather than oppositional in, say, the spirit of some of the 1960s 'happenings' and the work of the Living Theatre. Even so, a great capacity for surprise and delight lurks behind this infiltration of public space, and site-specific work builds, in different ways, immediate bridges between artists and public communities. We could well witness an age of robustly promoted 'alternative' work, in unusual environments, whose influence on the art of the twenty-first century might match that of the European independent theatres established towards the end of the nineteenth century by practitioner-managers including Otto Brahm, Lugné-Poë, André Antoine, J.T. Grein and of course Stanislavsky and Nemirovich-Danchenko.

Where are such enterprising latter-day producers to find the money for their projects? The easy clarion call is 'More money for the arts'. Of course most theatre practitioners lament the discrepancy between the lavish support accorded to creative industries in France and Germany and the comparatively slim pickings offered in Britain. That said, the situation has been transformed – salvaged, you might say – by the disbursement of cash generated by the National Lottery to the six 'good causes', of which the arts is one. (The first balls of the Lottery were drawn live on television on 14 November 1995.) There were initially five 'good causes' [the arts, charities, heritage, the millennium and sport], with the introduction in 1998 of health, education and the environment as a combined category. The Lottery is in effect a form of regressive tax, given its predominantly lower-demographic participants. With this in mind, it is true that the nation's new gambling habit has, at a stroke, reversed the erosion of funding for cultural activities.

In 1998–99 the arts received an annual revenue from the Lottery of around £200 million (consider, by way of comparison, that the Arts Council of England's budget for grant-in-aid for 1998-99 was a total of £184.6 million). There have been obvious teething problems with the distribution of this booty, most notoriously in the requirement that it should fund buildings, equipment and 'stabilization' rather than the generation of artistic work itself. The National Lottery Act of 1998 allows the Arts Councils to support a wider range of activities, and to do so in a strategic manner (soliciting applications on the basis of perceived needs, for example, and delegating some of its decision-making to the RABs). This, along with the internal reorganization of the Arts Councils instituted in 1998, should assuage many of the part-random and competitive mechanisms built into the funding machinery.

Such an evolution, alongside the steady consolidation of joint initiatives involving public and private sector bodies, suggests a move towards a highly legitimized arts scene overseen by a claque of mandarins or sponsorship executives. A more vibrant situation presents itself – as evidenced, paradoxically, by another funding scheme, Arts For Everyone. Launched in 1996, A4E was designed to increase access to artistic practices, especially by way of its subsidiary, A4E Express, which targeted youth and amateur groups, and which distributed over £21.5 million to 5353 projects.

These figures suggest a rash of amateur, youth and developmental work running under the surfaces of the legitimate mainstream arts practices in Britain, and the apparent health of this sector augurs well, if the door remains open for funding of its activities. The scheme as a whole concluded with the announcement in the autumn of 1998 of a last round of awards.

You might still surmise that the writing is on the wall for theatre *per se*. The fact that many more applications were received by the A4E commissars for Combined Arts than for Drama projects signals very clearly the priorities of aspiring practitioners. Drama's omission (along with that of Music and other artistic practices) as a foundation subject in the National Curriculum for schools, laid out by the Education Reform Act of 1988, is yet more significant. This denies, at a prime educational level, an experience of the sublimities offered by the performing arts, along with the capacity to understand how these work and why one might enjoy them.

Meanwhile, the Government's welfare-to-work reforms make it more difficult for arts practitioners to engage in unpaid or voluntary work (sadly necessary in the generation of a good deal of experimental theatre). Nonetheless, the Department of Culture, Media and Sport has begun to review the operations of the 'creative industries'. If its findings have any weight, the ministry could still broker a more benevolent relationship between government and the arts than was the case under the Thatcher and Major administrations in the 1980s and '90s. It might mark the shift by focusing concretely on 'enablement' – both of the young practitioner to 'practice', and of the audience to attend. This is not just a question of financial provision but of shrewd rejigging of legislation surrounding funding mechanisms, educational activities and the nature of artistic 'work'. The opportunity to reverse a number of Gradgrindian policies remains golden – unless we intend to breed a nation for whom the arts are an esoteric adjunct or an exercise in commodity management, and something done better by people in other countries.

I have described, in particular, a shift in the nature of theatre forms and processes of creation: the structures through which 'alternative' and experimental theatre are made. During our own *fin de siècle,* experimental and avant-garde practitioners investigated these structures. The result is an experimental field whose ground has been laid. Contemporary theatre can commune with a modern audience using new technologies, without being circumscribed by outdated customs or conditions.

In 1898 the Moscow Art Theatre presented Chekhov's *The Seagull*, an event so successful that the seagull was adopted by the theatre as its emblem. The first production of the play, two years previously, had been a disaster. Marie Curie was eventually killed by radium, irradiated by the substance she had discovered. Yet this luminous element, always in a state of spontaneous alteration, is used in radium therapy to treat cancer. The principles of change and transformation evident here apply no less readily to the subjects of this chapter.

In 1998 I looked, among other places, to a converted fire station in Quebec City, where Robert Lepage's company Ex Machina is based, and a converted terraced house in Clerkenwell, London, where Artangel has its office. There are doubtless other places where crucial experiments are being conducted – the places where I *should* have looked. But we do not know what lies around the corner of the next millennium. We do not know how the elements we describe will be used and transformed.

18

JATINDER VERMA

Sorry, No Saris!

Jatinder Verma was born in Dar-es-Salaam, Tanzania, and migrated to Britain from Kenya in 1968. He co-founded Tara Arts in 1976 and has directed, written and adapted most of their productions, which have ranged from contemporary plays to the classics of the world stage. In 1990 he directed Molière's Tartuffe, *with an all-Asian cast, for the Royal National Theatre. He is the originator and director of Tara's three-year Millennium project,* Journey to the West, *the story of East African Asian migrations. As well as making regular appearances on radio and TV, he has also contributed to several books, including* Contemporary British Theatre, Analysing Performance *and* Theatre Matters.

T HE CHALLENGE OF THE COMING MILLENNIUM, in society as in theatre, is to embrace the Other: to learn how to become neighbours across divides of colour, language and sensibility. If the theatrical enterprise is about the continual construction and reconstruction of a shared community – the dialogue between a given set of audiences and performers – then the question arises: how do we create the shared community with such diversity in our midst? And, as a follow-up, what sort of community or communities are we seeking to construct in the impending millennium?

In *The Satanic Verses*, Salman Rushdie's hero, Saladin Chamchawalla (who literally *fell* into England from the skies), wakes up one day in his flat in the East End of London to find that he has begun to sprout horns on his forehead and has hooves for feet. The demonization of the Other,

I think, was what Rushdie was alluding to as a characteristic of modern Britain – a demonization that achieved the stamp of political orthodoxy when Mrs Thatcher in one of her election speeches of 1979 invoked the fear felt by the host community of aliens 'swamping the country'. This notion of the Demon Other has been given horrendous expression as we hurtle towards the next millennium: the former Yugoslavia, Rwanda, India and, of course, Ulster, have provided some of the most graphic examples of the failures of multicultural experiments. Despite the veritable revolution in diet over the past thirty years (the only revolution we've experienced), the Demon Other lurks beneath the surface – as has been cruelly demonstrated by the Stephen Lawrence case. (Stephen Lawrence was a 19-year-old Black student who was stabbed to death by racist youths in a south London suburb in 1993. It took years for the police to admit that the killing was racist and they have yet to bring the perpetrators to justice.)

For me, the starting point – perhaps even the underlying premise – of modern multiculturalism is a sensibility of Otherness, of being an Outsider. Starting from this premise, there seems to me one of two choices: either try and become an Insider – join the Club, as it were – or try and change the rules of the game. After all, as an Outsider, you're not expected to be au fait with the rules. The former strategy, I believe, leads to attempts to conform, to integrate; the latter, to confront. Multiculturalism, I would argue, is about confronting or encountering the Other. A choice I found myself making in 1989, when invited to direct at the Royal National Theatre.

I had arrived in Britain in February 1968 as part of what the press at the time termed the 'exodus' of Asians from Kenya. Following the usual *rites de passage* through school and university – compounded in my case by an extraordinarily virulent racist atmosphere, where well-respected politicians like Enoch Powell (before he became the anti-racist bogey) spoke in reasonable terms of the threat posed by Asians. In one memorable speech he pronounced prophetically: '. . . it is when the Englishman looks into the eyes of Asia, he sees one who will dispute with him the possession of his native land.' In July 1976, following the murder of a 17-year-old Asian, Gurdip Singh Chaggar, two friends and I founded Tara Arts. Its objectives were simple: to find a public voice as and for Asians. In 1990 that objective was posed its sternest challenge when finally I came to direct at the National.

I had chosen to adapt and direct Molière's *Tartuffe*. This comic farce exposing the sham of religiosity seemed an obvious choice: barely a year had elapsed since the fatwa pronounced on Salman Rushdie and it seemed to me that *Tartuffe* offered a salutary reminder of the absurd actions that sometimes pass under the guise of religious fervour. While the political circumstances certainly played a part in choosing to work on this particular story, I found in Molière's comic genius equivalencies in other dramaturgies, most notably Bhavai – a form of theatre originating in western India (Gujarat). Bhavai's origins were as radical as those of Commedia dell'arte, which had inspired Molière's work. As a form, Bhavai was designed (and continues today) to poke holes in the great and the good of Indian rural society: priests, money-lenders, landlords, police.

It would have been perfectly possible to direct the play in accordance with existing conventions of English-language productions of Molière. My choice is best articulated by quoting from my production notebook at the time:

> I am setting out to translate a seventeenth-century French farce through an all-Asian company of performers. This entails a double translation: once from the French original to English; and secondly to an English spoken by Asian actors, who have their own history of the acquisition of English speech. In other words, who are themselves 'translated' men and women – in that they (or their not-too distant forebears) have been 'borne across' from one language and culture to another. In order then to lay bare the full dimension of 'translation', I must take account of the specificity of my performers (their history): by conveying Molière's original play-text into a form that allows the performers to make creative connections between their ancestral traditions and their English present . . .

The provocation of such a production, I would contend, is to stimulate other ways of 'seeing'. Is a French classic, with its history of translation into English theatre as a stylized comedy of manners, so bound within this defining convention as to be incapable of being seen as an

'Indian' play? Stylized according to an Indian vocabulary of gesture, mode
of speech, dress, music, theatrical convention? Theoretically, one should
be able to answer 'Why not?' In practice, however, the provocation of such
an act is not to be underestimated – a sentiment echoed by a critic writing
in the *Surrey Advertiser* during the tour of *Tartuffe* in 1991: 'Somewhere in
France this week Molière is turning in his grave . . . For me [the conception
of *Tartuffe*] was as valid as transporting *A Passage to India* to Paris!' What is
'acceptable' is here being confronted; what is being contested is the notion
of the 'authentic'.

In making the choice I did, the production text did not start from the
assumption of a 'shared community'; on the contrary, the axiom of such
theatre practice is that the 'community' is diverse, perhaps even mutually
exclusive. It is not, therefore, an attempt to display a myth of commonality.
Rather, it creates a situation where different communities share different
moments of engagement with a performance. Most interestingly, it creates
a dialogue *within* the audience: what was he saying? what's so funny? why
are people exclaiming? These are all questions I have heard white members
of the audience ask their Asian neighbours. These are moments of real
frisson, where one section of the audience has the feeling of not being 'in'.
Such production texts make great demands on dramaturgy: the place of
rhythm, tone, image, gesture, alongside speech, in the creation of a *total*
language of theatrical communication. The texts become a rich melange
of spoken (English, Urdu, Hindustani) as well as physical (Commedia
dell'arte, Bhavai, Kathak) languages. Bereft of a simple reliance on the
meaning of given words today, I was obliged to raid other disciplines of
communication – which include mime, dance, music and film.

Such dissolving of the borders between different artistic and
linguistic disciplines (in itself a legacy of nineteenth-century nationalism),
I believe is imperative if we are to face the challenge of the next millennium. It seems self-evident that if an audience cannot be involved in a
dialogue of creating a community, it cannot share in one. Hence the
demands on our dramaturgies to become more inclusive; where, for example,
a gesture may replace a spoken word or a real object, to facilitate a more
open dialogue of the imagination between performers and audiences. The
suggestive power of a fan (as in Noh) has more 'openings' for the radically
diverse audiences that now inhabit British cities than the 'literality' of a

realistic stage prop (which is never more than what it looks). The theatre, it seems to me, therefore, needs to regain its tradition of 'magic realism' – which in the latter part of this millennium has been largely appropriated by the novel – if it is to create the images, symbols, colours and gestures appropriate for our communities today.

There is a sense in which modern Britain is best characterized as a jungle: the gap between the lords of the jungle and their prey. Social Darwinism has had a revival over the past two decades, under the guise of 'market forces'. The ever-increasing gap between the rich and the poor, the enlargement of the hidden economy, the rise in power of marketeers and accountants in theatres as in other walks of life, the homeless dotting every city and town, the multiplicity of languages, faiths, diets, dress . . . of course, Britain was never a homogeneous society. But in former eras the facts of Empire and Whiteness at least kept alive a notional sense of 'One Nation'. Today all but naive politicians find this notion highly suspect. Issues surrounding gender and ethnicity alone (forgetting for a moment modern telecommunications) make contemporary society a multiplicity of 'nationhoods', bound within the geographical confines of this island. Brecht's 'jungle of cities' is a more useful way of viewing the nation today.

Loss, I've come to believe, is central to multiculturalism. That ever-present shadow alone lends depth to the gains of multicultural practice. Without that 'chip on the shoulder' the picture is flat. I suppose I have come to this realization because of the fact of migration. To quote Salman Rushdie again, when the character of Saladin Chamchawalla falls from the sky into England, 'there floated the debris of the soul, broken memories, sloughed-off selves, severed mother-tongues, violated privacies, untranslatable jokes . . . the forgotten meaning of hollow, booming words, land, belonging, home.' To put it another way, there are many actors today who stand in British rehearsal rooms or drama schools reading texts while the shadow of other texts cloud, confuse or beat upon their hearts. Take the word 'honour'. Individualized in modern English. But it also offers an approximate translation for the Urdu concept of 'izzat'. Izzat is familial, transmitted through generations, a treasure to be guarded jealously; where the gain by one is the gain of all, and so too for loss. Or take 'thee' – the ubiquitous word in the Shakespeare canon. Old English now; almost, dead

English. But offering me the only means of translating the concept of the honorific that is a structural component of all Indian languages. Speaking in Hindi, Punjabi or Urdu (three languages I do speak with relative fluency), I could not and would not address my elders or those I accord respect with the familiar 'you': that is reserved for those I consider my equals, or lower. Speaking in English to my mother, how do I say 'you' without violating some sense of myself – without feeling (as I always do when I've used the familiar word) as if I've sworn at her? When I first came to England, schooling in Manchester, I latched onto 'thee' as offering a way out – until I was reminded by my teacher whilst giving a talk on Gandhi (yes, in a geography lesson, of all things) that English had moved on.

All cultures are rapacious: it is the fuel to go forward, to change, to evolve. Empire, however, opened another chapter in cultural exchange: borrowing without acknowledgement. A borrowing that is ingrained in the very language we use today. Take shampoo, for instance. The word comes from the Hindi 'champa', meaning 'to massage with oils'. To quote an example from the *Oxford English Dictionary*, one John Forbes observed of a woman in India in 1813, 'She first champoes her husband, and fans him to repose; she then champoes the horse.' Thankfully, not many of us are called upon to do the latter nowadays – or the former, more's the pity. A similar etymology goes for the vehicles that plague our roads – juggernauts. The word is derived from the name given to Krishna in eastern India (Jagannath) and the festival in praise of him in the city of Puri, when devotees pull along a huge cart through the winding streets. Should the cart slip from the control of the scores of men pulling it, and trample devotees under its myriad wheels – which tends to happen often – it is considered a blessing. I'm not sure the families of the victims would feel they were blessed, any more than we would, if one of the modern-day juggernauts ploughed through our living rooms.

And this process of linguistic borrowing has not ended. Today, the most popular take-away food in Britain is Indian. Indeed, ready-made Indian foods, spices and other ingredients are now commonplace in most shops and supermarkets around the country. This is the revolution I spoke of earlier. When I first arrived in 1968 the smell of our Indian cuisine actively discriminated against our ability to rent rooms. Thirty years later those very same smells are voluntarily imbibed in homes by all communities of

Britain – biriani, gosht, kebab, pakora, samosa, poppadom are all popular items of food and have begun to be incorporated in the vocabulary of modern English. So, in a quite real sense, the development of multiculturalism is being led by the stomach.

Food, however, is not the only source. Politics has also provided some impetus. In the wake of the controversy surrounding Salman Rushdie's *The Satanic Verses*, 'fatwa' and 'jihad' are now common parlance for many English political commentators and journalists.

Jokes, it is commonly assumed, are among the most difficult things to translate from one language to another. I put this to the test in 1996 in a play I'd adapted and staged – another Molière, *Le Bourgeois gentilhomme*. The father, foiled by his son in his attempt to seduce a fashionable woman, rounds on him angrily and shouts: 'Why must you forever be a bone in the kebab?' To my amazement, this literal translation of a Hindi joke elicited hoots of laughter from a largely English middle-class audience. I shouldn't have been so surprised; we are all now familiar with the properties of a kebab, and know that a bone in a kebab is the equivalent of being a 'stick-in-the-mud'.

Such interlacing – what the pre-eminent cultural commentator Edward Said calls 'overlapping' – of texts and tastes is what I've come to call 'Binglish'. Yes, it means exactly what it sounds: not quite English. Food, popular music, dress are pushing this sensibility ever onward. We are, in a quite real sense, therefore, living in times of *dis*continuous narratives, where other lands, cultures, times and tastes seep into our present at a remarkable rate. Popular culture makes of such seepage a positive virtue – as in the modern London nightclub scene, where drum-and-bass rhythms sit beside flickering images of Indian gods and screen goddesses, with the occasional 'Indian' sound titillating the ear. In the modern phenomena of migrations – including refugees and asylum-seekers – we are witness to the most dramatic instances of leakage.

Though I accept that to 'eat' the Other does not necessarily obligate one to love the source of the food, nevertheless, faced with the babble that abounds in the modern Forest, the jungle that is England, can we ignore the creative challenge and possibilities of Binglish?

Thanks to modern telecommunications, English is rapidly becoming the world language, with its dominance assured as much by air traffic as the Internet. Increased globalization enforces a uniformity (ubiquitous Big Macs and Cokes) but, on the other hand, individuals and communities crave a distinctiveness – of language, of dress, of food, of mores. Glaswegian, Jamaican patois, Irish brogue, broad Yorkshire – all are, in the closing years of the twentieth century, zestfully deconstructing the notion of standard English that has ruled British theatre stages through most of the twentieth century. These and other varieties of English are constructing *other* sensibilities.

Binglish for me denotes more than modes of speech. If language is a way of structuring the world, then Binglish more accurately reflects the fractured world – the overlapping world – that is modern Britain; where English vies with a whole host of languages in our cities and towns. As is amply demonstrated in the works of the current masters of English literature – Salman Rushdie, Vikram Seth, Rohinton Mistry, Arundhati Roy. Indeed, I would suggest that literature is currently at the forefront of multiculturalism to an extent that theatre, certainly in England, has not caught up with. The great writers of today have realized that standard English is simply not capable of giving adequate expression to the fractured narratives of our times. It is by bringing what Salman Rushdie has called 'a different sort of noise' into English (or any other dominant language) that these writers have opened the world of literature to other voices and therefore other stories.

Binglish, by definition almost, is inherently *in*clusive. It is an expression of the Other in constant dialogue with the Self. (A modern paradox is that post-colonial societies consider the mark of 'modernity' the acknowledgement, even emulation of the West, whereas post-imperial societies characterize 'modernity' by the *denial* of the East . . . borne out of unvoiced shame of Empire.) This inclusivity tends towards a consensuality: attempts to make whole the fractures of oneself, like the Asian kid growing up in a Mirpuri-speaking household in Bradford, who is faced constantly with the need to negotiate between Yorkshire and the foothills of the Himalayas where Mirpur district is located.

Such consensuality perhaps suggests an alternative model to the conflictual one that has been dominant for so long. Our economic fabric is founded on the weave of Them and Us. Increasingly, however, economists and entrepreneurs are beginning to acknowledge that the most successful enterprises are the ones where the bosses work and eat with the workers and where lay-offs are not the only options available to sustain a decent enterprise.

This slow turn in economic thinking leads me to wonder whether, with the end of this millennium, the Aristotelian paradigm of drama that has conflict at its core, has also had its day. It is a paradigm that has acquired the status of a transcendant Truth, yet Indian and many other Asian dramaturgies of the classical period drive towards a consensual notion of drama. In Indian thought a central notion is 'sat-chit-ananda' – 'Truth is Joy'. Joy as Truth sounds quaint to our post-Freudian ears. What about Good and Evil? But life – certainly life in the Forest – is somewhat greyer (or browner) than that.

An Asian woman, dressed in a sari, walks onstage. Stops and addresses the audience. 'When we first came to work in England, we were told, "Sorry, no saris!"' She turns, back to the audience, and slowly removes her sari . . . revealing a pair of slacks and a blouse underneath. This sequence, from my production of *Exodus* – an epic play about Asians who arrived from Kenya in February 1968 – I would cite as an attempt to construct a theatrical moment that looks beyond the contemporary jungle of borders between nations, races, sensibilities. The sequence shatters the fourth wall convention, of course. Establishes a particularity (Asian woman, speaking a kind of English). In the silent, non-confrontational gesture (back turned to the audience, stripping off her garment), she enacts a moment of chrysalis: the birth of a new being, dressed in another convention (tight-fitting 1960s slacks and blouse). No explanations offered, no recriminations aired. In the silent transformation we are left to reflect on our own moments of change – childhood to adulthood, school to university, Glasgow to London, Kenya to England.

If for me the only valid challenge of the next millennium is the construction of theatre works that are passionately inclusive of our multicultural communities, it is fuelled by a despair as much as a sense of loss. The despair evidenced by theatre works of the past fifty years in Britain. Since the Second World War Britain has been transformed in colour, in sound, in taste by, specifically, non-European migrations. Yet our theatres as a whole, through their writers as much as their producers, have scarcely reflected this tectonic shift in the nature of the country. The number of theatre texts, for example, can be counted on a pair of hands. This suggests that the migrants who are now citizens of the country do not exist in the imagination of our David Hares, Michael Frayns, Tom Stoppards and the rest of the theatre community. To not be part of the imaginative universe is, really, to not exist. (Except as special 'ethnic' enclaves: a socio-political programme, at best; hardly an aesthetic one.)

In the works of our major contemporary playwrights the 'different sort of noise' Salman Rushdie refers to is remarkably absent. It is not unreasonable to ask if writers such as these can interact with other dominant European languages – French, German, Italian, Russian – why not with the languages that form part of the pulsating linguistic landscape of contemporary Britain?

To conclude: a journey into a millennium past may provide instructive lessons for the one to come. In an Indian eighth-century BC text on theatre performance, a disciple asks his guru to teach him the principles of theatre. The latter replies that before he can understand and appreciate theatre, he needs to understand the principles of space and gesture through mastering dance; and before dance can be mastered, the disciple needs to understand the principles of line and form from sculpture; and before line and form can be mastered, he needs to understand the nature of time through music . . . and so on. Perhaps then, the impending millennium offers the opportunity to go forward to our pasts, and recover the *unity* of all forms of knowledge . . . and begin to truly understand, following Shakespeare, that when we are cut we all bleed the same colour of blood.

Vera Gottlieb

Lukewarm Britannia

Vera Gottlieb is Research Professor of Drama at Goldsmiths College, London University. Publications include Chekhov and the Vaudeville, Chekhov in Performance in Russia and Soviet Russia *and the article* Thatcher's Theatre – or, After 'Equus'. *She has worked as a script adviser and consultant for the Royal Shakespeare Company, on Channel 4 productions, and in Moscow and New York. For Magna Carta Productions she directed and co-wrote* Red Earth *and* Waterloo Road *with Robert Gordon. In 1990 she translated and directed* A Chekhov Quartet *(two one-act Chekhov plays and two dramatized stories), which appeared in London, Yalta and Moscow.*

THE HISTORY OF THE TWENTIETH CENTURY provides grim material. If the aim of this book is partly stocktaking, then these are the figures for this century's unnatural deaths: 100 million from famine; 10 million in 'natural' disasters (floods, earthquakes); 25 million through road accidents; 150 million in war; 100 million victims of their own state or government, and 14 million from genocide – this last being unique to our century in scale and method. This does not detract from the 'ethnic cleansing' in earlier history, whether the genocide of the Native American, or deaths from black slave trafficking, or lynch mobs. It is not that previously there were no wars or genocide or natural disasters, but the *scale* – linked to real progress for a minority – is the major characteristic of the barbarism of this century. Statistics are always contentious but most historians of the period are agreed on the above approximations.

These deeply disturbing figures must be placed in the context of *some* areas of progress: declining child mortality; rising life expectancy; increased food and manufacturing production; new technologies which have enabled speed of travel and communications unknown before 1900, and – in the developed world – increases in literacy, and greater equality for women. The significant word here is 'developed': the progressive features have, in fact, improved the lives of only approximately 20 per cent of the global population. The rich have become richer, the poor – poorer; the world has become smaller given modern travel – and the speed with which images from the other side of the globe can now reach our living rooms.

Europe and North America have reaped the benefits of the century's progressive features, but viewed globally, the vast majority of the world's population in Asia, Africa and the Americas have remained largely untouched by progress yet nonetheless victims of the 'barbarism' of the century: malnutrition; overwhelming poverty; rates of life expectancy half those of the lucky 20 per cent of the population in the developed world; environmental disasters from deliberate destruction of the natural environment by property development and industry; continued illiteracy; and for women, the increased 'double bind' of domestic drudgery and underpaid work.

The period could equally be characterized as the 'century of dictatorships', whether the historical dictatorships of Franco, Mussolini, Hitler, Stalin, Batista, Amin, Pol Pot, or the more recent and contemporary, as in former Yugoslavia, or East Timor under the Indonesian occupation from 1975, or in Rwanda, Somalia, or some of the poorest countries of Latin America, such as Honduras or Panama.

In the light of such realities, it may seem ironic that at the end of the nineteenth century there were those in Europe and North America who viewed the future with optimism – and this might well apply to many of us now as we view the coming millennium. With hindsight and knowledge of our century, optimism has received a hefty blow: too much has happened in the name of science for us to retain an unquestioning belief, whether in science itself, reason, human enlightenment, or any global equality of progress. It is difficult, in this context, to acknowledge the progress brought by culture yet the developments in literature, theatre, music, sport, or the new media of cinema, radio and television have articulated many of the issues behind the statistics – and raised many of the issues affecting ordinary people in the context of crisis and conflict. It *is* difficult to write about theatre in the light of the statistics given above, and it is essential to remember how Eurocentric most of us are – a point Jatinder Verma makes in his chapter. It is salutary to remember that much of what exercises our thinking in this book may seem not only insignificant but positively frivolous. If, however, we still believe that a crucial aim of humankind at the end of this barbaric century is that more people should have *more*, that quality and equality are still aims worth preserving and promoting, and that fun, entertainment and the thought-provoking should be available to more than a small elite, then theatre – as one of the most powerful modes of communication – may offer a live experience which both can and sometimes does transcend the unequal boundaries of literacy, social position, economic and political circumstances, ethnic background, physical disabilities, gender and generation.

People may be reached by stories, the Western characteristic of literature and theatre, or by dance, song and the natural 'mixed media' of much Eastern literature and performance. But the 'barbaric' context may or may not be demonstrated by culture in general and theatre in particular; *how* theatre is regarded makes it more or less frivolous, and *the purpose* behind theatrical activity will also define its nature, and determine its effectiveness. There is nothing inherently frivolous in making people laugh or cry, in drawing them away from their daily lives into something else which may then enable them to return to their present circumstances with fresh perceptions, and new questions, all of which remind human beings that there is a civilized and progressive aspect some might wish to share with others, *and* that illustrate alternatives or possibilities which might enhance the quality of life for the majority, instead of the current minority. And theatre, like the other arts, may enhance a progressive and positive sense of quality by offering both fun and entertainment *and* the possibility of questioning directly themes or issues related to the lives of the audience. If theatre lacked such potential, it would not have been regarded with suspicion and unease by dictatorships of varying kinds, both in the twentieth century and before. It is worth remembering, for instance, that the Statute 'classifying' actors as 'Rogues and Vagabonds', which became law in the sixteenth century, has not yet been repealed.

It is this potential theatre can offer that makes the search for new audiences – a priority of today many contributors have mentioned – all the more important. It is theatre's potential ability to engage and enhance which gives it particular resonance in different and often extreme contexts. However appalling, grotesque or surreal, it says much about the human spirit and human need that in the death camps of Auschwitz and Bergen-Belsen, prison orchestras were ordered to play some of 'the audience' into the gas chambers – but, from several accounts, played brilliantly, while in some instances – largely for propaganda purposes – theatre performances were given to a starving audience by starving actors even as the death factory chimneys belched out the grey dust of what had been millions of human beings. Somehow, it is essential at least to *acknowledge* that the Auschwitz 'Angel of Death', Dr Josef Mengele, loved Mozart and Beethoven – and attempt, *if possible*, to understand that even monsters are multifaceted – and *made*. It may seem easier to understand the actions of 'butchers', but the actions of the 'cultured', or the educated or 'civilized' may seem harder to comprehend. Some of this was explored by Brecht in *The Resistible Rise of Arturo Ui* (1941) with Margarete Steffin; or his *Schweyk in the Second World War* (1943), or by Trevor Griffiths in his *Comedians* (1975); by C.P. Taylor's *Good* (1981), and other European plays of Brecht, Max Frisch, Friedrich Dürrenmatt, Rolf Hochhuth and – more recently – Joshua Sobel's *Ghetto*, a play directly about the Holocaust, staged by the National in 1989; or by Ariel Dorfman's *Death and the Maiden*, performed with Pinter's sketch *The New World Order* at the Royal Court in 1991.

Personally, I have problems with the 'reproduction' of the Holocaust or Hiroshima or Third World famine on stage, played invariably by white reasonably-fed British actors: the dilemma of reproducing the unspeakable, which can, all too easily, tip over into making the trauma of history palatable. But, as with any subject, it is the *treatment* which is decisive. Responding emotionally, none of this seems to me stageable when reminded of the statistics or carrying real images from television documentary and news. Reacting with hard-won objectivity, I would argue that theatre has the potential for the most direct and positive interrogation of 'the unspeakable', of barbarism *and* of opening a dialogue between the event and its audience.

Emotional need partly motivated the audience at a Chekhov production in blockaded Leningrad during the Siege of the Second World War: with the city surrounded by the Nazi armies of Germany and Finland, some of the starving citizens went to a performance of *Three Sisters*. The resonance of 'to Moscow' took on a unique meaning for Russians cut off from the rest of Russia, with 'Moscow' unreachable as the moon. At the end of the performance almost one third of the audience remained in their seats. They had died in those few hours. Literally starving, the dying and those who only just survived, tried to assuage their hunger by dining at a different table – a spiritual meal.

In these, and all too many other examples, the human spirit has found in theatre, and in making theatre, a means of communicating directly, simply and significantly. All it really requires is a space, an audience, performers – and 'the play'. But there is also a real danger that a wish for the artistic results of crisis, often the most powerful, will produce a wish for crisis itself. The price could never be justified. In a century of dictatorships, the classics – as Richard Eyre points out in his chapter – have frequently been utilized to carry 'coded' messages to audiences that otherwise would have been prohibited. The electricity of theatre owes much to its collective nature, to the immediacy of performance, and to the ever-changing osmosis between performers and audience. The only real threat to theatre-making comes from *its own* loss of identity, uniqueness and confidence when brought about by external factors which affect society as a whole. Or when, as with an individual, it forgets its *real* identity and prostitutes itself to get attention *or* to survive, while forgetting what it really is – and can offer. In short, when it loses its own integrity.

It has been hard for the British theatre to retain integrity given Tory policies under Thatcher. Whether in privatizing British Gas ('Tell Sid!') – the opening advertising campaign to 'sell' the notion of privatized utilities – or British Telecom, these represented the economic arm of the ideology of the New Right – while many of the words which hitherto had been associated with 'the Left' in British politics, were now annexed by the New Right: 'radical', 'revolutionary' or 'populist' (as distinct from 'popular'). And there are other phrases that became the currency of the Eighties and Nineties: 'nanny state', 'welfare scroungers' – or with reference to actors –

'whingeing luvvies', the latter a part of the populist culture of 'denigration' discussed by many contributors, and which also included attacks on academics, 'intellectuals' or 'the chattering classes'.

Part of the difficulty of opposition was that the New Right took over the *language* of opposition: *they* were the radicals, not those on 'the Left'; *they* had an agenda for a 'revolutionary' Britain, but – above all – the appeal of property and share ownership had been seriously underestimated by 'the Left'. And the media consistently characterized 'them', irrespective of variations and divisions, as 'the loony Left'.

By 1989 we were well aware that this was an ideological battle – with culture and education inseparable from 'monetarism' and the 'free market' as proselytized by Thatcher, Reagan and other advocates who formed an inner ideological 'think-tank' to push forward the radical Right's new policies. This was based on a return to Victorian values, to a particularly vicious kind of 'social Darwinism' related to 'the survival of the fittest'. The tone is perhaps best summarized by the line from the film *Wall Street*, when the highly successful 'monetarist' Gekko tells his shareholders: 'Greed is good!' The theatre can *dramatize* this as in, for example, Shakespeare's *Timon of Athens* or Marlowe's *The Jew of Malta*. What it cannot do is to have this value system as the *foundation* for and of theatrical activity: the collective and public nature of the theatre itself makes such a value system both paradoxical and contradictory.

We therefore found ourselves individualized and privatized, a point reiterated by most contributors, but the repetition of the issue relates to the fact that it was the first time the British theatre *itself* became politicized, as distinct from staging political plays – a politicization in response to threat, and as part of a larger battle for the values, conscience, and importance of those areas of a country's identity and life which could not be measured by monetarist criteria.

A critical part of Tory strategy was to end the old British appearance of 'fair play' by unashamedly attacking and disenfranchising local democracy by controlling and capping local government expenditure. This disenfranchisement also included the brazenly undemocratic 'quangos' which – for example – made BBC departmental heads *and* the Director-General of the BBC *overtly* political appointments, as were the appointments of successive Chairs of the Arts Council.

The broader political effects were explored in the theatre by Caryl Churchill who, perhaps more than any other writer, wrote the most stinging denunciation and feminist critique of Thatcherism in her *Top Girls* (1982), and then monetarism in her *Serious Money* (1987), set in the City with the Yuppies of the Eighties – a play which coincided with 'Black Monday', the worst international financial crisis since the 1929 Wall Street Crash and subsequent Depression. With hindsight, 'Black Monday' was probably the beginning of the end of that form of monetarism when it became evident that the market was not as 'free' as the monetarists had thought. Only World Bank intervention was able to save global markets and the major international currencies. This World Bank intervention began to show cracks in capitalism as the Berlin Wall was beginning to show cracks in the seemingly monolithic Soviet-style Socialism.

Some of this and related issues were reflected in our theatre. There was a clutch of plays on the break-up of the Soviet bloc: David Edgar's *The Shape of the Table*; Tariq Ali and Howard Brenton's *Moscow Gold* and Caryl Churchill's *Mad Forest* (all three in 1990). Stretching from *The Birthday Party* (1958) or *The Homecoming* (1964) to *Mountain Language* (1988) or *Ashes to Ashes* (1996), Pinter has continued to write political plays, albeit not always recognized as such. And David Hare's *The Secret Rapture* (1988), and his 'state of Britain' trilogy – *Racing Demon* (1990), *Murmuring Judges* (1991) and *The Absence of War* (1993) – explored the effects on Britain of Thatcherism and the new ideology. Edward Bond continued to write overtly political plays, as did Peter Flannery, Trevor Griffiths, Howard Brenton, Winsome Pinnock and Timberlake Wertenbaker, whose *Our Country's Good* (1988) debates the role and function of theatre – to mention the most political playwrights of the Eighties and early Nineties who *did* explore central issues arising from the end of the postwar consensus which Thatcher swept aside.

Over 1988/89 some action took place involving theatre's response. An article I wrote for *New Theatre Quarterly*, called *Thatcher's Theatre – or, After 'Equus'*, was followed by a Symposium written up in *NTQ* (Vol. V, No.18, May 1989), from which, in turn, followed a national conference, *Theatre in Crisis*, written up in *NTQ* (Vol. V, No.19, August 1989). Speaker after speaker forcefully talked about the needs of theatre, the threat to its survival, the dangers of sponsorship and the climate of *self-censorship* that it created. Opening the conference, Clive Barker remarked that the Chinese word for 'crisis' was a combination of words meaning both 'danger' and 'opportunity'. The feeling at the end was optimistic and resulted in a Conference Declaration which the editors of this book had drawn up, signed by several of the contributors here – Harold Pinter, Peter Hall, Genista McIntosh, Leila Jancovich – amongst 95 professionals who were present, *and* those who could not be present. The actual Conference Declaration is worth quoting in full:

> We believe that
>
> – the full and free development of every individual depends on the full and free development of all
>
> – cultural activity is an essential part of this social process in which theatre has a distinct and important role to play
>
> – for theatre to play this role it must be as diverse as the society it represents. It must be linked to and therefore accessible to that diversity of needs and interests whether they be national, regional, local, community-based, gender-based, ethnic, educational, rooted in class, age, sexuality, or stemming from physical circumstance
>
> – a free market economy and private sponsorship cannot guarantee the necessary conditions for theatre to fulfil its many functions
>
> – in the current climate of increasing authoritarianism and regulation, the health of the theatre along with cultural activity of all kinds has been seriously impaired and is under further threat
>
> – for theatre to retain and sustain its vigorous social role, for theatre to grow and be fully creative, the foundation of its funding at a level adequate for its basic needs and future development must be public, and that the management and distribution of that funding should be democratically organized and devolved.

The Declaration was also published in Australia and New Zealand in the same year, 1989, and attracted the interest and attention of many in the theatre who had missed the opportunity of adding their names. Since then there have been other conferences, debates and books extending some arguments and bringing others up to the present.

There were those at the time, of course, who considered that all this was 'out of tune' and belonged to Sixties' thinking, not Eighties' – and now Nineties' – realities. What they failed to appreciate, however, was the urgency in trying to find a language to oppose what was happening to the social and cultural life of the country – *and* to restate the values expressed so clearly by many in this book. Those values have become as pressing now as we reach not only the end of the century, but the millennium – values inseparable from the context. And the context of today, with New Labour in government, is that of 'Cool Britannia'.

In 1996 *Time Magazine, Le Monde, Newsweek,* and London's *Evening Standard* all described London as 'cool'; by 1998 media and public relations companies had turned the country into 'Cool Britannia' – a description utilized by Tony Blair's government of New Labour. Something new seemed to be happening, something as distinctive, it seemed, as 'the Swinging Sixties'. The media and the market 'named' something, then 'made' something – and subsequently 'claimed' something. Emanating from the sense of change *finally* brought about by the end of eighteen years of Conservative government, this new hype was initially used about 'Brit' pop and 'Brit' film (conveniently forgetting that Britain does not have a film industry as such), but this marketing ploy then extended into other aspects of society, culture – and theatre. Implicit is the sense of something new, sophisticated, reticent – and enviable.

In the theatre this term was used to label new plays, in particular Mark Ravenhill's *Shopping and Fucking* (1996), Jez Butterworth's *Mojo* (1995) and Sarah Kane's *Blasted* (1995). There is some critical controversy about whether anything actually new *has* happened – and if so, how significant. Although postmodernism has virtually succeeded in relieving us of the responsibility of making value judgements, I am swimming against today's tide in assuming criteria for assessment and would suggest that anything that has happened in the Nineties was less creative, positive or radical than some critics might concede, and of mixed significance. 'Cool Britannia' feels decidedly 'lukewarm'. We are in a period of transition in which little at this moment suggests birth or rebirth. On the contrary, we lack any clear direction, unable to find a new language to describe new phenomena, and seemingly still at the mercy of such international forces as the free market and global warming. We are witnessing an increasingly stark division between the developed and underdeveloped worlds, with a 'new' nationalism, even tribalism, which may be a reaction against the increased globalization of 'control'.

Crystal ball-gazing into the near future suggests more concern than reassurance, and less innovation in society, and thus theatre, in the Nineties than in the Eighties when opposition to the New Right stimulated *some* combative theatrical activity. The Nineties seem to me more worrying than the previous decade, given the politics and value system resulting from eighteen years of Thatcherism, and a new Labour government that has not, so far, demonstrated an articulated programme for improving Britain's public services. At this time, New Labour seems more of a continuum with what went before with Thatcher's 'populist' and 'radical' revolution. Even Clause 28, brought in by the Tories to ban public funding for the 'promotion of homosexuality', has yet to be repealed. Another rather obvious reason for some pessimism is the fact that the election of New Labour to power has removed the hope of a stronger opposition than we had under the Tories, and because so far New Labour has not started to implement any *radical* changes of policy, not least towards the arts.

Few local authorities can now afford to subsidize community theatre. The current situation is best exemplified by the demise of many Black or Asian or other 'ethnic' theatre groups, or women's, lesbian or gay companies, yet the audience is out there, as are imagination, talent and motivation.

Likewise, a new feature of the fringe has been the importation of a star to help offset financial difficulties. In October 1998 Nicole Kidman played at London's Donmar Warehouse – a fringe venue – boosting both profile and profits. One single ticket was literally selling on the street for £600. In November 1998 the Hampstead Theatre brought in Ewan McGregor, famous for his role in the film *Trainspotting*. This vividly illustrates both the media hype of today in selling 'stars' *and* the financial needs of such venues: new and exciting theatre cannot survive without assured subsidy. The result is loss of experiment, innovatory and lively theatre and the *closure* of repertory and touring theatres. Peter Hall raises another area of concern: he suggests that Covent Garden may be privatized – and then the other subsidized houses – bringing to an end *any* public subsidy other than through the Lottery. A crystal ball with a dark lens!

There is also the lack of *major* new writing which engages with our contemporary realities. The exception is Sarah Kane's *Blasted* – lambasted by many critics ('this disgusting feast of filth', as the *Daily Mail* put it), which contains scenes of female and male rape, defecation, blinding, cannibalism and masturbation. But Kane is drawing a serious parallel between Britain and Bosnia, albeit using the kind of violence we are more used to seeing in the cinema – or in Jacobean tragedies. There is the use of verbal violence as a stylistic feature. This is both a continuum of Howard Barker's verbal abuse – *and* also the theatrical equivalent of such films as *Pulp Fiction*, *Reservoir Dogs* or *Natural Born Killers*.

Some critics view the plays of Kane, Ravenhill and Butterworth as examples of a renaissance in British theatre. I do not see a renaissance. The virulance of the attacks on Kane seemed to have driven her into withdrawal, imitating the 'language'-based dramas of Pinter or Beckett, but without their often profound content. Equally, Butterworth seems to be strongly influenced by Pinter's language and style – but he remains essentially a stylist, lacking in content. Many of their images resonate from film, and from the plays of Edward Bond, Howard Barker and Howard Brenton – but since these three older dramatists come from within a more overtly *social* context, their use of violence is seemingly less gratuitous. In Kane's subsequent *Crave* (1998), her possible fear of being called 'naive' motivated a play which is essentially 'only' language. The attacks on Kane, and virtual hounding by the media, may not have happened had she been a male writer depicting such violence, and although speculative, this may well have been a factor in her shocking suicide, while only 28, in 1999.

As for Ravenhill's *Shopping and Fucking*, again the politics are *implicit* and the values seem to be represented by sexual obsession on the one hand – and consumerism on the other: both are 'neat' points about today, but it loses itself and a sense of direction by providing little challenge, debate or provocation on the level of serious analysis. In both *Shopping and Fucking* and *Handbag* (1998) Ravenhill's technical sophistication masks emptiness of content. And that is a waste of undoubted talent, given his ability to structure a play. Like Kane and Ravenhill, Butterworth strikes a real chord in *Mojo* amongst the 20–30 generation, but the root of it lies in the immediacy of his trendiness; his seemingly gratuitous use of language and violence intended to shock, and 'small-scale' issues compared with the broader ones treated by *Blasted*. All these writers are very much in touch with the malaise amongst their generation, all too aware of consumerism, but in effect the plays end up as 'products': the 'themes' of consumerism, drug culture and sexuality paralyse the plays. And yet they *do* speak to their audience, if only because of their referential use of pop culture, television and Hollywood films – the postmodernist emphasis on form as distinct from content. If the Eighties demonstrated a search for a language of opposition, then the plays of the Nineties seem to have moved even further away from the politically oppositional, and to have given up any attempt to engage with significant public issues.

This is not the case, however, with two major dramatists – one American, one Canadian – who *have* presented a 'global' view of our times: Tony Kushner in *Angels in America – Part One: The Millennium Approaches* (British premiere, NT, 1992) and the French-Canadian Robert Lepage in *The Seven Streams of the River Ota* (NT, 1996). Both of these works are immensely theatrical – *and* address some of the most important issues facing us today as we approach the twenty-first century, from Aids to Hiroshima. Kushner and Lepage demonstrate that theatricality and 'rule-breaking' can still produce social and political plays of immediacy, controversy and clarity.

Virtually all of our contributors have referred to these plays with relief and hope, and this optimistic view is reflected in their 'snapshot' of today. It is significant that in the final decade of the twentieth century several articles in newspapers and journals, and Richard Eyre in the Preface to his autobiography, *Utopia and Other Places*, quote Oscar Wilde's thinking in 1891. The resonance from one century to the other, *in spite* of the particular horrors of the twentieth century, demonstrates a continued need which spans period and history. In *The Soul of Man Under Socialism* Oscar Wilde wrote:

> A map of the world that does not include Utopia is not even worth glancing at, for it leaves out the one country at which Humanity is always landing. And when Humanity lands there, it looks out, and, seeing a better country, sets sail.

Selected Bibliography

The following selection provides a context to and a background for the chapters in this book. The list is not intended as an academic bibliography or a comprehensive review.

Beauman, Sally *The Royal Shakespeare Company: A History of Ten Decades* (OUP, Oxford, 1982)

Brook, Peter *The Empty Space* (McGibbon & Kee, London, 1968)

Brook, Peter *There Are No Secrets: Thoughts on Acting and Theatre* (Methuen, London, 1993)

Brustein, Robert *Who Needs Theatre? Dramatic Opinions* (Faber & Faber, London, 1987)

Callow, Simon *Being An Actor* (Methuen, London, 1984)

Callow, Simon *The National: The Theatre and Its Work 1963-1997* (Nick Hern Books & National Theatre, London, 1997)

Chambers, Colin *Other Spaces: New Theatre and the RSC* (Eyre Methuen, London, 1980)

Chambers, Colin & Prior, Mike *Playwrights' Progress: Patterns of Postwar British Drama* (Amber Lane Press, Oxford, 1987)

Craig, Sandy (ed.) *Dreams and Deconstructions; Alternative Theatre in Britain* (Amber Lane Press, Oxford, 1980)

Davies, Andrew *Other Theatres: The Development of Alternative and Experimental Theatre in Britain* (Macmillan, London, 1987)

Edgar, David *The Second Time as Farce: Reflections on the Drama of Mean Times* (Lawrence & Wishart, London, 1988)

Elsom, John *Theatre Outside London* (Macmillan, London, 1971)

Elsom, John & Tomalin, Nicholas *The History of the National Theatre* (Jonathan Cape, London, 1978)

Eyre, Richard *Utopia and Other Places* (Bloomsbury, London, 1993)

Eyre, Richard *The Eyre Review: The Future of Lyric Theatre in London* (HMSO, London, 1998)

FitzHerbert, Luke & Paterson, Mark *The National Lottery Yearbook* (published annually from 1993-94, Directory of Social Change, London)

Gaskill, William *A Sense of Direction: Life at the Royal Court* (Faber & Faber, London, 1988)

Goodwin, John (ed.) *British Theatre Design: The Modern Age* (Weidenfeld & Nicolson, London, 1989)

Hall, Peter *Making an Exhibition of Myself* (Sinclair-Stevenson, London, 1993)

Hall, Peter (ed. Goodwin, John) *Peter Hall's Diaries: The Story of a Dramatic Battle* (Hamish Hamilton, London, 1983)

Hewison, Robert *Culture and Consensus: England, Art and Politics Since 1940* (Methuen, London, 1997)

Hobsbawm, Eric *Age of Extremes: The Short Twentieth Century 1914-1991* (Abacus, London, 1995*)*

Hutchinson, Robert *The Politics of the Arts Council* (Sinclair Brown, London, 1982)

Hutton, Will *The State We're In* (Vintage, Random House, London, Revised Edition, 1996)

Hutton, Will *The State to Come* (Vintage, Random House, London, 1997)

Kershaw, Baz *The Politics of Performance: Radical Theatre as Cultural Intervention* (Routledge, London, 1992)

Keyssar, Helene (ed.) *Feminist Theatre and Theory: Contemporary Critical Essays* (Macmillan, London, 1992)

Khan, Naseem *The Arts Britain Ignores: The Arts of Ethnic Minorities in Britain* (Arts Council, Calouste Gulbenkian Foundation, Community Relations Commission, London, 1976)

Levitas, Ruth (ed.) *The Ideology of the New Right* (Polity Press, Cambridge, 1986)

Lewis, Justin *Art, Culture and Enterprise: The Politics of Art and the Cultural Industries* (Routledge, London, 1990)

McGrath, John *A Good Night Out - Popular Theatre: Audience, Class & Form* (Eyre Methuen, London, 1981)

Minihan, Janet *The Nationalisation of Culture: The Development of State Subsidies to the Arts in Great Britain* (Hamish Hamilton, London, 1977)

Moffat, Kate *The House: Inside the Royal Opera House, Covent Garden* (BBC Books, London, 1995)

Owusu, Kwesi *The Struggle for Black Arts in Britain* (Comedia, London, 1986)

Pick, John *Managing the Arts? The British Experience* (Rheingold Publishing, London, 1989)

Pinter, Harold *Various Voices: Prose, Poetry, Politics 1948-1998* (Faber & Faber, London, 1998)

Ponting, Clive *Progress and Barbarism: The World in the 20th Century* (Chatto & Windus, London, 1998)

Rowell, George & Jackson, Anthony *The Repertory Movement: A History of Regional Theatre in Britain* (CUP, Cambridge, 1984)

Schechner, Richard & Appel, Willa (eds.) *By Means of Performance: Intercultural Studies of Theatre and Ritual* (CUP, Cambridge, 1990)

Smith, Chris *Creative Britain* (Faber & Faber, London, 1998)

Tynan, Kenneth *Tynan on Theatre* (Penguin, Harmondsworth, 1964)

Walter, Harriet *Other People's Shoes: Thoughts on Acting* (Viking, London, 1999)

Wandor, Michelene *Carry on Understudies: Theatre and Sexual Politics* (Routledge, London, 1986)

Wardle, Irving *The Theatres of George Devine* (Cape, London, 1978)

Wardle, Irving *Theatre Criticism* (Routledge, London & New York, 1982)

Witts, Richard *Artist Unknown: The Alternative History of the Arts Council* (Brown, Little, London, 1998)

Annual Reports from the Arts Council/s (HMSO, London) and other reports emanating from them and the original Arts Council of Great Britain, such as *The Policy for Drama of the English Arts Funding System, The Glory of the Garden* and *Arts for a New Century: The Charter for the Arts in Scotland* (HMSO, London, 1993) and reports or studies from other sources, such as *Culture as Commodity* (Policy Studies Institute, London, 1995).

Index of Proper Names

Unless otherwise stated, theatres and other venues listed are located in London.

Also available from Amber Lane Press

Colin Chambers and Mike Prior
Playwrights' Progress: Patterns of Postwar British Drama

David Cheshire
Portrait of Ellen Terry

Richard Corballis
Stoppard: The Mystery and the Clockwork

Ben Francis
Christopher Hampton: Dramatic Ironist

Ronald Harwood
Sir Donald Wolfit

Sheila Yeger
The Sound of One Hand Clapping –
A Guide to Writing for the Theatre